"Fascinating reading." — B
Corporation)

"Not since John Naisbitt's ⎯⎯⎯ ⎯⎯
hit the mark so clearly." — *American Institute oj Architects*

"Nine Shift is mind blowing." — *Philip Badman, CityLit, London, UK*

"A most interesting book." — *Peter F. Drucker, internationally famous business guru*

"Please God, make Draves' and Coates' prognostications come true." — *Prof. David Calhoon, Black Hills State University, Spearfish, South Dakota*

"I haven't been able to stop talking about the book to everyone I encounter," — *Darlene Cullimore, Winnipeg, Manitoba*

"It was difficult to put down. While reading I came to realize the shifts are already happening and could find examples in my daily life." — *Drew Weilage, sophomore at the University of Minnesota – Duluth*

"A great contribution." — *Don Tapscott, author of Growing Up Digital*

Nine Shift

Work, Life and Education
in the 21st Century

by William A. Draves and Julie Coates

Published by LERN Books, a division of
Learning Resources Network (LERN)
P.O. Box 9
River Falls, Wisconsin 54022
U.S.A.

Phone: 800-678-5376 (US and Canada)
E-mail: *info@lern.org*
URL: *www.lern.org*

Manufactured in the United States of America

5 4

Library of Congress Cataloging in Publication Data
Draves, William A., 1949-
   Nine Shift

ISBN: 1-57722-030-7

Dedication

For Greg Marsello

Nine Shift

Work, Life and Education in the 21st Century

Table of Contents

Acknowledgments

We are indebted to many fine people who have made contributions to our work.

For the cover photo, we need to thank Yana Sergeevna Sletten, who kindly posed in the George IV or Lady's Phaeton carriage in the cover photo. The carriage is part of the private collection of Charlie and Anne Leck, and we appreciate their time and help in the cover photo session.

Family members who have contributed to our understanding of our past include Julie's father, Mr. Y.A. Taylor, who shared his experience in the transition from the agricultural age to the industrial age. Mrs. William A. Draves III and David Draves provided valuable insight into life in the first half of the twentieth century. Tim Draves sent us the 1907 department store brochure from Frankfort, Kansas, which started our exploration of *Nine Shift*. Family members who have contributed to our understanding of the future include Jason Coates, Willie Draves, and all their friends who 'hang out' in our house.

We are dependent upon and grateful for the support of LERN co-founder Greg Marsello, as well as the LERN staff, leaders and consultants who form the best organizational team of which one could ever hope to be a part. Proofing assisted by our longtime editor, Glenna Wilson, although all errors belong to the authors. Production was carried out professionally, as always, by Danita Dickinson.

Introduction

"I'm not a futurist. I only describe the present to the 98% of people who are not there yet."
— Richard Thieme, technology expert

In just twenty years, between 2000 and 2020, some 75% of our lives will change dramatically. We know this because it happened once before. Between 1900 and 1920, life changed. We moved from an agrarian farming way of life to an industrialized way of life. Now it is all happening again.

The way we work is changing. The way we live is changing. The way we learn is changing.

These changes are causing tremendous uncertainty, doubt, anxiety, and stress. Those of us who are adults grew up in the Industrial Age of the last century. We are now moving from a time in which we were fairly certain of the basic facts about life and of the rules that applied to it, to a time when we are not quite sure what is real and what is not real.

This ambiguity will be with us for another ten to twenty years. Living with the ambiguity, and feeling comfortable with discomfort, is not easy.

Our purpose in writing this book is to discover how our lives are changing, and to understand what lies ahead, by looking back at our great grandparents' generation, the generation that was alive during the last time society experienced such a dramatic change. We call this dramatic change in how we work, live and learn a "nine shift."

What *Nine Shift* Means

The term "nine shift" is used to describe the great changes taking

place in our lives right now. What we are experiencing in how we use our time and how we experience life derives from the phenomenon that nine hours in your day will be spent entirely differently in 2020 than they were spent in 2000.

There are 24 hours in a day. We have no real discretion with roughly 12 of those hours. We need to eat, sleep, and do a few other necessary chores in order to maintain our existence. That hasn't changed much through the centuries, so far.

That leaves approximately 12 hours a day where we, as individuals, do have some discretion. That includes work time, play time, and family time.

Of those 12 hours, about 75%, or 9 hours, will be spent totally differently a few years from now than they were spent just a few years ago. Not everything will change, but 75% of life is in the process of changing right now.

The same kind of change occurred between 1900 and 1920 as well. Frederick Allen called it "the big change" in his 1952 book by the same title.[1] We call it a *nine shift*.

What this means is that nine hours in your day will be spent entirely differently in 2020 than they were spent in 2000. That is an enormous change. That is a *nine shift*.

The last time we experienced this *nine shift* in society was between 1900 and 1920. The driving force of the last century, the 20th century, was the automobile. The automobile and the way the automobile was made — the mass production factory — shaped how people worked, how people lived, and how they learned, for the last 100 years. The auto is not a symbol for the 20th century. Instead, the car and the car factory literally changed most of life.

So many common features of life today would not have been widely present without the car. They include offices, suburbs, fast food restaurants, company organization charts, unified school districts, and many more aspects of life that are considered "standard" today.

People in society are so dependent on the car that to do without one for a week would be an enormous burden for the majority of us. We simply have no readily implementable back-up plan to working and living without a car, even for a week.

The car shaped and defined the 20th century. It had an almost negligible impact on the 19th century, and as we will see, the automobile is going into steep decline and will have a much reduced and non-dominant role in the 21st century.

Now there are arguably more important inventions than the automobile. Electricity and the printed book are two examples. But neither shaped the 20th century as the auto did. And neither were confined to the 20th century like the auto has been. Electricity had a much greater impact on society in the 19th century than the auto, and it will have a much greater impact on society in the 21st century than the auto. The importance of the printed book has continued for five hundred years, and even with the advent of digital communication it is unlikely that we will see its influence wane in the newest age.

As we will see, the Internet is behaving exactly the same way as the automobile did 100 years ago in its impact on society. The auto is not used here as an "analogy," which is defined as something "somewhat similar." Instead the influence of the Internet on our lives is exactly a replay, a mirror, of the influence of the auto on society 100 years ago. The outcomes will be different of course, but the forces and how those forces interact and change our lives, are the same.

This book is not really about the Internet. It is more about the consequences and changes of the Internet, about how the Internet is changing how we work, live and learn in this century. It is about the tremendous transition from one way of life to another that we are undergoing between 2000 and 2020.

To understand what has happened already in the 21st century, to understand what is happening today, and to understand what will be happening between now and 2020, all we need to do is to revisit the years 1900 to 1920.

Most all of the fundamental changes in our society in this century will take place before 2020. We know this because most all of the fundamental changes in 20th century society took place between 1900 and 1920.

In 1900 society was in the Agrarian Age. The predominant occupation was farming. A majority of people lived either on a family farm or in a small town (less than 2,000 people). We will explore more what life was like then, but most of us have little knowledge about life in 1900.

In just a short period of time, just twenty years, society went from being an agrarian society to being an industrial society.

By 1920, almost all of the major inventions of the century had seen the light of day. They included radio, movies, airplanes, the gasoline engine, and more.

About the only device to have a major impact on us that had not yet been invented was the television. Yet even there, "the visual language for television was established by 1920," according to television and communications expert Kathleen McMonigal .[2]

More importantly, by 1920, almost all of the major aspects of 20th century life had emerged. They include suburbs, commuting, offices, factories, the National Football League, women's right to vote, and possibly most importantly, the ubiquitous organization chart or pyramid.

So the time period to analyze is 1900-1920. Life in the 19th century before 1900 looked a lot like life in 1900. And life in the 20th century after 1920 looked fundamentally the same as life in 1920.

The leading business thinker regarding this metamorphosis from the Industrial Age to the Internet Age has been Peter F. Drucker, who invented the term "knowledge worker." Notes Drucker, "Both in its speed and its impact, the Information Revolution uncannily resembles its two predecessors within the past two hundred years, the First Industrial Revolution of the later eighteenth and early nineteenth centuries, and the Second Industrial Revolution of the late nineteenth century."[3]

Drucker notes, "The Next Society will be a knowledge society. Knowledge will be its key resource, and knowledge workers will be the dominant group in its work force."[4] And he concludes, "All this suggests that the greatest changes are almost certainly still ahead of us."[5] In this book, we will take two magical mystery trips. One will be back to the time of your great grandparents (give or take a generation, depending on your age). The other magical mystery trip will be forward just a few years. Both scenarios will be very unfamiliar, both are equally exciting and ripe for exploration.

There are two halves in the period of transition from one society into another. The first half, the first decade (2000-2010), is characterized primarily by the unraveling of the old society. The second half, the next decade (2010-2020), will be characterized primarily by the reformulating of society around the new way. At the juncture of the two decades, around 2010, is the turning point from the old society to the new society.

Here are the critical time periods we will look at:

1990-2000 and 1890-1900

Technology first introduced. Intellectual excitement and creativity.

2000-2005 and 1900-1905

New way grows; old way becomes dysfunctional, but is still dominant.

2005-2010 and 1900-1910

Conflict and chaos as the new way challenges the old way.

2008-2012 and 1908-1912

Turning point in society.

2010-2020 and 1910-1920
Old way gives way to new way.
2020 and 1920
New way is clearly dominant and accepted. The old way is clearly in decline.
Some of these changes in life are fairly fundamental. For the sake of symmetry, we will describe nine of the most important changes coming and going on right now.
What we know, and what many other technology and economic experts have widely documented, is that the Internet, and the World Wide Web in particular, is a profound new technology that has already fundamentally affected our economy. We know that we are moving from an industrial economy to an information economy. We know that the number of knowledge workers is dramatically increasing and will become a significant part of the workforce.
From this, we are alone, at present, in predicting that all of these nine shifts are occurring and will become commonplace by 2020.

Shift One. People work at home.
Commuting to an office will become a rarity, a thing of the past. A significant part of the workforce will work from home or telecommute.

Shift Two. Intranets replace offices.
Offices will diminish as primary work places. Intranets will replace physical offices for most businesses, companies and nonprofit organizations.

Shift Three. Networks replace pyramids.
The basic organizational structure of life in the last century, the organization chart or pyramid, goes into steep decline. It is replaced by a superior organizational structure, the network.

Shift Four. Trains replace cars.
The automobile, the dominant mode of transportation in the last century, loses its dominance and becomes a peripheral and supplemental mode of transportation. Trains and light rail become the dominant mode of transportation.

Shift Five. Dense neighborhoods replace suburbs.

5

Suburbs, and suburban sprawl, come to a halt and then recede. Towns and cities are reformulated around dense communities composed of shops, stores and homes within walking distance of a light rail station.

Shift Six. New social infrastructures evolve.

The increasing inequality in wealth between the rich and the rest of society comes to a halt. The issue of inequality of wealth in society is addressed and a variety of social reforms are implemented to restore more of a balance in income distribution.

Shift Seven. Cheating becomes collaboration.

New values, work ethics and behavior of the 21st century take over. Boys are leading the change in values and behavior, just as they did 100 years ago.

Shift Eight. Half of all learning is online.

The traditional classroom rapidly becomes obsolete. Half of all learning is done online, changing the nature of how we learn and how we teach.

Shift Nine. Education becomes web-based.

Brick and mortar schools and colleges of the past century become outdated. All education becomes web-based, providing a better education for both young people and adults.

We will explore each shift in detail. Each one is a logical outcome of a whole series and system of forces that are set in motion by the dominance of a new technology. That new technology for us right now is the Internet and World Wide Web.

For our great grandparents' generation, give or take a generation depending on your age, the same system of forces were set in motion by the dominance of a new technology, the automobile, exactly one hundred years ago.

While the outcomes, of course, are different, the forces and the way the forces impact our work, life, and education, are exactly the same.

Future Predictions

None of the nine shifts described in this book are future predictions. They are all taking place right now and we see them and experience them on a daily basis. Thus Richard Thieme's comment rings true for us.[6]

While much of this book may seem to be future predictions, it is a present reality to us, our family, our staff, our organization, and to a fair number of others with whom we communicate. Julie goes so far as to say that what we are describing is not the present, but the past. A recent past to be sure, but that these changes have already taken place. Most of us just do not know it yet.

About Us

Julie Coates has lived in all three ages, the Agrarian Age, the Industrial Age, and now the Internet Age. She grew up on a subsistence farm in the rural South, and experienced the extended family, home-grown vegetables, fall canning rituals, and going to church three times a week. She watched as her father made the transition from the farm to the factory.

As "the world's oldest baby boomer," Julie is also an authority on the demographics of learning. She currently teaches an online course called Generational Learning Styles.

William A. Draves grew up in a family that was involved in the creation of the Industrial Age. His great grandfather started several factories, one of which became a Fortune 500 company.

He works from a home office, has created a virtual office for his organization, and teaches online.

Julie and Bill, along with Greg Marsello, form the senior management team for the Learning Resources Network (LERN), the leading association in the world in lifelong learning. LERN is currently the largest online provider of professional development for professors in higher education to teach online.

Beginning in 1995, Julie, Bill and Greg initiated the transformation of LERN into a virtual organization. Thus our research has evolved out of three engagements: a) a personal and family history interest; b) our work in leading several thousand providers of lifelong learning and continuing education; and c) our own organization's transition to a virtual organization, and to a structure that is positioned to operate effectively in the 21st century.

About This Book

The purpose of our research is twofold:

1) Business.

Nine Shift is a business book. It describes how your own work organization should change and transition into the Internet Age in order to remain viable and successful. After reading this book, you will understand the major shifts your work organization must go through to remain successful in the 21st century.

2) Personal.

To help you individually in your personal and emotional journey through the current period of uncertainty and ambiguity. Our lives are moving from a reality with which we grew up to an entirely new and unfamiliar environment. We each will need to live with that ambiguity as our lives change. After reading this book, your comfort level will increase about that ambiguity and you will feel better about addressing the personal challenges ahead.

Welcome to our story. Welcome to *Nine Shift*.

Chapter 1
The End of the World, As We Know It

"And he who lives to scan the twentieth century
as it merges into the twenty-first may look back with
as startling comparisons as we now employ
in speaking of the nineteenth."
— *Oshkosh Daily Northwestern, December 31, 1900.*

It wasn't very long ago and we were in the 20th century. And in 1999, as we were about to enter a new century, a new millennium, we were two of those few people who believed that on January 1, 2000, the world as we knew it would end. During the last two months of 1999 our local public radio station played "The 20th Century is Almost Over," a Steve Goodman song written about the many familiar events, common appliances, and features of the 20th century that were disappearing into the past.[1]

We had just purchased a house from a retired university history professor, Clyde Smith. So we asked him about the turn of the last millennium. He related the story of how thousands of people gathered in St. Peter's Square in Vatican City on the night of December 31, 999. If the world was to end, as many believed, they wanted to be there. Others hoped that the Pope would be able to intervene and save the world from the destruction that would occur at the stroke of midnight, January 1, 1000.

As the church bells rang twelve times and brought in the new millennium, the crowd fell to its knees. Some people actually had heart attacks, unable to bear the fear and dread.[2]

One thousand years later, almost everyone believed that nothing would change as the clock turned to January 1, 2000. Yet at the same time there was also a huge feeling of dread and fear. The fear was that as the clock turned to January 1, 2000, that the digital clocks of the 20th century would break down and society would come to a halt. This was Y2K (Year 2 thousand, or K).

Computers controlled the civilized world, and because they were programmed to read 01/01/00 as January 1, 1900, and not January 1, 2000, all sorts of crazy things would happen. Airplane control systems would go berzerk. Municipal heating and water systems would shut down. The food supply chain would be disrupted. Employee payroll checks, welfare checks, health care reimbursement checks, all would not be printed and mailed, shutting down the financial system. Banks would close.

In the United States, the great millennial celebrations fizzled in advance as people erred on the side of caution. Hotel rooms went unclaimed. Events were cancelled. Huge numbers of police were called out in the few cities where celebrations were scheduled.

Insurance companies sent out notices saying they were not responsible for claims resulting from Y2K breakdowns.

As a result, most people stayed home on the eve of the new millennium. Many companies and cities required managers to be on alert at their offices in case the computer systems did break down. As one British reporter covering the story reported, "Essential personnel were ordered to be at their office desks. Anyone who was anyone was nowhere. And everyone else did not want to attend New Year's Eve parties because that would mean they were non-essential personnel. So no one went anywhere."[3]

As for us, we believed that on December 31, 1999, the world as we knew it would end. After some initial misgiving, we decided this was an event that required celebration. After considering various options, we decided to join a tour and go to London, England, to celebrate the dawning of the new millennium.

On New Year's Eve Day, we took our 14-year-old son down to the Thames River where there was an enormous family fair with multicultural exhibits and tents, bands, street theatre, food from different ethnic cultures and countries, and even new millennial construction projects for the kids. Later that evening we returned to the Thames River along with 2.5 million other people to see the largest fireworks display in history. The streets were blocked off and only pedestrians were allowed in the City Centre.

To the left of us was an eight-year-old girl from New Zealand and her mother. To the right, some people who must have been from Spain because they spoke only Spanish. Up close was a black Brit with a baby in his backpack. Together we watched, cheered and clapped for half an hour during the magnificent display.

We limped tiredly and emotionally exhausted back to our hotel. The next morning we awoke and went out in the streets. And behold, we were right. The world as we knew it had ended. The signs were everywhere. They were on the billboards. The top three billboards in London, England, on January 1, 2000:

- The first was an advertisement that said, "If we build it, they will .com" (a pleasant reference to the Iowa-based movie *Field of Dreams*).
- The second billboard was rather traditional, "Ring out the old, click in the new."
- And the third billboard was Julie's favorite. It featured a woman in bed with a laptop, and the headline read, "Shop until you drop off."

Indeed, the Industrial Age had ended. It was a symbolic ending, but about as good a symbol as one can get. We were not just in a new century. We were in a new age, the Internet Age.

As we look back on it, it was important to say good-bye to the Industrial Age. This was the age in which we grew up. It was all we had known. It was everything familiar to us. It was a wonderful century, a wonderful time. A time in which, overall, life became better for humankind. And yet it was gone. And it cannot come back. And it cannot be preserved. And we have to distance ourselves from it. As the great adult educator Jerry Apps says, we have to grieve the loss of old ideas. We have to grieve the loss of a whole way of life. And Apps adds, and we have to decide "what to leave behind, and what to keep." There are some things we do not need to give up. There are some things we can keep. Just not most things. We can only keep a few things.

And so we tell you the story of the new millennium because we all need to celebrate the last century, and then say good-bye to it. We have to separate ourselves from this past which is so familiar and so ingrained in us. We have to "unlearn" as Jerry Apps says.[4]

Once we say good-bye to that way of life, we can understand and accept that it is now an obsolete way of life. It is not "bad," but simply no longer relevant. And then we can be excited about starting over and looking forward to our new century, the 21st century.

The Wizard of Oz

For more than twenty years we lived in Manhattan, Kansas. But we did not grow up in Kansas. So we signed up for a class on the Wizard of Oz, the most famous American fairy tale ever written.

It turns out that *The Wizard of Oz* was written a little over 100 years ago, in 1900. The movie came out in 1939. But L. Frank Baum wrote the book at the turn of the last century.

The Wizard of Oz is about the transition society was going through at that time. Up until that time we were an agrarian society. Most people earned their living by farming.

Baum saw that things were going to be different, that we were going to move into what would become known as the Industrial Age. He knew that life would be totally different. He understood somehow that the attitudes and the values of the agrarian pastoral society, which people had known, and he had known, and which had made America wonderful and great — that all of that was going to change.

And he was against that. He thought that was awful. So he created the scarecrow and the tin man and the lion to represent the virtues of the agrarian society.

He set it in Kansas because Kansas was like California in the 1960s. It was the land of golden opportunity. He had never been to Kansas. But ten years before he wrote the book, a New York newspaper man named Horace Greeley said, "Go west, young man." And so a million and a half people moved to Kansas within about ten years. It was a huge migration. Kansas was a symbol of prosperity and the good life. And that's why he set it in Kansas because he was saying, "Even in Kansas this awful transition is happening."[5]

Baum was right, of course. Everything did change. The Industrial Age took people off the family farm, moved them into cities. And it changed not only our way of life, but our values and attitudes. Your great grandparents lived very differently. Today we don't grow up in extended families; we don't spend weeks every year canning fruits and vegetables for the winter. We don't get our fresh vegetables from the garden. We don't rest on Sundays; kids don't help with the chores at an early age; we didn't go to school with children of all ages and abilities; most of us don't hunt; we no longer view a handshake as a binding contract.

Now, 100 years later, we are going through another total and gut-wrenching change in society. It is not just the turning of the century to which we are witness. It is not just the changing of the millennium. But it is the moving from one age, the Industrial Age that all of us adults have grown up on and known, and moving into the next age, which is the Internet Age.

The Reluctance to Change

Now one hundred years ago, in 1900, there were similar great celebrations welcoming a new century. In the United States, the economy was at a high, having come out of a recession earlier in the decade, and people felt prosperous. The situation was very much like that a century later in the 1990s and the new millennium.

It was also a time of great predictions.

It is the nature, or business, of predictions that most of them do not come true. But a great many predictions do indeed come true. So it was in 1900. Many things, such as human travel to Mars, did not come to pass in the 20th century. But a great many others did indeed occur, right on schedule. The *Ladies Home Journal* at the time devoted a special issue to predictions about the 20th century. Some of them that were quite accurate. Here are a couple.

- About suburbs, life span, and commuting:
  "The American will live fifty years instead of thirty-five as at present — for he will reside in the suburbs. The city house will practically be no more. The trip from the suburban home to office will require a few minutes only."
- About fast food restaurants:
  "Ready-cooked meals will be bought from establishments similar to our bakeries of today. They will purchase materials in tremendous wholesale quantities and sell the cooked foods at a price much lower than the cost of individual cooking."[6]

The great educator and writer Henry Adams, writing in 1904, looked ahead and noted:

"Every American who lived into the year 2000 would know how to control unlimited power. He would think in complexities unimaginable to an earlier mind. He would deal with problems altogether beyond the range of earlier society. To him the nineteenth century would stand on the same plane with the fourth — equally childlike — and he would only wonder how both of them, knowing so little, and so weak in force, should have done so much."[8]

Adams was correct in his assessment. Even his forecast of "unlimited power," which we might not claim, would in his view come true, as microwave ovens, downloading files from anywhere in the world in seconds, getting on an airplane and going to Europe in six hours, and so on, were indeed unimaginable to the average citizen in 1900.

And yet most everyone did not believe these predictions. Most everyone believed that the agrarian society into which they were born and raised was the height of civilization. That nothing could be better. And that it would basically remain, with only some minor additions (such as the automobile and factory) and enhancements.

There was debate, to be sure. In the opening scene of *The Music Man*, the famous 1957 musical by Meredith Willson, two salesmen in the early part of the century are debating whether there are fundamental changes underway. The lyrics include:

" ...ya can talk all ya wanna but it's different than it was

No it ain't, no it ain't, but you gotta know the territory

Why it's the Model T Ford, made the trouble, made the people wanna go, wanna get, wanna get, wanna get up and go...

Who's gonna patronize a little bitty two by four kinda store anymore?

Gone, gone, gone with the hogshead cask and demijohn, gone with the sugar barrel, pickle barrel, milk pan, gone with the tub and the pail and the tierce..."[9]

The classic description of how people in the first two decades of the 20th century did not see the fundamental changes underway is told in *Main Street*, by Sinclair Lewis, named one of the top one hundred novels of the 20th century.

It was published in 1920, just 'moments' after the events in the book took place. And yet it described rural and small town way of life that was already in the past tense.

For the people in the book, living in the first two decades of the 20th century, there were no fundamental changes underway. As Lewis writes, "Main Street is the climax of civilization... Our railway station is the final aspiration of architecture... Such is our comfortable tradition and sure faith."[10]

From the first page, Lewis makes sure we understand this is not a description of one town, but of American society. He begins, "This is America — a town of a few thousand, in a region of wheat and corn and dairies and little groves. The town is, in our tale, called 'Gopher Prairie, Minnesota.' But its Main Street is the continuation of Main Streets everywhere. The story would be the same in Ohio or Montana, in Kansas or Kentucky or Illinois, and not very differently would it be told Up York State or in the Carolina hills."[11]

The people in *Main Street* were not isolated from the changes taking place, they were in the middle of them. One civic leader brags, "Bresnahan — you know — the famous auto manufacturer — he comes from Gopher Prairie." The town has a Ford garage, and a Buick garage, "The most energetic and vital places in town."

Yet, the people didn't get it. And they did not approve of the other vast changes in life that were taking place, from women teaching in schools after they were married, to driving on Sunday.

They believed:
- The auto was a conveyance for pleasure, not work. The doctor would drive the auto on Sundays, but of course only in summer because in winter the roads had deep frozen ruts and in spring were too muddy for passage. The concept of someone driving to work, or the grocery store, or school, would have been a fantasy.
- The factory was a fad, a trend, but certainly not a replacement of the family farm as the primary place of employment. At one point in the book, the people of the town try to recruit a factory to remain trendy and progressive and enhance their small town's image.

They finally recruit a factory, one that made automobile tires — out of wood. Even with the Industrial Age and the growth of the automobile pressing down on them, they still did not get it.

When the book ends, somewhere around 1910, the town's citizens are still stuck in the Agrarian Age. There is a vague uneasiness about change. There is a vague resentment of the growth of the big city a half-day's journey (60 miles) away. But the citizens maintain their 19th century values, their 19th century habits. And they maintain that their tiny town will remain viable and prosperous.

The heroine is optimistic and vaguely aware of the changes that are taking place for her new born daughter, but her husband doesn't buy it.

"'Think what that baby will see and meddle with before she dies in the year 2000! She may see an industrial union of the whole world, she may see aeroplanes going to Mars.'

'Yump, probably be changes all right,' yawned Kennicott."[13]

Once again, the majority of people are unaware of the fundamental changes underway. We cling to the old way of life, its patterns, behaviors, and values. Yet once again, we are in the middle of all the excitement.

Some people already understand the great changes underway. At a museum exhibition about the new century, visitors were asked "Does the changing of the millennium mark a new period in our history?" Some 67.4%, or two-thirds, said yes, while 32.6%, or one-third, said no.

- Will your children be better off in the 21st century? Yes, 60.2%; No, 39.8%
- Will the United States dominate the world? Yes, 46.4%; No, 53.6%
- Are the technology advances worth their societal and environmental costs? Yes, 50.0%; No, 50.0%.[14]

One hundred years later, from 2000-2005, the vast majority of people act and speak very much like the people of *Main Street*.

- The Internet is a fad, a trend, an experiment, or even a permanent addition and enhancement. But the Internet will not fundamentally change the way we live, they believe.
- People will always work in centralized offices, spend hours commuting, spend hours every day driving automobiles, and live in suburbs.
- College administrators ask us whether there will still be a role for the residential brick-and-mortar university, hoping and believing that while everyone else may have to change, their particular institution will not. Sometimes we lie and tell them what they want to hear, but the odds are the same as telling a school marm 100 years ago that there will always be a place for the one-room school house.
- It is "impossible" to have a transportation system in this country without the automobile being the central and predominant mode of transportation, one Minnesota legislator recently declared. And in Wisconsin, like other states, the Department of Transportation was told to make plans to widen a four-lane highway to as many as 12 lanes, able to accommodate traffic growth for another 30 years.[15]
- Authors harangue the new changes, writing popular books that appeal to a majority opinion. Working from home is assailed as an impossibility, doomed to certain failure because one cannot manage people from a distance, due to the "inevitably face-to-face side of management," because of the "frailty of technological systems." The home becomes an "isolated social setting" and the home worker is "renouncing society."[16]

This reluctance, this resolve to ward off the threatening "next big thing" gets played out again and again. And with good reason. Most technological changes do not bring major societal changes. Most hyped "things-will-never-be-the-same" products do not substantially change our lives. Even "the big change," or a *nine shift,* does not change everything. But every once in a while, there IS a big change, a *nine shift.* And right now most of us are trying to figure out, trying to decide, whether this is the time. And will I have to change, or just everybody else? This is the way history flows.

Eleven Miles

The driving force in society for the 21st century is the computer chip and the Internet. For the 20th century, the Industrial Age, it was the automobile and the factory that made the automobile. One hundred years ago the richest men in America were John D. Rockefeller, Andrew Carnegie, and others involved in oil and steel — the stuff that made automobiles and made them go. Today the richest people in America are Bill Gates, Paul Allen, and others involved in computers and the Internet.

Just as the automobile shaped society in the 20th century, the Internet is shaping society in the 21st century. The automobile was not just a transportation vehicle. It created suburbs, the nuclear family, greater freedom for women, shopping malls, community colleges, consolidated school districts. And the factory that built the auto created an organizational structure based on the command and control pyramid of hierarchy. The computer chip and Internet are having a similarly dramatic and significant impact on all aspects of life in the 21st century.

We don't know yet all the ways the computer chip and Internet will influence our lives. But we do know already that the computer chip and Internet increase the need for knowledge and information. The need for current information, knowledge, and knowledge skills is so great that lifelong learning will be at the center of society, including the workplace, for at least the next hundred years.

To remain competitive and profitable, every business will increasingly rely on updated knowledge and skills from its people. So we know now that lifelong learning, which has already grown tremendously in the last 25 years, will increase even more dramatically in the years ahead.

To understand how the Internet is changing work, life and education in the 21st century, we go not to Bill Gates' house, not to Silicon Valley, but to Kansas, and to Frankfort, Kansas, in particular.

We have driven through Frankfort many times. It is about eight blocks long. There's nothing really there. There's a public school. The only store that's ever been open when we've driven through is a combination convenience store, gas station, soda grill, grocery store and youth center.

But a few years ago Bill's brother, who lives in Texas and frequents antique shops, found a brochure from 1907 for a department store in Frankfort. When he gave us the brochure, we could not believe that Frankfort ever had a department store of this magnitude. It was called Heleker's Department Store. It had more clothing and goods than any store you could possibly imagine in 1900 in the town of Frankfort, Kan-

Main street in Frankfort, Kansas, around 1900. The authors have never seen as much activity in Frankfort as there was 100 years ago.

The first cars in Frankfort, Kansas, during a cross country tour sponsored by the American Automobile Association in 1909.

sas, population 1,200. The store was like Nieman and Marcus. There was probably not a store in Washington, D.C., or Los Angeles that had more than Heleker's department store in Frankfort, Kansas.[17]

At Heleker's, they had 150 ladies' capes. They had shoes, shoes from the best line on earth. They had shoes for men, boys and youth, women, misses, and children. Here are just some of the shoes they had just for infants: Baby Budd shoes; infants' silk trimmed moccasins; infants' soft-solid button shoes. Today one cannot buy shoes at all in Frankfort.

Soon after receiving the brochure we decided to go to Frankfort again, because we wanted to find out why there was a department store there in 1907, and what was going on in 1907 in Frankfort. So we called up the library. It was closed. So we called the police station. We got an answering machine. Finally we found someone and they told us about June, the librarian, and we called June and she invited us up to the Frankfort library that afternoon.

So we drove on up. The Frankfort library today is a one-room library. And we said, "We're interested in knowing about the department store that was here in 1907." And June said, "Which one?" It turns out there were four department stores in Frankfort back then.

So we asked her what life was like in Frankfort in 1907. She said Frankfort in 1907 had six banks. It had four department stores. There were two opera houses. Frankfort had an African-American community. It had a racetrack. It had a newspaper. Not just a newspaper, but a daily newspaper. In the daily newspaper you can see the train schedule of the daily train going from Frankfort, Kansas, to New York city. The bankers were millionaires who imported marble and stained glass for their homes from Italy. It turns out there were thousands of people who came to Frankfort to do business, shop and attend cultural events.

Frankfort was a pretty special place, we thought. "Well," we asked June, "where was the next town where there was an opera house and millionaire bankers?" June said, "Eleven miles away in Blue Rapids, Kansas."[18]

It turns out Frankfort was not unique. This was how America lived. This wasn't just Frankfort. This was all of America. Because in the early 1900s, a majority of people in society farmed. We were in a rural, agrarian economy. And a large farm back then was 80 acres.

When you fly over the country, look down on the ground and you will see little squares. Those are each one square mile. It is called a section. There are 640 acres to a section. Today Kansas farms and ranches are thousands of acres. A 10,000 acre farm is not unusual.

Page from Heleker's Department Store advertisement, Frankfort, Kansas, 1907.

But in the early 1900s, a farmer had 80 acres if he was lucky. An 80 acre farm was about as much land as one family could farm with the existing technology of the horse. And so all around Frankfort were hundreds and thousands of people who were farming, and they all came to Frankfort to buy goods, be entertained, and to visit. And then something happened. They invented the automobile and they invented gasoline. The first automobile was sold in 1896, just a few years before *The Wizard of Oz* was written.

Two years after the brochure from Heleker's Department Store was published, in 1909, the first automobiles rolled into Frankfort on a cross country tour of small rural towns. And within ten years Frankfort, Kansas, was in decline. The opera houses closed. Heleker's Department Store went out of business. The millionaire banker went bankrupt and went back to Scotland where he died penniless. People left town, moved to the big city, went to work in the factories.

What did Frankfort do wrong? It did nothing wrong. Instead, the automobile, gasoline, the factory and the Industrial Age changed everything about the way people lived. But we don't think people woke up in 1915 and said, "My grandfather farmed. My father farmed. I think I'm going to go to the factory and assembly line in Kansas City or Omaha and get a job."

We don't think that's what happened. We think a more important use of gasoline powered engines than the car was the tractor. The reason the largest farm was 80 acres was because that was what a horse could plow. With a tractor one could plow more land. One could plow 160 acres, 320 acres, 640 acres, 1,280 acres and more. And the tractor could plow deeper than a horse-drawn plow, so there was more yield per acre. Which meant there were fewer farms.

So the invention of the tractor caused people to have to move off the farm and into the cities. Today we would call it "downsizing." People had to get different jobs. And a whole way of life changed.[19]

Think of your area of expertise, your work or 'business' if you will, as an 80 acre farm. We are all running little 80 acre farms. And the tractor — in the form of the Internet — is about to change how we work, live, and learn.

We tell you the story of Frankfort, Kansas, because once again life is changing. By 2020 we will no longer be living in the Industrial Age of the 20th century. Work, life and education will be very different.

The turning of the century was not just the turning of the clock, but it signaled in the most symbolic way possible the transition from the Industrial Age of the last century into the Information or Internet Age of the current century. We have to say good-bye to that former way of living in order to welcome the new way of living, and while not everything will change, most things will. The old ways were not bad ways. The attitudes and values of the Agrarian Age were good and relevant and useful to the times. But they were not appropriate for the Industrial Age. Likewise, the attitudes, values, and behavior of the Industrial Age were good, but they are not appropriate for the Internet Age.

Just like 100 years ago, the majority of people in the first decade of the century are reluctant to change or to see the full extent of the changes taking place. But like your great-grandfather's generation, that change is happening quickly and soon will significantly change our lives.

Chapter 2
The Auto and the Internet

"Now candidly, wouldn't you like to know what sayers will be saying, thinkers thinking, writers writing, doers doing, and plotters plotting at the end of the next hundred years."
— *Platteville (Wisconsin) Journal, January 11, 1901*

Every once in awhile, a technology comes along that is so influential that it changes the way we live. Work, life and education are reorganized around the technology, and it defines a given age. Such is the case with both the automobile and the Internet.

There are more important inventions, to be sure. Electricity, the printing press, and probably trains are a few. But their influence spans the centuries, and does not define a particular age. Electricity has been equally valuable in the 19th, 20th and now 21st centuries. The printing press has played a critical role in society for the past 500 years.

There are many inventions that have become universal, but yet have not changed how we work or live. Movies, television, radio, airplanes are a few examples. The airplane, for example, changes how we travel, but has not changed how we shop, where we live, or the basic nature of our jobs.

From Technology to Values

A transformative technology changes how we live. Here's how it happens.

- The technology changes the economy, including the means of production, how we build things, buy things and sell things.
- The new economy then changes the job structure, including what jobs are valued and available.
- The new job structure then changes the work place, and how we work.
- How we work and earn a living are so central to life that home and family are impacted.
- The new living situation then determines the nature of our local community.
- The new economy, new job structure, and nature of work also determines how we prepare young people for the workplace, and so education and schools are redesigned.
- And finally, all of the above changes lead to a new set of values and attitudes.

The changes are not totally sequential. Many of them occur concurrently. And the changes do not occur totally. They may take several decades to play themselves out. But all in all, this is how it happens.

Here's how the sequence of change played out in the 20th century.

- The automobile created a mass demand, and its cousin the tractor created a decrease in the number of farmers needed. This led to a significant increase in the output of factories (led by gas refineries and iron, steel, and automobile factories) and mass production of goods.
- The increase in factory output led to a dramatic increase in factory and office jobs, and the decline of farm jobs.
- The factory and office led to the organization chart and the behavioral norms and expectations of the factory and office. A few examples include the 40 hour work week, first, second and third shifts, starting work at a precise time, hourly wages, middle managers, and so on.
- The industrialized work situation led to greater family mobility, the nuclear family and the decline of the extended family.
- The nuclear family led to suburbs.
- The factory and office led to mandated universal high school education, the consolidation of schools, age-grades, and schools that look and function like offices and factories.
- New values and attitudes set in. They include shopping on Sunday, women's right to smoke and drink, the showing of the ankle among ladies, and many more.

The 20th century is widely called the "Industrial Age" because industry jobs (factory and office) rose to constitute half of all the jobs in the economy during the century. The Industrial Age is not the Industrial Revolution, which took place in the early 1800s. The factory was created in the Industrial Revolution. But factory jobs did not surpass farm jobs until the 20th century, the Industrial Age.

The same scenario is playing out now with the Internet, impacting work, life, and education changes once again.

Here's how it is playing out in the 21st century:

- The Internet has created a different kind of economy, one in which mass customization is possible, information and knowledge is critical, distance is no longer a barrier (and sometimes is an advantage), intangibles such as speed, design, and customer service rise in importance, and technology takes over an ever growing number of routine tasks from people.

- At the same time, the resulting technology allows manufactured goods to be produced by fewer factory workers, as well as in countries where labor is less expensive, causing a huge decline in the number of people employed in manufacturing.

- The technology creates knowledge jobs, those jobs which utilize a person's thinking skills to a high degree. Knowledge jobs are the only jobs that add value in an advanced society.

- Knowledge workers grow in number, and find that they not only can do their work at home, but that they can do it better from home.

- With a workforce now working from home, companies find that not only are physical offices a liability, but that intranets can accomplish what the office used to do, and the intranet can do it better.

- With people working from home, they become linked to each other in relatively small business units that are more flexible and efficient than in large departmental structures. Organizations are thus refigured into networks instead of the pyramid of the organization chart.

- With time being the principle resource of a knowledge worker, time becomes far more valuable. Consequently people desire shops, stores, clubs and centers to be close to home. Thus communities become much more dense.

- Commuting becomes unnecessary and driving wastes too much time, so knowledge workers switch to trains and light rail for transportation, able to work while they are traveling.

- Social structures, government policy, federal and state "safety nets" are all redesigned around the new economic reality of the 21st century.

- To save time, tap into the expertise of the world's foremost authorities, and engage with similar professionals around the globe, half of all learning is done online.
- To prepare young people for this new work environment, schools and colleges become web based, as do other nonprofit institutions serving society.

Each one of the changes, these nine shifts, is a logical and necessary outcome of people working in a new environment.

The Internet was created in the 1970s. The Internet is the vast number of computers linked to each other. The Internet was invented by scientists and others working for the defense department in the United States government, along with researchers in universities. The Internet was invented by people in the nonprofit sector.

The World Wide Web was invented around 1991 by Tim Berners-Lee. He worked for a nonprofit organization in Switzerland called CERN. The World Wide Web is the common language that allows us to understand the information stored on another computer.

While we understand the difference between the Internet and the World Wide Web, in this book we will generally use the word "Internet" as a vernacular term to describe either or both the Internet and World Wide Web.

At about the same time that Berners-Lee invented the World Wide Web, the economy in advanced or industrialized nations began to change. Before that time, the advanced nations were indeed "industrialized nations." But sometime in 1991 or so economists say that the annual investment capital in information technology: computers, software, and related items, became greater than the annual investment capital generated by equipment, or hard goods. To give an example, more of the cost of an automobile produced today is for information technology than it is for steel, metal, seat covers, and the other hard goods that go into a car.

Thus, economists point to the early 1990s as the first years of what they called the "Information Age." For those of us in the post-industrialized nations of the world, we are now in an economy where the information required for economic life constitutes the most important aspect of economic activity, whether it be service, manufacturing, retail or even agriculture. Just about every expert says we are in an Information Age for the long haul, with no end in sight. No one forecasts that this will change.

By 1996 the first financial transactions were taking place on the Internet. Buying and selling and business had come to the Internet.

The 1990s were also a period of intellectual fervor and productivity related to the Internet. John Hagel III and Arthur G. Armstrong wrote *Net Gain* and introduced us to the concept of virtual communities.[1] James Martin authored *Cybercorp* and noted how computers and technology perform a number of economic functions better than humans.[2] Bruce A. Pasternack and Albert S. Viscio wrote *The Centerless Corporation* and popularized the notion of business units replacing the pyramid structure.[3] Dan Sullivan wrote *The Great Crossover* and showed us how the organizational structure, or pyramid, had permeated our lives in the 20th century and formed a framework for not just our work lives but our social and community lives as well. Sullivan helped us understand that as the pyramid declines, we go through a personal and emotional transition that can be very difficult.[4] Stacey Horne "lived" online and shared the first experiences of what online culture is like in *Cyberville*.[5]

Much of what is taking place and will take place was envisioned by these thinkers during the last decade.

The Undisputed and Irreversible Trend

At the same time, a more fundamental and irreversible change became more widely known and documented. The percentage of people employed in manufacturing went into decline. This had been happening for awhile. But it was only in recent years that the situation became publicized. One overt sign was of jobs moving to the developing nations. Another symptom was the number and amount of imports of manufactured goods into the United States. Army hats and even American flags were no longer made in the United States, for instance.

We need to separate manufacturing employment from manufacturing productivity or output. Manufacturing productivity or output may increase. But the definitive line that is moving us in this great change, this Nine Shift, is the irreversible decline in the percentage of our workforce engaged in manufacturing and factory jobs.

Manufacturing employment during the middle of the 20th century rose to 50% of the workforce or more.[6] It has since declined to less than 20% of the workforce. Some figures say lower.[7] What is critical is that the line is heading downward. And no economist, politician, businessperson or corporation predicts that manufacturing employment will even stabilize, much less rise again.

The only forecasts are that manufacturing employment will continue to decline.

Manufacturing employment at the beginning of the 20th century was less than 25% of jobs. In 1900 about 50% of employment was in farming. About half of us in 1900 worked on a family farm. As society back then moved from an Agrarian Age to the Industrial Age, the percentage of workers engaged in farming went into decline, a long slow but steady and irreversible decline. By the end of the 20th century, employment in farming was less than 2% of the workforce, and may still be declining.[8]

One hundred years ago, manufacturing employment was growing and sometime between 1910 and 1920 surpassed farming as the leading employer of the workforce. Thus, we had passed from the Agrarian Age into the Industrial Age.

"The blue-collar worker in manufacturing industry and his union are going the way of the farmer," writes management guru Peter F. Drucker. "The newly emerging dominant group are 'knowledge workers.' Knowledge workers amount to a third or more of the workforce in the United States…"[9]

This is the indisputable and irreversible force that is at the base of the current transition in which our lives will be transformed. There is no decision to make. There is no choice. There is little argument to be made.

We can emotionally refuse, deny, or ignore this transition. We can be unaware of it. We can hold on to the Industrial Age in our behavior, attitudes, and values.

We know that sometime between 1910 and 1920 the number of industrial jobs in the economy surpassed the number of farm jobs. The lines on the chart crossed, signaling a new era. And work, how we live, and education all changed in accordance with the new Industrial Age.

During the 20th century, the lines on the chart did not cross. Industrial jobs rose, and then fell, but no other sector of jobs exceeded industrial jobs. So we stayed in the Industrial Age.

Today, manufacturing jobs show the same decline as farm jobs did 100 years ago. And no one has predicted that this trend line can or will be reversed. At some time, and it looks like between 2010 and 2020, Information Age or knowledge sector jobs will exceed industrial jobs. The lines will cross again. Life has to change again, in accordance with the new Information or Internet Age.

Employment determines where we live, how we live, what we are able to do in much of our non-work time, and much more. Just as it was nigh impossible for the majority of us to work in a factory job and then return at night to the family farm, so it is nigh impossible for the majority of us to work in the information sector, the knowledge sector, and to return at night to a life embedded in the Industrial Age.

Suburbs, commuting, malls, television and two week summer vacations were just some of the products of the Industrial Age. And as we move out of the Industrial Age into the Information Age, what may be more appropriately called the Internet Age, these features of a past society will fade as well. This is a nine shift.

What's a Phaeton?

To find out how this nine shift occurs, how this transition is accomplished, we can look back 100 years to the timeline and way in which the car replaced the carriage.

As the twentieth century opened, the horse and buggy were the dominant means of transportation for most people in society, next to walking. Even as late as 1913, very few people foresaw that the automobile would replace the horse and buggy. And yet, as we know, within 20 years the horse and buggy became obsolete, replaced by the automobile.

When the twentieth century opened, there were only 13,824 automobiles. As F.L. Allen writes in *The Big Change*, "For in 1900 everybody thought of automobiles as playthings of the rich — not merely of the rich, but of the somewhat adventurous and sporting rich: people who enjoyed taking their chances with an unpredictable machine that might at any moment wreck them."[10] There were no paved roads, no gasoline stations, no handy mechanics in the neighborhood.

Today, similar charges are made about the Internet. The Internet is not a necessity, it is an enhancement. The technology breaks down frequently. Each person has to be his or her own "techie." Not many people in the world have broadband connections (paved roads).

Just as people in fifty years will look back on 2000 as a more primitive time when there were thousands of offices, millions of cars, and homes spread out in unwieldy suburbs, so too we look back at 1900 with the same view. As Allen tells us,

"Horses were everywhere, pulling surreys, democrats, buggies, cabs, delivery wagons of every sort on Main Street, and pulling harvesters on the tractor-less farms out in the countryside.

"The sights and sounds and sensations of horse-and-carriage life were part of the universal American experience: the clop-clop of horses' hoofs; the stiff jolting of an iron-tired carriage on a stony road; the grinding noise of the brake being applied to ease the horse on a downhill stretch; the necessity of holding one's breath when the horse sneezed; the sight of sand, carried up on the tires and wooden spokes of a carriage wheel,

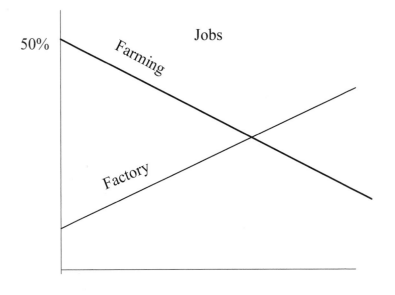

50%

Jobs

Farming

Factory

1900   1920

One hundred years ago, the percentage of people employed on farms went into steep decline from about 50% of the population in 1900. Somewhere in the second decade the percentage of people employed in factories, manufacturing and offices exceeded the percentage of people employed on farms.

Source: Statistical History of the U. S., Fairfield Publishers, p. 74

spilling off in little cascades as the wheel revolved; the look of a country road overgrown by grass, with three tracks in it instead of two, the middle one made by horses' hoofs; the special male ordeal of getting out of the carriage and walking up the steeper hills to lighten the load; and the more severe ordeal, for the unpracticed, of harnessing a horse which could recognize inexperience at one scornful glance."[11]

It was impossible for people to think of a society without horse drawn vehicles, just as it is impossible for most people today to think of a society without the car as the main source of transportation.

In 1903, Henry Ford's own banker said, "The automobile is just a fad. The horse and buggy is here to stay." Over the next several years, the auto gained recognition, but not much. In 1904, the Family Educator noted, "While there will not be a time when horses will no longer be used to draw vehicles, the automobile has attained such success that it is no longer a mere experiment."[12]

In the same year of 1904, the Republican Governor of Wisconsin, Robert M. LaFollette, began to use an automobile to campaign around the state. One of the state's largest newspapers, the *Milwaukee Sentinel*, opposed the use of a car. The newspaper charged the governor with endangering the population and causing horses to get out of control by driving.[13]

By 1908, the automobile was fairly well established. And yet people still did not believe it would replace the horse and buggy. In that year, an encyclopedia noted, "It is impossible to say what further changes [in buggies and carriages] may be introduced by the automobile."[14]

And this was probably the most ironic example of how the general public did not understand that the auto would replace the horse and buggy. In the city of Hartford, Connecticut, a local man named Alexander Pope became a pioneer in the invention of the automobile. He was famous and lauded widely. When he died in 1913, the city decided to honor him by building a memorial in a downtown Hartford city park. And so they built the memorial, a big, beautiful — horse trough.[15] They simply did not get it.

One day in an antique store we ran across an encyclopedia from 1908, and looked up carriages. We were astounded to read about the diversity of buggies and carriages. There were:

"Gig, sulky, and go-cart; chaise, calash, cariole, coupe, hansom, and jaunting car; coach, brougham, barouche, rock-away, landau, and victoria; buggy, phaeton, and surrey; cab, hackney, fiacre, and drosky; drag, carryall, and tally-ho; wagonette, barge, stage, and omnibus; dray, express wagon, and van; cart, truck, and farm wagon

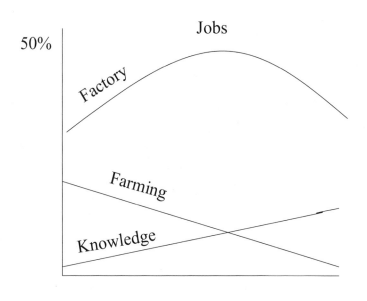

Most adults today grew up experiencing these trends. The percentage of people employed in manufacturing peaked at around 50% in mid-century and then went into a decline. The percentage of people in farming continued to decline to below 2% of those employed. Knowledge work, which was not categorized as such, grew somewhat.

Source: Statistical Abstract of the U. S., 1996, National Data Book, p. 410

— there is no end to the classes, styles, and variations."[16]

We loved the word phaeton. We wanted to find out what a phaeton was. Prior to 1900, buggies and carriages were too expensive for many people. The situation was documented in the popular song *Bicycle Built for Two*, where "I can't afford a carriage, but you'll look sweet on a bicycle built for two." In the second verse, Daisy responds that she will not marry someone who cannot afford a carriage. Before the turn of the century, most people walked. The advance in manufacturing drove down the price of a buggy or carriage, and enabled companies to make more of them.

Bill's great grandfather Thorkelson helped run a buggy company called the Beebe Cart company. The Beebe Company specialized in two wheeled carts that could more easily go through mud without getting bogged down. With a flexible axle, it could go over logs and rough spots in the road without breaking.

The first automobile was sold in 1896. And in 1901 Ransom Olds built the first automobile assembly line.

The introduction, development and growth of the automobile in society followed the exact same path as the introduction, development and growth of the Internet today. To understand the changes today, we need only look back exactly 100 years.

1. Most new players do not make it.

Many people dismiss the Internet by pointing to the thousands of failures of Internet businesses, the dot.com crash. Yet the same situation took place with the automobile. In 1903, for instance, some 57 companies began making cars, while 27 others went out of business.

In all, some 2,200 companies made automobiles at one time or another. By 1920 there were 80. By 1940 there were 40. And by 1970 Americans spoke of the "Big 3" automakers.

2. Initial decline is slight.

The sales of buggies and carriages did not immediately decline upon the invention of the auto.

The 1910 Census enumerates the following numbers and types of horse-drawn vehicles produced in those years.

Year	Carriages	Wagons	Public Conveyances
1899	904,639	570,428	2,218
1904	937,409	643,755	2,711
1909	828,411	587,685	2,243[17]

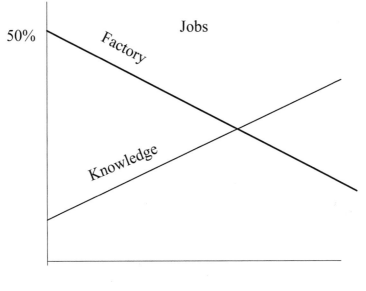

50%   Factory   Jobs

Knowledge

2000   2020

In the 21st century, the same employment transition is occurring as 100 years ago. The percentage of people engaged in manufacturing has declined from 50% down to around 15% already and continues to decline. The percentage of people engaged in knowledge work is increasing. The percentage of the work force engaged in knowledge work is likely to exceed those engaged in factory work sometime between 2010 and 2020.

Around 1 million carriages were sold every year in the first decade of the twentieth century. Sales declined only about 10% during that ten year period. The price also came down, so that a buggy could be purchased via mail order from Sears-Roebuck for as little as $16.

"After 1909, production of horse-drawn vehicles declined drastically. In 1919, only 216,000 carriages, buggies and sulkies and 324,000 farm wagons, trucks and business vehicles were produced."[18]

The turning point in the manufacturing and sales of buggies and carriages was 1909, after which they went into steep decline. Great grandfather Thorkelson retired from his carriage business in 1908, probably not a coincidence.

3. Mergers and adaptations occur.

In the second half of the first decade, there were mergers and adaptations going on. Carriages took on some features of automobiles. Automobiles, or horseless carriages, of course, took on many aspects of the carriage, from the rumble seat to the running board to the wooden siding in a station wagon.

"In 1909," says the 19th Century American Carriages book, "there were 14,908 carriages, 42,112 wagons and 104 public vehicles produced by firms engaged primarily in the manufacture of products other than carriages. Conversely, carriage and wagon manufacturers produced 174 automobiles in 1899, 199 automobiles in 1904 and 544 automobiles in 1909."

"Obviously this was a period of transition and experimentation for those in the business of producing road vehicles."

The authors of the carriage book continue, "By 1908 the impact of the automobile is readily discernible in the Sears Roebuck advertisement of an automobile seat top buggy described as 'A high class stylish up to date automobile seat top buggy' with a 'special design automobile bent front wing dash.'"[19]

During this time some carriage companies began making cars. Studebaker, a famous car company known for its high quality, was a carriage company at the start of the century. John Deere, the well-known tractor company, made wagons at the start of the century. Great grandfather Thorkelson's carriage company was sold to the John Deere company sometime just before 1910.

In the years after 1910 most of the companies that made both horse-drawn vehicles and motor vehicles dropped the manufacture of their horse-drawn vehicles and made only motor vehicles. This was often accompanied by a name change of the company, or simply dropping a few words from the company name.

4. Obsolescence takes decades.

Horse drawn vehicles did not disappear quickly from the scene, and years later were held in high regard, even while in steep decline. Farm animals and wagons continued to be in use on farms until the tractor made them completely obsolete decades later.

The most lingering example of the vestigial use of the horse was in the military. In 1939, the United States Army still believed that men on horseback could do battle with Hitler's tanks. In that year, President Franklin D. Roosevelt went to Alabama to see the preparations for the coming world war. When he saw the cavalry, he immediately dismantled the units.

5. Infrastructure is different.

The switch from horse drawn vehicles to motor vehicles was not a simple transition for some businesses. While an individual or family could simply sell the horse and buggy and buy an auto, it was much more complicated for a business. For a business, the transition could involve changing jobs and employment, contractors, side industries, investments, and an entirely different infrastructure.

6. Some advantages are lost.

There were some advantages that were lost with the transition from the horse to the horseless carriage. The auto was not superior to the horse drawn vehicle in all respects. Milk delivery businesses, for example, were reluctant to switch from horse drawn wagons to trucks for one very good reason. The horse, once trained, would move forward to the next house without a command or driver, and stop at the next house while the delivery man deposited the milk bottles at one house and went to the next. A truck couldn't do that.[20] And of course, the automobile created an enormous annual death toll ranging from 30,000 to 50,000 people a year, depriving society of many talented people of all ages.

The decline of the carriage illustrates several key features about how a new technology, even a dominant one, takes over. It is not immediate and not immediately recognizable. It has its ups and downs. The previous technology merges with it and contributes to it. Then the previous technology fades, imperceptibly at first, and even the eventual decline takes decades. Clearly, the growth of the Internet is taking the same path.

And what is a phaeton? Look up "phaeton" on the Internet, and one finds something other than a type of carriage. Look the word up in the dictionary, and one might find the Latin root, but no carriage. We raced Bill's mom to find out what a phaeton was, and she won.

A phaeton was a model of carriage. The George IV or Lady's Phaeton was a beautiful carriage for the well to do, and not just the well-to-do man, but the well-to-do woman as well. It was like a Lexus or Rolls Royce. It was top of the line. It had headlights, powered by gas, as there was no electricity in carriages then. It had beautiful leather seats. It had shock absorbers, something rare for horse-drawn vehicles. It had a convertible top. It had thick cushions on the seat. The Lady's Phaeton, to our view the grandest carriage of them all, had a graceful swooping line along each side of the carriage. The low cut sides had two purposes, other than being so beautiful. One was to make the step up into the carriage more manageable for the ladies. And the other purpose, oh what a purpose. It was so everyone on each side of the street could see the fabulous gown the lady was wearing as she rode in the phaeton down the street. It was like a one-person Easter parade whenever a lady rode in her phaeton. To stand on the side of the street and watch this beautiful carriage come down the street, and then see whatever wonderful gown the lady was wearing, was always cause for excitement. Oh what a sight it must have been!

The phaeton has faded into history, first as a carriage and now a century later, even as a recognizable word. But it did not fade without first bringing the classic style, grace, name and image to the automobile. For during the 1910s and 1920s there were high-priced luxury automobiles called phaetons.

The *New York Times* recently ran the obituary of a man, noting, "His father, the owner of a printing company, was so prosperous that he bought a Phaeton Studebaker with disc wheels in 1924."[21]

The automobile shaped life in the 20th century. The Internet is shaping life in the 21st century. Just as the 1890s were a period of intellectual fervor, new ideas, and the first commercial sale of the automobile, so too were the 1990s a decade of intellectual creativity resulting from the creation of the World Wide Web. The first e-commerce transaction took place around 1996, 100 years after the first automobile was sold.

To see how the new technology takes hold of the economy, we can study the decline of the carriage and other horse drawn vehicles in relationship to the rise of the automobile. The same characteristics of the transition from carriage to car can be seen being played out today with the transition from the Industrial Age to the Information or Internet Age. The timeline of this transition from 1900 to 1920 gives us a guidepost to the transition going on today in our society.

Chapter 3
Your Pyramid is Collapsing

"In times of change, the learner will inherit the earth while the learned are beautifully equipped for a world that no longer exists."
— *Eric Hoffer, American philosopher, 1902-1983*

We all work in an organizational pyramid, a pyramid that is collapsing. For almost all of the 20th century, from approximately 1910 through 1999, most of us have worked in organizations. And those organizations have had structures. They are organized like a pyramid. We understand our workplace pyramid. It is called an organization chart.

Some three-fourths of people reading this book have a boss. Many of you have a boss who has a boss. About one-quarter of those of you reading this book have people reporting to you. Most of you have people "above" you on the organizational chart, and someone "below" you on the organizational chart. That is a pyramid.

There were few organizational pyramids 100 years ago. Some 50% of our great grandparents worked on a family farm. They did not have an organizational pyramid. They had an extended family. Some had a hired hand, but they did not have a boss. Another percentage of the population worked in shops and stores, churches and schools, in small towns. And they did not have bosses, or people reporting to them, either.

In the early part of the century, as people moved from farms into the pyramid structure of the factory and office, they had to be told about the organization chart. As one source explains, "The success of any business enterprise rests on a combination of plant and organization. No business can succeed unless emphasis is placed on workers belonging to both groups."[1]

The organizational chart is not the only similarity between the office and the factory. A history of the office on the Smithsonian web site notes, "By the 1920s any real difference between some office work and the factory production line had disappeared. The office, like the factory, was tedious and stressful for the worker and closely monitored by the manager."[2]

The organizational pyramid was very functional for the Industrial Age of factories and offices. But it does not work in the Information Age. It is in the process of collapsing as the nature of work is changed by the Internet.

Here are the top ten things people say when their pyramid is collapsing:

10. "I can't make that decision."
9. "We've always done it that way."
8. "Our computer can't do that."
7. "That's not in my job description."
6. "We can't get that information from our computer (or computer department)."
5. "They won't give us the staff to do that."
4. "We have to serve everyone. We have to....."
3. "I'm overworked."
2. "They'd fire me if I tried that."
1. "My boss should be hearing this."

Forty years ago, one did not hear these comments. Because forty years ago the pyramid worked. Forty years ago people did not say "My boss should be hearing this" because then the boss was the only one going to seminars and conferences, so the boss was hearing whatever was being said.

The pyramid, the organizational structure of the "bricks and mortar" Industrial Age of offices, has become dysfunctional. It no longer works.

As we will see in a later chapter, networks composed of "business units" are replacing the organizational pyramid.

Whether you will need to be part of the transition from the organizational pyramid to the network in your workplace depends on when you plan to retire.

If you plan on retiring around 2005, you don't have to change. If you are still in the work force between 2006 and 2010, you will have to face the problems as your organizational pyramid collapses. If you will be in the workforce between 2010 and 2029, you will have to change. You also will have to lead the change in your company or organization. And if you do not plan to retire until 2030 or later, you probably have already changed. That is, you probably understand even now why the pyramid is outmoded, and you will easily accept and work in a network structure.

In the workplace, there will be two types of companies and organizations. One type will undergo the transition from a pyramid structure to a network structure. The other type will not change. In either case, you as a worker have no choice. You will need to change.

If your company begins transforming itself into a networked organization, then you will need to become a knowledge worker and function as part of a business unit in that network. Employees who cannot change will not be needed anymore. Employees who cannot change will be a burden on the company.

If your company is resistant to being restructured into business units and wants to remain with the pyramid structure, it likely will not survive very long. Thus, you will need to seek work in another organization, most likely one functioning with business units in a network.

The 40-acre family farm did not survive in the 20th century. Not even larger family farms succeeded very well. So if your organization stays in the pyramid mode of operation, it will crumble, which means you will need to look for work.

At the time of this writing we are in a period when the dysfunctionality of the organizational pyramid is becoming apparent. People spend too much time in staff meetings. We spend too much time commuting. We spend too little time getting input from front line staff. We spend too much time making decisions that can be determined better by computer analysis or a front line person closer to the situation. Technology is used too little.

When we spent a week in a hospital following an operation, we had a different nurse come into the room four times a day. Every time the nurse would try to turn down the temperature, and we would have to explain that the doctor wanted the room to be warm in order to speed Julie's healing. With technology, the doctor's orders could be verified in advance by every nurse attending to us. Instead, relying on outmoded forms of communication for information transfer, such as paper and pen and verbal instructions, time was wasted, and the chance of error increased. At the same time, when face-to-face communication is used for information transfer, we don't have the time for the very valuable communication that can only take place in-person.

Sometime around 2010 we will see an increasing number of companies begin to transition from the pyramid structure to networks. This transition is taking place alongside the other shifts we have cited.

Led by a change in the nature of work, and the nature of one's job, and then the nature of one's organizational structure, these nine shifts are occurring: slowly, with some backward motion as well as forward motion, with little publicity, with resistance. But moving nevertheless.

By looking back to the years from 1900 to 1920, we can see the timeline over the next two decades for the changes in our work, living, and learning.

The Coming Conflict

At the time of this writing, we are moving out of the first stage in the transition, from 2000 to 2005, and moving into the next stage in the transition, between 2005 and 2010.

In the time between 2000 and 2005, we have all agreed that the Internet is here to stay, that we are moving into the Information Age from the Industrial Age.

But the dominant thought is still that essential elements of the Industrial Age will not change: we will still drive automobiles for travel; still commute to offices; still mail letters; still meet face to face; still send our children to a school building for their education; still live in suburbs.

We are soon to enter a period of domestic conflict over the Industry Age and Information Age.

Since 2000, the primary conflict has been external. It has been "Us" versus "Them." Americans perceived "the enemy" as being among foreigners. The United States has even viewed such traditional allies as Europe and Japan with wariness.

We now move into that time period when there will be serious conflict between the old ways of the Industrial Age and the new ways of the Internet Age. It is no longer "Us" versus "Them." It will soon be "Us" versus "Us."

There are only so many resources. The fight over resource allocation will pit the 20th century against the 21st century.

- We will continue to build buildings and spend more money on physical plants than on technology.
- Advocates of cars and automobiles will argue for more highway funds.
- Car advocates will call for "freedom to drive" laws, such as raising speed limits, eliminating car pool lanes, and allowing drivers to use cell phones.

- Mass transit advocates will want restraints on the number of hours overworked truckers can drive their trucks. They will want curbs on cell phone use by drivers. They will want tougher drinking and driving laws. They will not want televisions, Internet connections and other diversions installed in cars.
- Automobile manufacturers will install Internet connections, GPS, e-mail, PDAs, computers, and other high technology gizmos in automobiles in desperate and failing hopes of turning the car into a roaming office.
- Real estate agents and construction companies will continue to build and plan more suburbs.
- We may see legislation prohibiting downtown office buildings from being turned into condominiums and apartments.
- We will see laws trying to govern the Internet, from sales tax laws to employment laws to copyright laws to intellectual property laws. We will see companies move to other countries to avoid these laws.
- Some companies will restrict or even prohibit workers from working at home. Other companies will encourage or even mandate their employees to work from home.
- More software will be built to help organizations create virtual offices. Wireless systems will make work much more mobile.
- Some states may act against home schooling, online schools, online courses. Others may encourage and fund online courses and online schools.

During this time frame, the lines will be drawn. There will be choices to be made. For example, should taxpayers build a new professional sports stadium, or buy laptops for every child in the school district?

In the period from 2000 to 2005 we thought we could have both. We could have both online courses and suburbs, both virtual offices and automobiles, both buildings and technology.

In the next time frame, we will understand that choices have to be made. This will create conflict.

The conflict will come in the form of legislation and laws. It will come in the form of an attack on values and beliefs of the other side, and the defense of the values and beliefs of our side. It will come in the form of tough fights over funds, government subsidies and government priorities.

Here are some of the lines of conflict:
- Zoning laws permitting or encouraging people to work at home.
- Funding of trains and light rail transit.
- Funding of highways.

- School attendance as requirement for graduation.
- Education taking place in one building (versus distance learning).

The period 1905-1910 was also a great period of conflict. The forces for the Industrial Age were gaining strength, and sensing that the new age could take over. Those people favoring the Agrarian Age were increasingly threatened, sensing that the new age could take over. Those supporting an agrarian way of life were not easily dismissed. They fought on all fronts.

- In Pennsylvania, the farmers' union, understanding that the automobile would destroy the family farm, encouraged its members to shoot at passing automobiles.
- Laws were passed. Oh, laws were passed. Automobiles were required to stop and pull over to the side of the road when a horse passed.
- The Colorado Supreme Court declared the eight-hour work day unconstitutional.[3]
- The International Workers of the World (IWW), nicknamed Wobblies, were formed in 1905 and began strident pro-labor organizing efforts against corporate owners.
- There was conflict over the running of cities. Cities were run by politicians noted for their favoritism, nepotism, and corruption. Government of our cities was, in the judgment of James Bryce, "the one conspicuous failure" of the American democracy.[4] In response, Dayton, Ohio, in 1908 became the first American city to have a "city manager."

Another form the conflict will take is that of humor and sarcasm. The Internet and the Information Age will be ridiculed and put down. The period 1905-1910 showed similar humor and sarcasm with regard to the automobile.

"Get a horse!" was the first reaction of someone who saw an automobile because they scared the horses. People took great delight, and felt reassurance, in seeing pictures or cartoons of horses pulling an auto out of a muddy ditch, with the horse team owner having a somewhat satisfied look on his face.

There were jokes about the new technology. Henry Ford and his Model T received the most jokes, but then he said he didn't mind as long as he sold the most cars.

Here are some of the popular jokes of the time:

"I don't own a car. I own a Ford."

"I hear they are going to magnetize the rear axle of the Ford."
"What's the idea."
"So it will pick up the parts that drop off."

"After all, the Ford is the best family car. It has a tank for Father, a hood for Mother, and a rattle for baby." (Ford cars tended to rattle a lot)

"I understand you have just bought a Ford."
"Yes, I saw seven of them chasing one pedestrian the other day, and I decided that I was on the wrong end of the sport."

"Can I sell you a speedometer?"
"I don't use one. When my Ford is running 5 miles an hour, the fender rattles; at twelve miles an hour, my teeth rattle; and at 15 miles an hour the transmission drops out."

"Have you heard the last Ford story?"
"I hope so."[5]

The Turning Point

The turning point in the transition from the Industrial Age to the Internet Age is likely to come between 2008 and 2012. It is during this period of time when it will become clear to a majority of people that the ways of the Industrial Age are behind us, and the ways of the Internet Age are here to stay for the remainder of the 21st century.

The actual point at which numerical superiority of the Internet Age exceeds that of the Industrial Age will not come for another few years, around 2015. For example, the number of people employed in knowledge work will exceed those employed in manufacturing sometime around 2015. The number of people telecommuting and using an intranet for an office will become dominant around 2015.

But by 2010 or so it will be clear to most decision makers in society that the downward trendline of the Industrial Age is irreversible, and that the upward trendline of the Internet Age is also irreversible. During this time period society as a whole will come to accept the Internet Age and then rush to establish, extend and expand the infrastructure for the Internet Age.

We know this because the turning point in the last century came

The Organizational Chart is a Pyramid

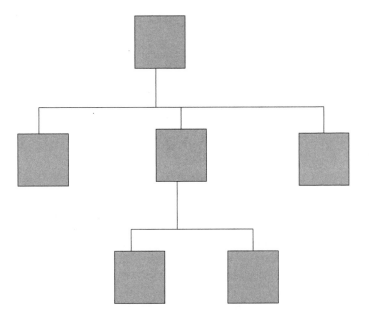

Most people in the 20th century recognized the organizational chart, the pyramidal way in which people were organized in the last century.

between 1908 and 1912. Here are some of the things that happened during that time period:

- The first cross-country automobile tour demonstrated the auto to small town America. In 1909 the American Automobile Association (AAA) organized several cross-country tours to show rural Americans what an automobile was. After they had seen an automobile, more and more Americans wanted one and purchased one.
- Companies dropped the manufacture of carriages. Many companies that were producing both carriages and automobiles began dropping the horse drawn vehicles during this period.
- The downward trend of farm employment, and the growth of industrial employment, became obvious and documented.
- The population in small towns peaked, and then went into decline, as people moved off the family farm and out of the small towns to cities to be closer to employment in factories and offices.
- Social reform was at its height. The social reform movements, which led to the infrastructure necessary to support the Industrial Age of the 20th century, reached its greatest height during this time period.
- The value of manufactured products of the country in 1909 surpassed $20 billion for the first time.[6] The number of women in college surpassed 100,000 for the first time. The percentage of workers in the industrial or manufacturing workforce who were women hit 20%.
- The political mood of the country changed. During this time enough Americans switched from an old order mentality politically to favoring policies and politicians who would move the country more quickly into the Industrial Age of the still new 20th century.

Of the political turning point, historians are quite clear. William Howard Taft won election as President in 1908. While some historians say he was mildly progressive, he was not progressive enough for the American public. By 1910 Americans had not experienced enough change from their government, and it was clear that Taft had lost the confidence of the general public. Historian David Saville Muzzey wrote, "Mr. Taft moved forward; but as he did not move so fast as public opinion, he seemed to be moving backward..." He lost the presidential election of 1912 to Woodrow Wilson, who represented the new policies of the 20th century and moved the country more quickly towards policies that would support and reinforce the Industrial Age. Taft had his chance. In the first two years of his term, there was a golden opportunity to seize leadership and move the country forward, but he did not take it.

Muzzey continues, "The election of 1910 marked a sharp division between its halves. During the years 1909-1910 the administration had the opportunity to satisfy the popular demand for reform by an honest revision of the tariff and a hearty espousal of progressive policies. During the years 1911-1912 it was powerless to resist the rising tide of opposition..."[7]

The election of Woodrow Wilson in 1912 symbolized the turning point.

Historian Paige Smith writes, "We can perhaps best understand Wilson as a transitional figure in the emergence of the new consciousness. The unbending devotion to righteousness which was often touched with self-righteousness, the faith in Providence, and dogged individualism, his belief in the common man and in democracy — all were conspicuous features of the old consciousness.

"On the other hand, Wilson's faith in the ability of modern scholarship, especially in the area of the social sciences, to describe and impose order on society was a conspicuous element in the new view of the world."[8]

Wilson's acceptance speech after being elected President also recognizes this turning:

"Citizens of every class and party and prepossession sit together a single people, to learn whether we understand their life and how to afford them the counsel and guidance they are now keenly aware that they stand in need of.

"The Nation has awakened to a sense of neglected ideals and neglected duties...

"...Plainly it is a new age. The tonic of such a time is very exhilarating.

"Our task is to effect a great readjustment and get the forces of the whole people once more into play."[9]

The top song of the year 1912, added fuel to the change, being titled *Everybody's Doin' It, Doin' It.*

Many, if not most, people failed to recognize that these years were a turning point until well after they occurred.

The turning point in the 21st century is also likely to occur between 2008 and 2012. A number of experts have already predicted the year 2010 to be a 'turning point' for changes in their fields during this time. They include:

- Computing power equal to brain power. Peter Cochrane, lead technologist for British Telecom, the large telephone company, says that Moore's Law indicates that computing power in 2010 will be about 1,000 times greater than in 2000, and will equal the brain's processing power by then.

He does not imply that computers will be able to think, make judgments, replace humans or be superior to the brain, simply that the power of computers will be sufficiently great and the cost will be sufficiently low that:
- 90% of communication over phone lines will be between machines, as compared to 45% in 2000.
- Objects will communicate. Computer chips will be located in light bulbs to indicate when they will burn out; in refrigerators to indicate when they need repair; in pacemakers to suggest the wearer may have a heart attack coming and should seek care, and so on.[10]
- Tele-emersion becomes a reality. The creator of virtual reality, Jaron Lanier, notes that by 2010 tele-emersion will be sophisticated enough and affordable so that two persons at a distance will be able to meet in virtual space and conduct a meeting without having to physically travel to meet. He indicates that air traffic congestion will be so bad by 2010 that tele-emersion will have arrived just in time to alleviate gridlock in air space.[11]
- Workers will be sent home. Our estimates are that around 2009 major companies will begin sending their workers home. Time Magazine, in a feature story in 2000, predicted this would happen in 2010.
- Home delivery becomes marketable. In 2001 the home delivery grocer WebVan filed for bankruptcy. The company delivered groceries to people who ordered them online. In its analysis of the demise of WebVan, National Public Radio interviewed an industry analyst who suggested that by 2010 home delivery of groceries would be attractive to enough people to be an economically viable business.
- Cars slow to 11 miles per hour. James Glick, in Faster, quotes sources that indicated that in 1990 cars averaged 30 miles per hour, given commuter congestion. In 2000 cars averaged 20 miles per hour, and Glick's sources estimated that in 2010 cars would slow to 11 miles per hour, practically an impossibly slow speed.[12]

It could be coincidence that the year 2010 keeps coming up in these predictions. It could be that projections are usually ten years in advance, and these predictions were made around 2000. Or it could be that we will actually see a convergence of influences and forces, driven once again by employment and the need for our home, community, social and cultural life to revolve around our economic environment, that will, once again, make the period between 2008 and 2012 a turning point in our transition

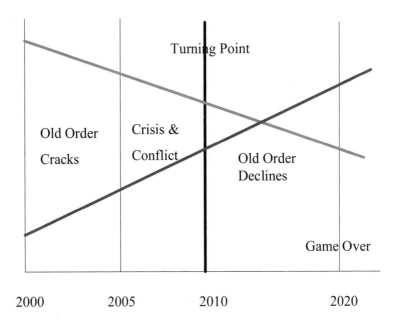

The changing employment lines create distinct time periods during the 20-year transition from one economic era to the next.

to the Internet Age. It is very likely that during this time period we will not recognize the signals, just as most of us did not in the past.

New Society Emerges

The years 2010-2020 are the years during which society becomes reformulated around the new reality.

There will be greater agreement in society that we are moving irreversibly into the Internet Age. There are still arguments about issues related to the new age, but the overall direction is accepted by a majority of people, and more importantly, by decision makers in society.

During this time period:

- Business and corporations, especially those that are either successful and/or more closely aligned to the Internet economy, move more strongly to becoming web based, having their workers work at home.
- Sometime between 2010 and 2020 the percentage of people employed in knowledge jobs becomes greater than those employed in the manufacturing sector.
- Many people will still feel as though little has changed. Around a third of people will still not acknowledge the passing of suburbs, the automobile, malls and other features of the Industrial Age.
- Automobile production goes into decline. There will be a few years of trying to rescue the automobile. Look for the auto industry and its supporters to try to:
  - incorporate the Internet in cars
  - accommodate cars into some kind of mass transit pattern that is emerging
  - seek legislation to sustain highways and automobile usage.
  - ask for new highway funding.
- Leading automobile companies will recognize they are not in the automobile business, but in the transportation business. A company such as General Motors will invest heavily in its locomotive, train and light rail divisions.
- New highway construction will come to a standstill in many states and areas.
- Government will stop building newer and bigger buildings. Instead, government will invest in technology and human resources.
- Educators and educational organizations will begin to create separation between the old unified school and the new web based

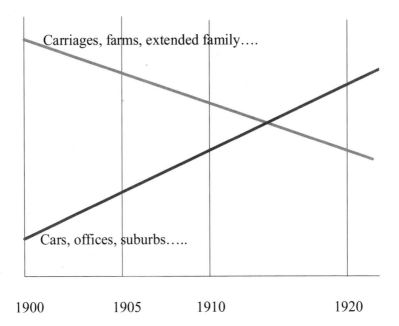

Carriages, farms, extended family....

Cars, offices, suburbs.....

| 1900 | 1905 | 1910 | 1920 |

In the last century, the demise of the carriage, as well as other characteristics of the Agrarian Age, followed the same declining timeline as the falling percentage of people engaged in farming.

educational system. There will be research, studies and denunciations of the building-based education system of the last century as being inadequate and faulty.

- There will be big building and/or renovation sprees in downtown initiatives to build apartment buildings and to convert office buildings into condominiums and apartments. Generation Y (born between 1980 and 2000) and the Baby Boomers will compete to live downtown close to light rail lines, restaurants, and theaters.
- With the Industrial-Age causes and labels of "liberal" and "conservative" rendered meaningless in the new reality of the 21st century, political parties will look to new themes, causes and labels around which to organize and advocate.
- Social reforms are enacted. Look to action on universal higher education and universal medical coverage as two infrastructure cornerstones necessary to support the knowledge worker sector of the workforce.
- Business actively encourages and supports the formation of community organizations, clubs, and municipal planning areas in order to provide access to neighborhood social and face-to-face outlets for workers.
- Online shopping makes a comeback. Home delivery services grow.

Between 1910 and 1920, these mirror transitions took place.

- Urbanization gained speed. The rate of its increase in the decade 1910-1920 was more than seven times the rate of increase in the rural districts, according to historian Muzzey.[11]
- Women were firmly in the workforce in a diversity of occupations. During the decade 1910-1920 women workers in the automobile factories increased 1,408%, while the same decade showed a decrease of 1,500,000 women farm laborers.[13]
- As noted elsewhere, companies that made both horse-drawn vehicles and gasoline powered vehicles stopped producing the horse-drawn vehicles. In 1915, for instance, John Deere quit manufacturing carriages and wagons.[14]
- Businesses established associations, in part, to increase face-to-face communication among professionals, in response to the increasingly impersonal communication engendered by the new technologies of the telegraph, telephone, and radio.

As did our ancestors in the second decade of the last century, another characteristic of the 2010-2020 time period will be the distancing of ourselves from the previous Industrial Age of the 20th century.

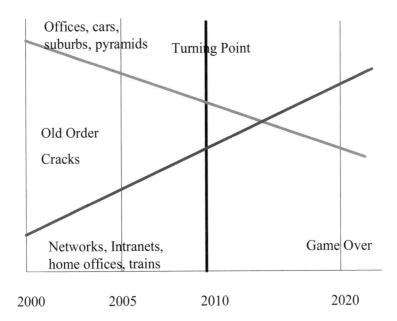

Offices, cars, suburbs, pyramids

Turning Point

Old Order

Cracks

Networks, Intranets, home offices, trains

Game Over

2000   2005   2010   2020

Today, the characteristics of the Industrial Age show the same declining timeline as the falling percentage of people engaged in factory work.

The Ballgame is Over

By 2020, the ballgame will be over. The Internet Age, including the nine shifts described in this book, will be preferred over the way of life in the Industrial Age of the 20ᵗʰ century.

We know this because in the last century by 1920, the ballgame was over. This was the last year in which the Agrarian Age existed, and the first full year in which all of society was firmly and entirely in the Industrial Age.

In 1920, chautauqua, those great cultural and educational programs that traveled from rural small town to small town, bringing history, music, and entertainment to an agrarian society, had its largest attendance. Some 25 million people were said to have attended a chautauqua that year. The following year they folded, never to put up a chautauqua tent again.

In 1920, the urban population was 51.5% of the population, the first time in history it was a majority of the population.

In 1920 women could vote.

In 1920 the National Football League was established.

In 1920 we had suburbs, commuting, offices, radio, motion pictures, airplanes.

Every conceivable aspect of rural and small town life in the Agrarian Age was in steep decline, never to return. That included the number of farms, people employed in farming, number of wagons and carriages sold, opera houses, small town population, train routes, and other defining characteristics of agrarian life.

The 40-hour work week was on its way in. Union membership was on its way up. Child labor was on its way out. Universal high school and compulsory education to the age of 16 was on its way in; rural one room school houses were on their way out.

Around 1920, two great American novels were being written. Both were named to the list of top 100 novels of the century in 1999. We have talked about *Main Street*, by Sinclair Lewis. The other was *The Great Gatsby*, by F. Scott Fitzgerald. In *The Great Gatsby*, the Industrial Age had arrived. There were suburbs, automobiles, gas stations, independent women, women smoking, commuting to jobs, office jobs, and a value and attitude system with which we would be familiar throughout the rest of the century. The Industrial Age had arrived, and we would celebrate it in the Jazz Age throughout the decade of the prosperous 1920s.[15]

By 2020 not everyone will be a knowledge worker, working from home, and traveling by rail. But by 2020 the new way of life will clearly be seen as superior to working in an office, commuting and traveling by car. By superior we mean that knowledge workers working from home and using virtual offices will be seen as more time effective and able to make more money. They will be able to spend more time with their families, and be able to have more and better quality leisure time. Given a choice, a majority of Americans in 2020 will choose a knowledge job, working at home, and traveling by train. By 2020, the last of the Baby Boom generation will be on the edge of retirement, with Gen X and the Net Generation dominating the workplace. The nation will be firmly in the Internet Age.

Throughout the last century, people in advanced or industrialized societies functioned within a pyramid structure. The organization chart is the most familiar example of the pyramid structure, although it is also present in church and voluntary organizations, schools and colleges, local, state and national government, and most everywhere else that people gather in a social or work context.

That pyramid structure, once valuable and useful, is now obsolete. Twenty-first century organizations are being organized in networks, not pyramids. The collapse of the organizational pyramid, and the transition into the Internet Age, is coming in stages of time between 2000 and 2020. At the time of this writing, we are entering a period of domestic conflict over the Industrial Age versus the Internet Age. Between 2008 and 2012, the tide will change and there will be a turning point. Enough of a majority of the population will recognize the inevitability and value of the new forms of social organization that changes will become more popular. And between 2010 and 2020 structures and behaviors of the old Industrial Age will go into decline. By the year 2020 the transition will be largely over, and we will be totally in the Internet Age.

Chapter 4
Homer Simpson and
The Gibson Girl

"Computers are useless.
All they can do is provide answers."
— Pablo Picasso

We look now at how women, men, boys and girls deal with a tremendous change in society, how we adapt or cope with enormous uncertainty, and how we each can approach these great changes.

Each of us as individuals can choose and respond in our own personal way. How we react is in no sense predetermined. Yet women, men, boys and girls each have certain differentiating characteristics that influence how they respond. When one looks at how others are responding, we see that, in part, they are responding based on their circumstances and experiences. In this chapter we look at how people react to change, and at who responds first to the changes in society. We will see that adults respond differently than youth, and that boys are actually leading society into the Internet Age.

Between 1990 and up to the time of this writing, Homer Simpson has been the best recognized male personality on television in the country. Our son's favorite emoticon is an image of Homer.[1] Homer is not a real person, but a cartoon character. He is not real bright. Looking over his son Bart's shoulder as Bart types on his keyboard, he says things like, "Wow, the Internet is on computers now." While this is technically true, we all can see that Homer doesn't get it. His wife

Marge is smarter than he is. His kids are smarter than he is. Most of all, however, Homer is a wimp.

Homer is not alone. Men are wimps today. Look at just about any television ad, any television show, and men are clearly wimps. Men have not always been portrayed as wimps. But exactly 100 years ago, men were also wimps.

From The Gibson Girl to The "It" Girl

In 1900 the role model or ideal woman was "The Gibson Girl," so named after the artist Charles Dana Gibson, who did drawings and artistic cartoons with The Gibson Girl.

The Gibson Girl was attractive, of course. But she was also intelligent, strong, and assertive. By contrast, men in 1900 were portrayed as wimps, the same as they are portrayed today. The Gibson Girl was often accompanied by a man. But the man was smallish, passive, and relegated to a secondary indecisive role.

In one drawing, The Gibson Girl and her man are in a carriage. The Gibson Girl is sitting upright, reins in hand, driving the carriage. The man is beside her, bent over, holding a small, pampered lap dog.

In another drawing, a group of Gibson Girls are standing around, taking turns looking through a magnifying glass. Through the magnifying glass they look toward the floor where, in the middle of the group, there is a miniature man. This is social commentary.[2]

But The Gibson Girl in 1900 would never think of drinking or smoking in public, taking a walk by herself, going on a date unchaperoned, going without a hat in public, cutting her long hair, showing her ankles, or getting a job. She might dream about voting, but she could not.

The Gibson Girl was an idealized woman, up on a pedestal, protected. Her clothes were a symbol of both her idealized status, and the tight binding by which society kept her on top of her pedestal.

In *The Big Change*, F.L. Allen details what the typical woman in 1900 wore:

"Pull out today a photograph album of the year 1900 and your first impression will be that even at the seashore or in the mountains all the women are wearing city clothes. At any season a woman was swathed in layer upon layer of underpinnings — chemise, drawers, corset, corset cover, and one or more petticoats. The corset of those days was a formidable personal prison which did its strenuous best, with the aid of whalebones, to distort the female form into an hour-glass shape. Dresses almost invariably came in two pieces, and the discipline begun by the corset was reinforced by the bodice part of the dress, which was stiffened to complete the hour-glass effect. The bosom was compressed as nearly as possible into a single structure, and the correct posture called for a rearward-sloping 'straight-front' effect from this eminence downward; the fashion-plate artists represented the well-dressed woman as almost falling forward — despite the counterbalancing effect of an unsubdued posterior — in the effort to achieve the perfect stance."[3]

Women in 1900 were bound by their circumstance, which for the majority of women was life on the family farm. The agrarian way of life required that women be supplemental, if partners, to their husbands on the farm. They had little freedom to choose another way of life.

Even getting a job was frowned upon. If a woman held a job, it meant her father was not able to support her, and this was a blemish on the family name. Those young girls who worked, as nurses, one-room-school teachers, or maids or house servants, were often from lower classes where the father indeed was not able to care for his daughters.

Between 1900 and 1920 all that changed. As young men left the farm to go to work in the factory, so did young women.

As more women moved to the city, they adapted a more urban and independent lifestyle.

- By 1909 women were driving across the country in automobile caravans. Several such caravans were composed totally of women.
- By 1912 Margaret Sanger had won several battles in her fight to provide birth control options and sex education information to women.
- Mother Jones fought against child labor.
- Women, including one of our grandmothers, joined the peace and freedom movement, parading in Washington to keep the United States out of World War I.
- Women, including another of our grandmothers, owned and ran their own businesses.
- In 1919, the first woman to sit on a federal court graduated from law school.

The summit was reached in 1920, when Congress passed the Nineteenth Amendment giving women the right to vote.

The Gibson Girl, the ideal woman of the Agrarian Age, was no longer the role model. By 1920, The Gibson Girl had decisively been replaced by the ideal woman of the new Industrial Age, the "It" Girl.

Movie star Clara Bow was the classic "It" Girl. She cut her hair to just above shoulder length, a symbol of women's new-found freedom. Not only did she show her ankles in public, but sometimes her shoulders as well. She drove. She smoked cigarettes. She drank liquor in public. She worked. She voted. As Frederick Allen notes, "The use of cosmetics is no longer, 1919, considered *prima facie* evidence of a scarlet career."[4]

She did just about everything, in fact, that women for the rest of the 20th century did. What did the "It" of the "It" Girl stand for? "It" stood for personality.[5] Before the Industrial Age, women were prevented from pursuing their own wants, prevented from having their own individual personality. The "It" Girl had personality. She could be who she wanted to be. Not entirely true by the standards of today, of course, but by the standards of 1900, just 20 years earlier, it certainly was a dramatic change.

As a whole, women benefited greatly from the transition from the Agrarian Age to the Industrial Age. They are likely to gain greater equality once again from the shift from the Industrial Age to the Internet Age.

But for many adult men, the transition was difficult and painful. If we look back 100 years ago, we see the experience was emotionally traumatic for men. Mr. Y.A. Taylor of Black Mountain, North Carolina, lived in a part of the country that saw the transition from the Agrarian Age to the Industrial Age take place later than the rest of the country, so we were able to interview him about the changes from farm to factory jobs. He told us in an interview:

"The small farmer sort of disappeared. One day they were just gone. The large farmer stayed on the farm, and it became more mechanized with not so many mules and horses. When people lost their farms, adults took it hard. They often became distraught. It was very difficult for them."[6]

The decades of the 1890s and 1990s were very similar, according to historian H.W. Brands. "Fear and resentment pervaded the politics of both decades. Each time, the sense of sliding over a cliff into an alien future prompted unprecedented efforts at heel-digging, and it produced a conspicuously conspiratorial brand of political rhetoric. In the 1990s, the mantra was traditional values... In the 1890s, the mantra was also traditional values, which in this case meant the way of life of American farmers, those sons and daughters of the soil who had nurtured the nation from its youth and who still represented its last best hope for the future."[7] He adds, "Something happens at the end of a century. Rules are altered, boundaries are breached, fundamental attitudes are changed."[8]

The difficulty was documented in the literature of the time as well.

The difficulty in emotional adjustment to the Industrial Age is evident in the great classic novel, *Lady Chatterly's Lover*, by D.H. Lawrence, which takes place in the first decade of the 20th century.

Lady Chatterly is talking to her lover about modern people, and he replies, "Their spunk is gone dead. Motor-cars and Cinemas and aeroplanes suck that last bit out of them. All the modern lot get their real kick out of killing the old human feeling out of men... Pay money, money, money to them that will take spunk out of mankind, and leave 'em all little twiddling machines. Let's drop the whole industrial life and go back."[9]

And later he says:

"I feel I've swallowed gall... I'd wipe the machines off the face of the earth again, and end the industrial epoch absolutely, like a black mistake. But since I can't, an' nobody can, I'd better hold my peace, an' try an' live my own life: if I've got one to live, which I rather doubt."[10]

Living in a rural setting rapidly becoming industrialized, Lady Chatterly's lover tries to figure it all out. "He went down into the darkness and seclusion of the wood. But he knew that the seclusion of the wood was illusory. The industrial noises broke the solitude, the sharp lights, though unseen, mocked it. A man could no longer be private and withdrawn. The world allows no hermits.

"The fault lay there, out there, in those evil electric lights and diabolical rattlings of engines. There, in the world of the mechanical greedy, greedy mechanism and mechanised greed, sparkling with lights and gushing hot metal and roaring with traffic, there lay the vast evil thing, ready to destroy whatever did not conform. Soon it would destroy the wood, and the bluebells would spring no more. All vulnerable things must perish under the rolling and running of iron."[11]

Lady Chatterly herself "had clung to the remnants of the old England. It had taken her years to realize that it was really blotted out by this terrifying new and gruesome England, and that the blotting out would go on till it was complete."[12]

So adults, and in particular men, went through an emotionally wrenching experience of transitioning from one world into another, from the Agrarian Age into the Industrial Age. What we take for granted, what we regard as good, to them was foreign and not very welcome at all for many men and women.

Boys, however, reacted very differently from their fathers to the advent of the Industrial Age.

Y.A. Taylor, whom we interviewed, himself was a young man when the job opportunities shifted from the farm to the factory. He grew up on a farm and worked long hours on the farm. But when he and other young men had an opportunity to work in a factory, they took the factory jobs without hesitation. He described the attraction to us:

"Young men in a factory could earn 10 cents an hour. On the family farm you weren't paid money. And, in a factory job, you were paid in cash on pay day at the end of the week, so you saw the money on a weekly basis. Construction paid 15 cents an hour."

"On the farm there were long hours, but also the weather was often poor, so you were working in the hot sun, or in the rain, or in the cold. For factory jobs, it was almost all inside work."[13]

Boys were characterized as being "bad" for their Industrial Age behavior. In the famous musical *The Music Man*, Professor Harold Hill tells the parents of River City, Iowa, what they already know, that their young boys have been exposed to new and immoral influences.[14]

Oh, we got trouble. Right here in River City, and around America. But boys did not just play pool and say awful words like "swell." They also got bad grades in school. And then they dropped out of school in huge numbers.

The reason there is a war against boys today is because boys are leading our societies into the Internet Age. Like they did 100 years ago, they are developing the necessary skills to perform in the new society. Today they are developing the skills they need for the knowledge jobs they will be doing after their schooling.

We know that young men were responsible for founding almost all of the 2,200 companies that produced automobiles in the early part of the 20th century. Likewise, we know that young men are responsible for most of the hardware, software and Internet inventions today. And when one asks for technical assistance, there is a four-fifths chance that a man will help you.

A society and school system still rooted in Industrial Age mores and values see boys today as "bad." Thus, many young men drop out of higher education and go into the workforce. Instantly, the "bad" young men in school become valuable workers. Young men in technical jobs perform so well they are in high demand in today's economy. In a recent article, columnist Bob Weinstein says that boys are succeeding in the workforce, particularly if they have a computer certification.[15] Technically oriented young men recently found 7 jobs for every 1 qualified candidate. Technically oriented young men are so much wanted in the workforce today that the United States Congress passed legislation allowing up to a half-million technical workers from other countries to work in the United States.

Boys are demonstrably more competent with new technology than girls. In several different studies in several different countries, boys score much higher on computer subjects, as well as the related math and science subjects. Boys are more into new technology than girls. Dr. Judith Kleinfeld, a professor at the University of Alaska at Fairbanks, in her groundbreaking article, *The Myth That Schools Shortchange Girls*, provides the documentation on why this is so.[16]

She says boys have a greater variability in many human characteristics than do girls. So boys and girls have different bell shaped curves to describe their variability. Both curves have the same averages, she notes, but they have different peaks and slopes.

Girls have a much higher peaked curve than boys, putting girls more in the middle or being similar in terms of human characteristics.

Boys, on the other hand, show a bell-shaped curve with much more variability, according to Kleinfeld. Thus, at the leading edge of the curve one finds more boys than girls. Applied to technology, there are more boys than girls engaged in the new technology and the accompanying behavior required in the new economy of the Internet Age. Males are also to be found in greater numbers on the other end of the curve, which might explain why many men have a harder time adapting to changes in society than do women.

Men often are more visible in opposing changes. Author and speaker John Seely Brown has gained popularity with Baby Boomer adults by attacking telecommuting and other social changes accompanying technology. In another such attack on change, Morris Berman lashes out at online learning in a recent book. He writes, "For every jackass of a dean who is ecstatic about 'distance learning' and who makes no distinction between higher education and marketing, there are a very few faculty members willing to stand up to her and tell her that there is no substitute for direct personal involvement and painstaking intellectual apprenticeship."[17]

Like Grandfather, Like Son

By coincidence, our son, William A. Draves V, or Willie, was born exactly one hundred years after his great grandfather, William A. Draves II. The other similarities between WAD II and WAD V are not coincidental, however.

Both were 14 at the turn of the century. Both were boys during the transition period from one age to another. And thus both have similar characteristics.

WAD II was a happy boy who loved to play. From his diary, we learn that he would often wake up late, by his own account. And he would often come home from high school and play with Dan, the family horse. He also liked to play and build with his "dynamo," an early engine. So grandpa was into technology.[18]

Grandpa went to the university, but he dropped out just before graduation. His circumstances were similar to several million boys of today in that he could get a job in industry without the university credentials.

For grandpa, the automobile was first and foremost something with which one played. He saved and collected his license plates, each one with his initials for the plate number. He had a special, customized metal logo put on the front of his car. He would joke that before he got married, he drove a Cadillac, and after he got married, he drove a Ford.

He lived in Milwaukee, and the main thoroughfare there is Wisconsin Avenue. At the time street cars had the right of way, so every time a street car came along, all the automobiles had to pull over to the side of the street to let it pass. So grandpa rigged up his car horn to sound like a street car, and drove down Wisconsin Avenue, beeping his horn and having all the cars pull over to the side to make way for him as he drove unimpeded down the main street.

He played with movies. This was before television, so the way people received picture news was with movies. He got a newsreel of the coronation of the Queen of England and spliced himself into the movie, so that the family was astonished and then amused to be watching the coronation of the Queen and then all of a sudden see Grandpa in the coronation.

As he was growing up, the auto was a leisure vehicle for the well-to-do. Grandpa picked up a beautiful red-headed girl in his auto, and she later became our grandmother. He was not alone in courting from a car. During the first half of the twentieth century, a shaving cream company found a unique way of advertising by putting up six signs that composed a poem along the highway. Driving only 30-40 miles per hour, people could read the poems easily. One of their all-time most popular rhymes was: "A man. A miss. A car. A curve. He kissed the miss. But missed the curve. Burma-Shave."[19]

A trip of 1,500 miles was an awfully long trip for an auto in those days. One time grandfather took Bill's dad, then a boy, on a trip out west. Before they left, Nana told him to write. So grandpa went out and bought a rubber stamp that said, "Having a wonderful time. Wish you were here.

Love Bill." And every day nana received a post card with a different date and city but with the same rubber stamped message. She did not think it was funny, but everyone else did.

Our son Willie is growing up a century later, a mirror time period from that of his great grandfather. He displays few of the characteristics of his father and grandfather, both entirely products of the Industrial Age after it was well established. But he has many of the same characteristics as his great grandfather. His circumstances, environment and situation are very similar to his great grandfather's.

And Willie is not alone. As we look around at his friends, at boys online, at newspaper accounts of trends among boys, we see the same characteristics as probably one to two million other boys his age.

He loves to play. He plays with our dog, Frisbee, like his great grandfather played with the family horse. He plays on the computer, for hours on end. One of the popular T-shirts in Hot Topics and other stores the past few years says, "Girls are no substitute for a PlayStation." He likes technology. He is into technology. He works with technology. Or rather, he plays with technology.

How Kids Perceive Online Reality

For adults, computers are often objects or impersonal robots with a secretly sinister agenda and undermining of the human spirit. For children, however, computers are a new and wonderful link with other people, says Jaron Lanier, inventor of the term "virtual reality."

Lanier is lead scientist for the Tele-Immersion Institute, a project of Internet II, a coalition of 161 universities working on a newer and more powerful Internet. Lanier's project takes us beyond virtual reality and places two people cybernetically in the same room, where they are able to interact with each other.

So Lanier is on the cutting edge of technology, to put it mildly. Here's what he says about computers, the Internet, children and education.

"Youth today have a fundamental fascination with the Internet. They say, what is this digital thing and how do I interact and use it? They have a fundamental fascination of co-exploring interactive spaces with other people."

"All young children have a confusion at an early age of distinguishing fantasy from reality. They cannot tell in many instances whether a giraffe is real or imaginary. This is a delightful state. It rewards imagination.

"If you can imagine it, it pops into existence. It is an amazing state to be in. A child is all-powerful in this nether world of fantasy and reality. But it is also somewhat insulated and isolated from other children and other people.

"As one grows older, the distinctions between reality and fantasy become clearer. One is able to tell which is reality, and what is fantasy. Reality hits, and it is not pleasant. It is an insult, a profound demotion. The child used to be king of the universe, and now she or he is totally powerless. Next to understanding mortality, it is one of the most bitter pills we experience in growing up.

"Some kids resist it. So when they encounter computers, they understand computers very differently than adults do. For young people, a computer is a path through their fundamental dilemma, which is retaining a sense of fantasy and imagination and power over their lives.

"So the computer becomes a profound step on a spiritual journey. The world inside the computer is the only place where the two — fantasy and reality — come together. So what the computer does is to bring us closer together. It bridges the interpersonal gap. It is a link to other people.

"We must never forget that the main actor is interactive space. Some of the most successful web sites on the Net are hollow structures filled with content from users. Computers are a bridge between people," he concludes.[20]

Lapping

In terms of learning technology, the children of the 21st century are likely to always be ahead of those adults who were raised in the last century.

Donald Tapscott, author of *Growing Up Digital*, calls this phenomenon "lapping." He writes,

"When it comes to understanding and using the new media and technology, many parents are falling woefully behind their children. We've shifted from a generation gap to a generation lap — kids outpacing and overtaking adults on the technology track, lapping them in many areas of daily life.

"Austin Locke, 15, sums it up perfectly, 'For once in our civilization, children are educating older people. Children are more adept at using computers. Parents, teachers and other adults are looking to children for information and help with computers and other computer-related stuff.'"[21]

What the "lapping" phenomenon means is that by the time an adult learns some technology, a child will have learned 2-3 times as much.

Thus, most adults can never catch up to their children.

We experienced lapping ourselves. When Bill wanted to learn how to do PowerPoint presentations, he took a four-hour class from an excellent teacher, and still couldn't do PowerPoint. So our teenage son tackled the problem and learned PowerPoint in about five minutes. Now Bill knows how to create PowerPoint presentations, but he is still learning some of the advanced techniques. Our son, however, is on to Flash and Java and has effectively "lapped" us.

The Digital Divide

There remains some opinion that the so-called digital divide should be a reason not to proceed with employing the Internet in our work and education. The "digital divide" is the phrase used to describe the condition of some or many people in a given society not having a computer and not having access to the Internet.

There are two aspects to the digital divide. The first concern is over those low-income families in advanced countries who do not have access to the Internet. The second is concern about large populations in countries and regions of the developing world who do not have access to the Internet.

There are millions of low-income families in advanced countries such as Australia, Canada, the UK and the United States without access to reliable Internet connections. Yet there are forces at work that will eventually provide reliable Internet service to most everyone in these societies.

The first force is business, and especially the large retail corporations. Business wants to sell products, and low-income people represent a large buying public for retail and consumer goods. Computer prices are already coming down. And Internet access is already becoming widely available. However, prices will come down and access will go up even more as business recognizes the enormous commercial potential of selling goods and services to this market. Computers and Internet access are likely to become as common among low-income families as television sets are in 2004.

The second force is the public sector. The community and society at large has a huge interest in assisting low-income families to gain access to the Internet. We can see this happening already. In early 2003 the first low-income housing project in the U.S. was wired so that every family in the complex could have wireless access to the Internet. Public libraries have been the leading institution in providing Internet access for people

Illustrations of The Gibson Girl portrayed the model woman as strong, and men as wimps.

with low incomes. It has been reported that hobos, homeless people who travel across country by hopping freight trains, get free e-mail accounts and then communicate with each other from computer stations in public libraries. Large numbers of other low-income adults and children also use the public library for Internet access. As we will explore more fully in a later chapter, within two decades schools will ensure that every student has a laptop and access to the Internet, just as schools in the last century ensured that every rural student had access to bus transportation to school, and every student had textbooks, paper and pencils.

Internationally, the problem is more complex, but even more intriguing. Recently a university in poverty-stricken Bangladesh became the first postsecondary institution in that country to provide Internet access for all its students. In rural India, providing Internet access has become a small family business. In a village, one family will get Internet access and, for a few rupees, rent time to other villagers. In China, hundreds of thousands of people have access to the Internet in Internet cafes. In Africa, the BBC reports that the number of cell phones is reaching the millions. The reporter concluded that while fiber optic cables are unlikely to be found in rural Africa, that towers for cell phone access are being built in rural areas on a financially feasible basis. Millions of Africans are likely to gain Internet access from their cell phones.

Technologically, one intriguing possibility is that developing countries may be able to bypass a wired infrastructure and establish a more cost effective and geographically encompassing wireless system of Internet access. Some scientists, for example, are working on a plan to provide low-level satellites around the globe, thus providing the entire world with wireless Internet access.

Then, too, it may be that workers in the developing world may not need the same amount and variety of information as workers in advanced societies, whose occupations are now totally dependent on access to information. The best economic growth in the developing world is likely to be manufacturing and agriculture, or some combination of both. Workers in the agricultural and manufacturing sector do not need as much access to information as knowledge workers. As only 15% of the world's population has access to running water, there are other possibly more important infrastructure improvements for those in an agrarian or manufacturing economy.[22] People in those societies can make significant gains in their standard of living by working in farming and manufacturing.

If you are interested in closing the digital divide, you can. Simply go out and buy a computer and Internet connections for just one low-income minority child or youth. Computers are coming down in price very quickly. You can probably do this for around $500 at the time this book was published. If you are reading this, you have that kind of money. You will learn more about literacy, culture, education and human nature than you will be giving. And you only have to do it for one child or youth to make a major impact on the lives of many people.

However, your real contribution to closing the digital divide will not be just your gift of a computer and Internet connections. Your real contribution will be how you help that child or youth to use the Internet. The real digital divide is not access to hardware, software and connections.

Julie grew up poor in a small Appalachian town. When she was a small girl her family did not have indoor plumbing, a telephone, television, or a water heater. Today poor people in Appalachia have indoor plumbing, a telephone, television, cars and hot water. But they are still poor. What we know is that poor people do eventually get many of the technological inventions. But what keeps them poor is lack of access to education and good jobs.

The digital divide is a reality at present. But concern over the digital divide has also been used as an excuse. It is used as an excuse by some people who do not want to change, for not entering the 21st century. And it is unpardonable when this excuse is used by professionals for not adopting new behavior and change that will enable children from all backgrounds a better life. There is no excuse for holding back our nation's children and depriving them of needed educational access to the Internet.

Another question is whether children from low-income and low-income minority families can learn online skills as readily as children from middle-class backgrounds. On this issue we have some anecdotal evidence which is reassuring.

In mentoring Tristan, a minority teenager from a single-parent family, we gave him a computer. Several weeks later when we asked Tristan how the computer was working out, he reported that his brother Devon had broken it. We cheered. Because Devon had not broken the computer with a hammer. He broke it by taking it apart and trying to "fix" the hard drive. What that told us is that low-income minority kids respond in very similar ways to kids better off financially.

Our adopted African American son's children are being raised in modest economic circumstances, yet Markell and Xavier, in early childhood, exhibit the same interest in computers as middle-class kids.

This is not to suggest that children from low-income and minority families do not need the same resources as middle-class youth. They do need additional resources, time, attention and mentoring. But given the same opportunity, they can achieve the same level of accomplishment.

Like every generation before them, children are responding to their own generation, not their parents'. The oft-heard phrase from parents, "where did we go wrong?" is often accompanied by a lament about changing values in their children, despite the parents' best teachings and example.

To illustrate, we as part of the Baby Boom generation will pick up a dime off the street. Our parents would pick up a penny. Our parents, part of the World War II generation, sometimes spend more money driving to a distant gas station to save a penny per gallon on gas, than they ultimately save. But our children will not stoop down to pick up any change, no matter in what denomination or what quantity. Julie once picked up five dollars in change off our son's bedroom floor.

When it comes to changing behavior and attitudes, the environment of their own generation is much more powerful than that of their parents' generation.

The Neutral Zone

Adults have the most difficult time going through the transition. For anyone born after 1985, there is no transition. They are already in the Internet Age. It is said that something is only "technology" if it was invented after one was seven years old. Even the oldest of adults do not regard the telephone as technology, because it was invented before we were born. The World Wide Web, invented in 1991, is "technology" only for those of us born before 1985.

William Bridges is one of the foremost authorities on helping people and organizations manage change and transitions. He says that as we move from an "ending" to a new "beginning," we have to move through what he calls a "neutral zone."[23]

In that 'neutral zone' period of time we are not quite sure what is real, what is not real, what is the old that we leave behind, and what is the new that we should be embracing. We are unsettled. There is a little vague uneasiness in the pit of our stomachs. It doesn't go away completely during the 'neutral zone' period. What we try to do is to live with that ambiguity and uncertainty until we make it through the neutral zone into the new ways. For anyone making the transition from the Industrial Age to the Internet Age, this gut level feeling of ambiguity and uncertainty is a constant presence.

Dow Jones Index

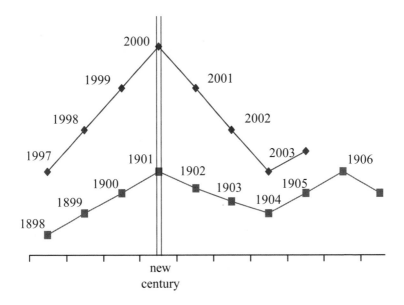

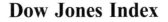

For the three years preceding and following the new century in both the 20th and 21st centuries, the Dow Jones average showed the same direction and approximate slope. Charting the Dow Jones average at the beginning and end of each year found that in the three preceding years before each new century, the Dow went up about 75%.

After the new century, the Dow declined about 25% in the 20th century and around 28% in the 21st century. In the fourth year after the turn of the new century, the Dow went up in the 20th century and, as of press time for this book, was also rising in 2003. Note that the 20th century was celebrated on January 1, 1901 and the 21st century on January 1, 2000.

Source: www.dowjones.com

New Values

The goal, the underlying value, the universal belief, of people living in the Agrarian Age was best summed up by Dorothy in the Wizard of Oz, "There's no place like home." While we can endorse that sentiment today, we cannot understand the depth and reality of that sentiment for those living 100 years ago.

One hundred years ago "home" meant owning 40-80 acres of land, land which either had been in the family for generations, or was expected to be in the family for generations. Most people would grow up, live and die in the same community, never leaving home. "Home" meant dividing up your land when you retired and giving a parcel to each of your sons so they could start their own farms.

"Home" was not just family, but the extended family. It was aunts and uncles, cousins, grandparents, unmarried sisters, and anyone who needed to be taken care of. "Home" meant providing for your parents after they retired or were too weak or infirm to earn a living for themselves.

When Horace Greeley wrote, "Go west, young man," he was talking only to those unable to prosper at home, preceding the famous phrase with "The best business you can get into you will find on your father's farm or workshop. If you have no farm or friends…"[24]

"Home" was where you worked, where your family income came from. "Home" was where you played. Moving as few as eleven miles meant moving away from home.

The universal belief that "there's no place like home" expressed itself in the national pastime of the 19th century, baseball. In baseball, as comedian George Carlin has noted, the goal is to go home. Whoever goes home, wins. In a "perfect" baseball game, no one goes anywhere.[25]

The goal of people living in the Industrial Age of the 20th century was not to go home. It was to leave home. Recently General Motors donated some money to the Smithsonian Institution for setting up a transportation museum. Officials at General Motors reportedly suggested that the theme for the museum be "America on the move." This is not only apt for the transportation museum, but as a theme for Americans in the Industrial Age of the 20th century overall. "See the USA in your Chevrolet," as popular singer Dinah Shore once exhorted, was an end in and of itself.

But it went beyond that. Keeping the extended family together was no longer a value. Instead, young adults broke away from their families to form their own nuclear families, families that excluded everyone but their children.

Upwardly mobile men in business were transferred several times during their careers to locations all over the country. A person who had "get-up-and-go" was highly valued, as was the person who was a "go-getter."[26]

People moved out of the "old neighborhood" and moved into suburbs. The farther the suburb from work, the more status it had. Commuting a great distance was a plus in social status.

"America on the move" was also expressed in the national pastime of the 20th century, football. Once again, it is no coincidence that the National Football League (NFL) was formed in 1920, the first year in which society was completely in the Industrial Age.

Football teams are the ultimate pyramid in organizational structure. The entire offensive line must act in unison to prevent the quarterback from being sacked. Draw the Xs and Os on a drawing board, and both the offense and defense looks exactly like a pyramid before the start of each play.

The goal of the football team is to be on the move. There is the ground attack. And there is the long bomb. The team marches down the field. Its travels are measured by the yard.

Once again, values are changing. In the Agrarian Age, shopping and driving on the Sabbath — whether a horse-drawn carriage or an automobile — was immoral. In the Industrial Age, driving a car on Sunday was not immoral, and by the end of the twentieth century Sunday was the second busiest shopping day of the week.

It is a little early in the Internet Age to know exactly what values are changing, but we already know many of the attitudes and values that are.

We each have the choice of how we want to respond to the new Internet Age. Yet we know in large measure how the majority of young people, older adults, women, men, boys and girls will respond differently based on their age and sex.

Women are likely to benefit from the Internet Age, getting the opportunity to both work from home and be with their families, and have another chance to close the salary gap between women and men. Men, who often value themselves in terms of their work, have much invested in Industrial Age values, work and businesses. Many of them will find it difficult to adjust. And boys are leading the transformation from Industrial Age behaviors and values. Boys are not only more likely to be techies, nerds and geeks with both hardware and software. They also have pioneered such new work behaviors as collaboration, intergroup collaboration, the discovery method of learning, hacking, and exploring the virtual world with play.

Chapter 5
Somebody Does Something

"Somebody has got to do something.
It's just incredibly pathetic it has to be us."
— Jerry Garcia of the band The Grateful Dead

In the early part of the 21ˢᵗ century, one of the glaring social realities is the gap between the rich and the poor. As John Cassidy wrote in *The New Yorker*, "The gap between rich and poor countries has turned into a chasm."[1] Since 1990, the number of people living on less than two dollars a day has risen by more than a hundred million, to three billion.

"Globalization today is not working for many of the world's poor. It is not working for much of the environment. It is not working for the stability of the global economy," notes Joseph Stiglitz, Columbia University professor, Nobel Prize winner in economics, and former chief economist of the World Bank.[2]

Americans, just 4% of the world's population, now own 25% of the world's wealth and resources. According to the United Nations, only 235 people have the same amount of wealth as 40% of the world's population.

Inside the U.S., there is not much more equality of wealth. Between the 1970s and the mid 1990s, only 20% of the population saw their incomes and assets go up, while "the bottom" 80% saw their income and wealth decline. The top 2% of Americans saw their wealth increase even more, and the top one-half of one percent saw astonishing gains in wealth.

The situation 100 years ago was exactly the same. It was badly skewed toward the rich. In 1900, some 250,000 people, or just .35% of the population, owned 75% of the wealth of the country.[3]

- Just 9% of American families owned 71% of its wealth.[4]

- The 125,000 wealthiest people averaged fortunes of $263,000 and owned more wealth than the 12,125,000 families of the other 99% of the population.
- The poor, those making less than $1,650 a year, made up 88.1% of the population.[5]

The average annual earnings of American workers were $400 to $500 a year. Shopgirls earned $5 to $6 a week.

There has always been a gap between rich and poor, of course. But in the United States, that gap was much smaller for most of the 20th century.

- In the Great Depression of the 1930s, for instance, a corporate executive made 12 times what a worker made.
- In the 1960s, an executive made 20 times what a worker made. (Peter Drucker cites this ratio as being the maximum or economic-ideal ratio in order to maintain a substantial middle class and democracy. Advocates of the rich have shied away from noting the ideal ratio for a healthy economy.)
- In 1980, a corporate executive made 40 times what a worker made.

And in 2000, a corporate executive made 400 times what a worker made. So in our two time periods of great change, 1900-1920, and 2000-2020, we see the greatest imbalance of wealth.

In both eras, the richest people were those engaged in the new technology of the time. In the early 1900s, the richest people in the world included people like Andrew Carnegie and John D. Rockefeller, involved in steel and gasoline that went into automobiles. In the early 21st century, the richest people in the world included people like Bill Gates and Paul Allen, involved in software and computers that run the Internet.

Other parallels between now and 100 years ago are also striking:

Long Hours

In the early 1900s the average working week was 60 hours. At the time the International Ladies Garment Workers Union was established in 1900, the hours of this trade were 70 hours a week.[6]

Today Americans now work longer than the workers of any other nation, some six weeks longer than Europeans. Americans have unseated the Japanese as the greatest workaholics in the world. Americans also work longer today than at any other time since the 1920s. [7]

Poverty

Poverty in 1900 was between 10 million and 20 million people, out of a population of 100 million. Today, poverty rates have crept up since the

War on Poverty of the 1960s, and now stand at pre-1960 levels.

Health

Unsanitary and filthy living conditions abounded in the early part of the 20th century. There was no food inspection, no regulation of drugs and medicine. Today we face a health crisis with more than 40 million people lacking health insurance.

And yet within just two decades in the last century, between 1900 and 1920, enormous and incredible social changes were made to the fabric and structure of our society. The changes were so great they were literally unimaginable at the turn of 1900.

What the new technology of the automobile, and the mass employment in the factory did, was to throw the balance of society out of whack. There was an imbalance in wealth. Laws that worked in the Agrarian Age were hopelessly outdated for dealing with the new economy. Traditional behavior, such as having children help out on the farm, simply did not transfer to the new environment of the factory and the office. To make the benefits of the new economy available to the majority of people, and to maintain democracy, something had to be done to restore the balance in society.

The new technology of the Internet has created similar imbalances in society, and in the world, for this century. Once again, that balance needs to be restored. To see how that is happening, we can look back to the first two decades of the 20th century. What is happening today mirrors what happened 100 years ago.

In the early 1900s, business had run amuck, monopolizing whole industries, making huge profits, beholden to no governmental regulation, and providing appalling lack of quality and terrible working conditions for their employees.

Those journalists trying to expose such corruption were called "muckrakers." One of those industries was the meat-packing industry, which made its workers perform in intolerable conditions, producing meat products for sale to the general public that were often unsanitary and unfit to eat.

In one expose, scholar Emory Elliott recalls the "embalmed beef scandal" in the effort to gain clean meat. Spanish American war hero Theodore Roosevelt himself testified before a Senate Committee, yet because of the powerful meat industry lobby, a bill to enforce meat inspection standards and protect consumers failed to get passage in the U.S. Congress in 1905.[8]

A socialist newspaper then commissioned Upton Sinclair to investigate the Chicago meat-packing industry. By dressing in ragged clothing and carrying a worker's pail, Sinclair spent seven weeks infiltrating the plants.

The result was the famous 1906 book, *The Jungle*. Elliott says, "Not since Harriet Beecher Stowe's *Uncle Tom's Cabin* had there been a book that would affect such a large part of the American people and move them to action."

In spite of desperate denials by the meat industry, within six months the Pure Food and Drug Act and the Beef Inspection Act were passed.[9]

Businessmen justified their enormous wealth in both economic terms, and religious terms. Their wealth, these rich men argued, was given to them by God and was theirs by divine right.

Yale's great teacher of political economy, William Graham Sumner, in his book *What Social Classes Owe to Each Other* (1883), said "You need not think it necessary to have Washington exercise a political providence over the country. God has done that a good deal better by the laws of political economy." John D. Rockefeller stated flatly, "God gave me my money."[10]

Coal mine owner George F. Baer, during a 1902 mine strike, sent these famous lines of assurance to a worried resident of a coal mining town, "The rights and interests of the laboring man will be protected and cared for — not by the labor agitators, but by the Christian men to whom God in his infinite wisdom has given control of the property interests of their country."

In the decade leading up to the turn of the centuries, business was booming. During both the 1890s and the 1990s, business prospered. The new century was welcomed in with a high note of business optimism throughout the country. And government during both decades pursued a policy of laisse faire, in which government was seen as part of the problem, not part of the solution.

That all changed in September of the first year of the new century.

- In September 2001, there was a terrorist attack on the nation in the state of New York.
- In September 1901, there was a terrorist attack on the nation in the state of New York.

Aside from these coincidences, what is important is that after both events, the role of government in society changed swiftly and decisively.

In September of 1901, President William McKinley, a conservative Republican, was assassinated by an anarchist in Buffalo, New York, during a world's fair. "When he died a week later," notes Charles Sellers and Henry May, "the young and dynamic Theodore Roosevelt became president. This tragic incident is often taken to be the beginning of a new period of progressive reform which lasted until World War I."[11]

In September of 2001, the President remained the same, but the policies of his administration shifted dramatically. Now government was called upon to protect the nation's airplanes and air space. Now government was called upon to protect the pensions and retirement savings of Americans. Now, the for-profit sector, once heralded as the savior of supposedly ineffective nonprofit institutions such as prisons, hospitals and schools, retreated from such bold and unfounded assertions. And we have not seen the last of government reforms yet in this century.

As President George W. Bush repaired for a week of vacation and reading following Christmas, 2001, it was not without coincidence and irony that the book he chose to read was "Theodore Rex," the biography of Theodore Roosevelt. While the pundits argued about whether President Bush resembled at all the president of a century earlier, the essential mirror is not the men, but the fundamental likeness of the times in which they governed.

In both centuries, the veracity and trustworthiness of government itself was called into question. "In no period after the Civil War," says Professor F.A. Ogg, "was the American system of government more clearly on trial than in the opening decade of the present (20ᵗʰ) century."[12]

In both centuries, the seemingly abrupt change in government involvement was a product of inequities built up over time. As Sellers and May note, "Actually, of course, the Progressive Era was not brought on by the assassin's bullet. Its sources lay deep in the economic, social and moral history of the country."[13]

A variety of people's organizations gained steam to pressure for change by the government. They included journalists and the press, huge and growing labor unions, socialists, third party Progressives, and the women's peace and freedom movement.

As a result, more changes in the social structure of society, and in its governance, were made during the period 1900-1920 than any other time during that century. As early as 1910, the famous journalist from Kansas, William Allen White, wrote, "Indeed, the growth of fundamental democracy in this country is astonishing."[14]

The great legislation passed in Franklin Delano Roosevelt's first term in the 1930s, the New Deal Legislation, was built on the "Square Deal" legislation of the first part of the century, and completed the restoration of balance and economic democracy for the rest of the 20ᵗʰ century.

The resulting changes in the laws of our country between 1900 and 1920 are amazing. The most significant included:

- Taxation of the profits of corporations
- Graduated income tax

- Direct election of senators
- Eight-hour work day
- 40-hour work week
- Child labor abolished
- Factory working conditions improved
- Workmen's compensation
- The first minimum wage law
- Women's right to vote

And there were other improvements in our social infrastructure which we take for granted today, including:

- City manager
- Pure Food and Drug Act
- Secret ballot
- Recall
- Referendum
- Abolition of private corporate militias
- Postal-savings bank
- Parcel post
- Commerce court
- Inspection of factories
- Tariff board

Not everything moved forward in this time. The civil rights, economic rights, and physical safety of African Americans took significant steps backward, even as (or because) African Americans made significant contributions to society in science, education, music, sports and other endeavors

Yet in 1900, citizens — even white male citizens with the right to vote — did not vote directly for such legislators as U.S. Senators. And citizens could not vote privately so others would not know how they voted. Women did not vote at all. William Allen White, again in 1910, relates the transition:

"Thirty years ago the secret ballot was regarded as a passing craze by professional politicians. Today the secret ballot is universal in American politics.

"Ten years ago the direct primary was the subject of academic discussion... Now it is in active operation in over two-thirds of our American states, and over half of the American people use the direct primary as a weapon of self-government.

"Five years ago the recall was a piece of freak legislation in Oregon. Today more American citizens are living under laws giving them the power of recall...

"The referendum is only five years behind the primary."[15]

In 1904, the Republican Governor of Wisconsin (and later U.S. Senator), Robert M. LaFollette, was a progressive fighting for the rights of the common people. At that time people in the general public were unaware of how their legislators voted. Many legislators ran for office saying they were going to serve everyone, and then voted in the interests of big business and special interests. LaFollette took to reading the votes of the legislators while speaking before crowds of citizens.

This was regarded as impolite, to say the least. It also made the legislators very uncomfortable, and those who were on the stage with LaFollette often walked off when their voting record was being recited. It was not until 1933 that *The New York Times* started publishing the voting record of New York congressmen.[16]

But change came from more than just a few leaders. Change came from thousands of groups. Advocating, proposing, pushing, striking, legislating, publicizing and fighting for the new social infrastructure of the 20th century were hundreds of thousands of people from the middle class and working class in America.

There was the labor movement, workers and labor unions who fought for the forty-hour work week, the eight-hour work day, and decent working conditions. There was the socialist movement, advocating for a greater role of government in the economic sector and for such new ideas as public education for children and public parks in the cities.

This was the Progressive Era, but not everyone advocating change came from the "left" on the political spectrum. There was a Republican president who advocated change. LaFollette, the leader of the Progressive movement, was a Republican. The progressive journalist William Allen White of Emporia, Kansas, was a Republican. The changes were not right/left, liberal/conservative. They were a necessary adjustment to the new industrial society. At the beginning of the 20th century, neither the Republicans nor Democratic parties endorsed the changes that would be coming. And fifty years later, the changes were so commonly accepted that both political parties took them for granted.

Changes occurred in social services and education as well. The first public city parks were created, some in cities such as Milwaukee led by socialist mayors. They were sometimes referred to as "sewer Socialists" because they were more interested in public works such as installing sewers rather than broad political ideology.

The great naturalist John Muir gave President Roosevelt a tour of the West, which led to the formation of the first national parks, national forests, and state parks and state forests.

Universal high school education came into being, as did free public education being made available to all. The first public school 'night schools' provided literacy and basic education for immigrants. The first community college was started in Joliet, Illinois, in 1906, after being proposed by the great president of the University of Chicago, William Rainey Harper, some ten years earlier. National and state associations burgeoned. The first modern university extension service was started by the University of Wisconsin in 1907, with the goal of serving adults across the state with continuing education experiences.

These changes did not go unchallenged. The Colorado Supreme Court declared the eight-hour work day unconstitutional.[17] The capitalists disliked Theodore Roosevelt, the Republican President, for "equality before the law."[18] But change did happen.

Change also occurred in the status of women. In 1900 women had few privileges. Women could not vote, could not travel alone without escort, show their ankles, go out in public without a hat, cut their hair, use make up or hair dye, drink or smoke.

Women were discouraged from working. Middle-class women could be nurses or school teachers, but generally only until they married. To be employed was a family disgrace. It meant that your father, or husband, was incapable of supporting his family. Lower-class women worked. And farm women worked. But this was, of course, out of necessity, not choice.

Yet in the first two decades of the 20th century women were a major force for social change as well. They campaigned against child labor and intolerable working conditions in the factory. Margaret Sanger began running her famous birth control and sex education clinics. Jane Addams started Hull House in Chicago, housing and helping immigrants, leading to the profession of social work in America. Mother Jones organized against child labor. Women marched in Washington, D.C., for peace and staying out of World War I. And women fought for their own rights as well, finally gaining the right to vote in 1920.

By the end of the first decade of the 20th century, all of these forces had gained momentum. Fighting hard by losing out were those holding on to the traditions of the last century, and those holding on to the new privileged state of inequality of wealth brought on by the automobile and Industrial Age. After serving as President from 1901 through 1908, Roosevelt stepped down. And William Howard Taft was elected President in 1908.

"It was a far different country that Mr. Taft was called to govern on March 4, 1909, from the country which Theodore Roosevelt found at the beginning of the century," notes historian David Saville Muzzey. "It was

America awakened, seething with social unrest. A general house-cleaning was in progress. The writers of the "literature of exposure" seemed almost to gloat over our shameful untidiness and squalor. The voices of reformers were crying 'Lo!' here and 'Lo!' there. The advocates of change were proposing a score of plans for our political and social redemption."[19]

Taft, unfortunately, was too rooted in the 19th century and its agrarian values and traditions to move the country into the Industrial Age. And by 1909, enough people in society recognized either the desirability (it would have been seen as such by people then) or inevitability (one looking back can see it as such) of the Industrial Age over the Agrarian Age. And this growing sector of the public saw enough of the dysfunctionality of the old way, enough of the promise of the new way, that it wanted things to change. Indeed, things had to change, for employment in farming had declined so far and employment in factories and the office increased to such a point, that industrial employment would soon overtake farm employment. The social structure, including the federal government with the President as chief executor, needed to respond to the needs of the industrial society. Before 1910, the forces to create a different social foundation for the new Industrial Era had to battle against the majority. After 1910, the forces to create a different social foundation were in the majority.

Conscious decisions to change and embrace the Industrial Era may be argued. But unconscious and unaware of the economic forces as people may have been, clearly they were influenced, no directed, by the impending economic shift. For, as we have seen, sometime between 1910 and 1920 the number of people employed in factories and offices overcame the number of the people employed on farms. After 1910 carriage sales went into steep decline, never to return to their previous levels. Sometime between 1910 and 1920 carriage makers merged with automobile makers. And sometime near the middle to end of that decade the automobile makers stopped making carriages.

Now a majority of people sensed these changes, and felt the need to have a social infrastructure that responded to the new way of life. While every change had opposition and resistance, and not every needed change was made, enough changes were made so that the new social structure, and the governing laws of the land were significantly different from those just a few years earlier. And they occurred because the Industrial Age demanded them.

Once again, we will see the rules that worked so well for so long undergo a significant transformation. Fundamental changes in the social structure and governing laws will be required in order to respond to the new realities and requirements of the Internet Age.

It is in this area of social policy where nations will have a choice. Advanced post-industrial societies do not have a choice about most of the Nine Shifts occurring right now. People in Japan, Russia, Europe, Australia, New Zealand and North America all will be working from home, using virtual offices and taking trains, for example. Just as workers in all those countries moved from the farm to the factory 100 years ago.

But how those nations responded in the area of social policy differed greatly. Japan created a system of lifetime guaranteed employment. Russia sought a workers state in its 70-year experiment with communism and state-run industries. Europe chose a democratic socialist approach, with worker benefits much different than those in the United States. And the United States saw the expansion of labor unions and a different set of laws and benefits for its citizens.

To illustrate the difference, we can take a look at the simple case of speeding fines. In the United States rich and poor people alike are fined the same dollar amount for speeding. A rich person caught speeding hardly notices the fine. In Finland, by contrast, a person is fined a percentage of their income, thus making the financial pain the same for rich and poor. So a Nokia telephone executive was caught going 11 miles per hour over the speed limit recently, and the fine amounted to $100,000.

Societal choice is also illustrated in the number of hours people work in a week. While not regulated by law, the differences between Europe and the U.S. are also startling. In the U.S. workers now work over 2,000 hours a year. Many workers get two or perhaps three weeks of vacation a year. In European countries such as France and Germany, workers work 6 weeks less a year. They get four to eight weeks of vacation a year.

In creating a new social infrastructure for the Internet Age, people in advanced societies will again participate in influencing decisions and making choices. Somebody will do something. To be sure, the increasing global interconnectivity of economics, the greater ability of knowledge workers to move, and the intangible nature of information flow all may influence a common social infrastructure. And yet cultures are still differentiated, people have preferences, new demarcations other than the nation-state for a "society" may emerge. And while we all may be thinking globally, we continue to live locally. Amsterdam is still a very different place than Denver.

The old infrastructure of the Industrial Age is being re-examined and will be found wanting. There will be a necessity to restore balance in society. Governmental tax policy will shift so that the middle class can be restored again to its former size, allowing the majority of people in society to participate in the rewards of the technology society.

Chapter 6
People Work from Home: Shift One

"Never mistake activity for achievement."
— John Wooden, basketball coach.

The technology of the Internet has created a new type of employment, and a new place of employment — the home. Former managing editor of Wired Magazine, Peter Leyden, says, "The Internet is a transformative technology. It changes how other people make money, do things and changes their jobs. It is not so much the invention itself, but the effect of the invention on all work and business."[1]

Management guru Peter Drucker was the first person to coin the term "knowledge worker." A knowledge worker is not simply an office worker. Throughout most of the last century, office workers functioned very much like factory workers. The necessary level of education to work in an office was a high school degree. Office workers were managed by supervisors, just like factory workers. They kept fairly strict 8-5 or 9-5 office hours, just like factory workers. They were paid on an hourly basis. Their productivity was measured by the hour.

"The newly emerging dominant group are 'knowledge workers.' The majority of knowledge workers are paid at least as well as blue-collar workers ever were, or better. And the new jobs offer much greater opportunities to the individual. The blue-collar worker in manufacturing industry and his union are going the way of the farmer," Drucker notes.[2]

"But — and it is a big but — the new jobs require, in the great majority, qualifications the blue-collar worker does not possess and is poorly equipped to acquire. The new jobs require a good deal of formal education and the ability to acquire and to apply theoretical and analytical knowledge. They require a different approach to work and a different mind-set. Above all, they require a habit of continual learning."[3]

Some office workers today are knowledge workers. Some office workers today are like factory workers and not at all knowledge workers. And some office workers today are part knowledge workers, and part factory workers. But by 2020 only knowledge workers will be valued, knowledge workers will predominate, and office workers will have diminished as a significant sector of the workforce. Most importantly, it is knowledge workers that create monetary wealth in an advanced society.

In the last century, a manufacturing worker was valued because she or he, by virtue of the products produced by the factory, brought in money from outside the local community. This created four additional local jobs. While retail stores merely cause money to change hands within the community, the manufacturing plant brought in new and additional money from outside the community, and thus manufacturing jobs were prized. That's why communities built Industrial Parks and why Chambers of Commerce recruited factories to their communities.

In the 21st century, the knowledge worker brings in outside money to the community. So knowledge workers are not only becoming the most prevalent sector in advanced societies, they are also the most prized workers.

Knowledge workers differ significantly from office workers. Knowledge workers:

1. Are paid by their outcomes, what they produce, not by the time they devote.
2. Are only paid for products or projects that are valuable to the organization for which they work.
3. Bring something unique to the organization for which they work. Their value is not in being like other workers, but in being different.
4. Have a marketable set of skills.

This set of characteristics are so different from office workers that they change the entire environment in which knowledge workers function, and how organizations are structured. It is difficult to imagine how different unless one is actually a knowledge worker. But here are some of the characteristics of the optimal work environment for knowledge workers.

Peak work time is critical.

Knowledge workers are oriented towards a project deadline, which is usually a weekly or monthly deadline. Thus the time of day in which a knowledge worker is engaged in active productivity can vary. The organization does not care when the knowledge worker is working as long as the person is in communication with other members of the organization. In fact, it is in the organization's own best interest that the knowledge worker function at her or his peak productivity times.

The knowledge worker wants to produce the best product or project, and this is entirely dependent on the knowledge worker's intellectual capacities. As different people work best at different times of the day or night, knowledge workers are at work during all 24 hours of the day, by choice.

Computers are everywhere.

Computer labs are on their way out. They were a transitional feature of the last quarter of the last century. The first computer lab used for continuing education was created by our friend Dennis DuBe in Boulder, Colorado, in 1976.

In 2000, Milwaukee technology guru Richard Thieme compared the usefulness of the computer lab to a fictional "pencil lab" that might have been created in the early days of the 19th century following the invention of the modern pencil in 1795.

Computer labs served a valuable purpose. But it is now clear that computers belong everywhere.

Work environment is important.

Just as working during the best hours of the day increases productivity, so too does having the optimal work environment increase productivity for knowledge workers. But the optimal work environment is different for each different knowledge worker.

Some people work best in a room with other people, some work best alone. Some work best staring at the ocean, others staring at mountains. Some work best in an urban environment, others in a small town. Some work best close to their small children, others work best with their small children in day care. Some work best with music playing, others in silence. On and on.

A centralized office environment provides one work environment, not the multiple choices that knowledge workers need to be most productive. So knowledge workers can and need to create their own most optimal work environment.

For these and many other reasons telecommuting is growing steadily in advanced societies, and will continue to do so. "Telecommuting" is one of those transition words, like "horseless carriage" or the "wireless" (early term for radio). By 2050 few people will recognize the activity of "commuting," and that word will likely come to mean something entirely different, or fade from our vocabulary.

"Telecommuting" is the same as "working from home" or "telework," and there may be other terms in use for the same work phenomenon. We like the phrase "working from home," keeping in mind that "home" may be any number of places. For many knowledge workers, home will be their own house or place of domicile. But for others, "home" may be the neighborhood juice bar, the public library, a neighbor's house, a community center, or even a rented office in the neighborhood.

The difference between a neighborhood office and today's office is that in a neighborhood office few if any of the workers are engaged by the same company or organization. In today's centralized office, everyone is in the same company or organization. No one outside of that company is allowed to work there.

And some people will work on the beach, at a cabin, in the woods, or on a boat. Thus "working at home" is really working at whatever place one chooses.

The Growth in Telecommuting

A telecommuter is a worker with a company or other organization, working from a site at or close to home, instead of commuting to a central office with fellow co-workers from the same company or organization.

"Worker" may refer to an employee, full or part-time, or someone working under contract, for an organization. The person may be temporary or long term, although we are referring primarily to permanent or long-term workers. The person may have previously been either a salaried or hourly worker.

"Organization" refers to the business, company, corporation, non-profit, or governmental agency for which the person works. This includes both organizations in the for-profit sector and nonprofit sector. Instead of using numerous terms, or varying the terms, we will refer to all such organizations as an "organization" here.

"Working from home" refers to the site or location from which the telecommuter works. While most telecommuters do work from their residence, others work in nearby locations, such as a personally rented office. Our definition of telecommuter is NOT about:
- Being self-employed
- Running a home-based business
- Being a consultant.

Most telecommuters work in organizations that have tens, hundreds or thousands of other workers.

People have always worked from home. Prior to the 20th century, most people worked from home or next to home. Working from home declined significantly in the 20th century, of course. But even during the last century, there are industrial tales of multinational companies being started out of the founder's garage. And during World War II, President Franklin Delano Roosevelt often did his best work from home. He would occasionally sneak out of the White House and travel by train to his home in Hyde Park, north of New York City, where he felt more comfortable.[4] Working in a centralized office became a value of the last century, so that today it is against the law in some cities to work from home without a permit. Some cities prohibit having someone else working in one's home.

Since 1980, and certainly gaining speed and momentum since the invention of the World Wide Web, a growing number of people have found it beneficial, necessary or more successful to work from home while employed or under contract to an organization.

Rough estimates for the first few years in the 21st century indicate:
• Between 3 and 10 million people telecommute.
• The numbers of people telecommuting have grown 25% between 1990 and 2000.
• The phenomenon is not confined to small companies or organizations. Signet insurance company, for example, was reported to have 43,000 employees in 2002, of whom 9,0000, or almost 25%, telecommuted.
• Telecommuting is most often found in the growing information sector, but is not limited to a specific number of occupations or professions. There are doctors who telecommute, even 'factory' workers engaged in manufacturing, who work from home.
• In 2001 the first U.S. Senator became an advocate for more telecommuting.

The estimates on the numbers of people telecommuting vary, but they all show an increase.

- A study by the Society for Human Resources Management showed that 37% of companies offered telecommuting as a benefit to employees in 2002, a big jump over 25% of companies just four years earlier.[5] The U.S. Census reported the number of Americans working at home three or more days a week grew nearly 23%, from 3.4 million in 1990 to 4.2 million in 2000.[6]
- The estimated number of Americans who telecommute at least some portion of the week jumped more than 42% in two years, from 19.6 million in 1999 to 28 million in 2001, according to the International Telework Association and Council.[7]
- The number of telecommuters rose to 23.6 million in 2000, up from 4 million in 1990, according to data collected by Joanne H. Pratt Associates, a Dallas firm that has studied telecommuting.[8]

One indication of the growth and influence of telecommuting in the work world came a couple of years ago when the Occupational Safety and Health Administration (OSHA) tried to make regulations about the home work environment for telecommuters.

OSHA passed regulations with requirements for the home work environment, and then indicated that companies would be responsible for insuring those standards were met. Obviously totally unworkable, the regulations were not well received and OSHA heard immediately from the public. The regulations were rescinded in less than a day, just three hours after being made public. The incident also illustrates what *Nine Shift* is all about: how our society — including our regulations — has to be radically altered to respond to our new environment.

Benefits to the Organization

We often think of telecommuting as primarily benefiting the individual worker. And the perception is that the impetus or initiative for telecommuting is coming from the individual worker.

Telecommuting equally benefits the organization. And we may well see the initiative for telecommuting in the next 5-10 years coming more and more from the organization rather than the individual worker.

Thus telecommuting is a win-win situation for both worker and organization.

Here are some of the benefits to the organization:

1. Greater productivity.
2. Employees work longer hours.

3. Retention of superior or valued workers.
4. Retention of workers who move.
5. Unlimited geographical recruitment of workers.

There may be less tangible benefits to the organization, such as higher morale, happier workers, longer staying workers, and lower training and recruitment costs because of the longer terms of employment. Here we have focused more on the tangible and definable benefits.

Benefits to the Individual Worker

Here are some of the benefits to the individual:

1. Saving an average of two hours a day in commuting time.
2. Increased energy due to a decline in commuting and driving.
3. More time for family, leisure or other outside activities.
4. Greater productivity, feeling of satisfaction resulting from greater productivity, and opportunity for work enhancement and challenge stemming from greater productivity.
5. Opportunity to engage in a positive, non-work activity or responsibility from home.

This last might include spending more time with children who are in school, having a hobby, taking care of a parent, etc. This is often a primary motive in becoming a telecommuter.

Studies show that telecommuters spend more time:

- Engaged in civic and community organizations.
- Involved in church, mosque, synagogue or other religious or spiritual organization.
- Exercising.

An initial and immediate question might arise as to how a telecommuter can both work longer hours than in a central office, and also have more leisure or free time. The answer is that the person is not spending an average of two hours a day commuting. Split equally, for example, there is one extra hour a day for work, and one extra hour a day for non-work activity.

Why People Telecommute

There are numerous reasons why people want to telecommute. Just a few:

- To spend time with young children not old enough to go to school.
- To move with a spouse who has taken a job in another city.

- For people with physical disabilities, simply the opportunity to work.
- To avoid three hours of commuting time and traffic.

And many more.

Our personal experience with working from home has been rewarding. Bill has been able to spend time with our son, time not available when he was working in the office, time that will be remembered for the rest of our lives.

One telling survey is that more than two-thirds of telecommuters say they are more satisfied, or much more satisfied, with their jobs since they began working at home, according to Tim Kane, president of the International Telework Association and Council.[9]

Of more than 1,000 people taking an MS-NBC online survey, 50% said they wish they could telecommute. Only 5% said it is not right for them (the survey was not scientific, or random).

Companies also report positive experiences with telecommuting. Some of them include Empire HealthChoice, Morgan Stanley, and Procter & Gamble.[10]

At IBM, 87% of telecommuters believe productivity and personal effectiveness has increased significantly. The International Tele-work Association says telecommuting enhances worker productivity by 22%.[11]

At Sun Microsystems, on a given day, nearly 30% of its employees around the world are not working at their desks. At 55 of Sun's field offices, when workers need a desk for the day, they make a reservation.[12].

Such shared desks have become known as "hot desks."

The numbers of people working at home will continue to increase for the foreseeable future. In the years 2005-2010 there will be a heightened awareness not only of the growing numbers of people working from home, but of the benefits of working from home.

By 2010 companies will begin to recognize the benefits to the organization of having people work from home. And beginning in that year, companies will start to send their workers home.

Why Companies Will Send Workers Home

The change will occur as CEOs and decision makers come to realize that in the Internet Age, work is an activity, not a place, as British Telecom lead researcher Peter Cochrane notes.

Since knowledge workers use computers, and increasingly laptop computers, they can do their work wherever they are most productive.

Increasingly, that means working at home or in one's local neighborhood rather than commuting long distances to an office.

People who work from home (or, as our 25-year-old son prefers, the neighborhood juice bar), are more productive, work longer, and require less supervision than people who work in an office. People who work from home also have more leisure time, and more time for family, community and church.

Here is why business will be sending its employees home beginning around 2009-2010:

1. Save money on office space.

This is the least important reason, but it adds up to millions of dollars a year for a larger company. Between 1990 and 2000 the amount of office space allocated to the average office worker decreased by 25%.

2. Save on supervision.

This is an important concern. Businesses can no longer afford to have their best employees spending a significant amount of their time just making sure that other employees are doing their work. Valuable staff time spent on supervision must necessarily decline in order for business to make the best use of its most talented people, and to remain competitive.

As we will see later, supervision will be done much more efficiently and effectively online by using a virtual office or company intranet.

3. Continual employee turnover.

Bill's father, who worked in the information economy as a newspaper man, worked for one company for 40 years. Employees today change jobs about once every 5-10 years. But in 2010 and beyond, employment experts say people will view jobs more like "projects" and have a new job on average once a year.

The needs of business will change so rapidly that flexibility in workforce will be a plus for the business. And your needs as a worker will change so that you will benefit from the new experiences, locations, contacts, and lateral or vertical advancement that annual new projects bring.

So by the time a business gets the office repainted for the new employee, puts a sign on the door, puts her birthdate into the staff celebration schedule, and does some staff bonding to welcome the new person, she will be on the way out to her next job/project.

4. Save two hours a day per employee.

Now we are talking big dollars. The average worker spends two hours a day commuting to work. Except in the Washington, D.C., area, where they spend 82 hours a year stuck in traffic — not going anywhere, just waiting.

The average worker is worth between $200 and $500 an hour to a company. That's not how much you make, but it is how much the company can gain in income per hour of your time. On average, let's say that is $50,000 a year per employee. If a company has 100 employees, that's $50 million a year.

And we're not even talking about the stressed-out lowered productivity level with which a person arrives at the office after a commuting experience.

This is simply unaffordable. Two hours a day is 25% of a knowledge worker's time. And that makes the difference between profit and loss, competitiveness or uncompetitiveness.

5. The best people won't move.

Compounding the issue is the biggest reason of all: the best people won't move. Companies will need the best people to remain competitive. The best people don't have to move. In fact, their high level of output and outcomes would probably fall if they were taken out of the environment in which they are most productive. So you don't really want to move productive people anyway.

Without the best people, companies fall behind. Getting the best people to move, whether it is to another city, another country, or simply another suburb or another six blocks, will shift from being difficult to becoming next to impossible. The best people will simply work for businesses where they don't have to move.

This is the single greatest reason why companies will send their workers home. So they can recruit and retain the best workers, regardless of where those people live.

6. Young workers will simply refuse.

Around 2010 the Net generation, the baby boomlet 80 million strong, will begin moving into the workforce. They will be Net savvy. And they won't commute.

The Net generation, the first generation in history which cannot remember a time when there was not a computer in the house, will simply not understand and not be willing to spend two hours a day to get to something (a laptop) that they have in their own apartment.

We know this because it happened before. In the middle of the twentieth century, people used to go downtown to watch the news. They would go downtown to the movie theatre, and before the movie began, there was a newsreel with the latest news. Until television was invented, when people said, why should I go downtown to watch something that I can get in my living room? The same will be true for work.

At the time of this writing, the U.S. census bureau does not even have a category for knowledge worker. Just as 100 years ago, the U.S. census bureau did not have a category for manufacturing and factory workers.

But by 2020 the number of knowledge workers will have grown so much in terms of numbers, and become recognized as the primary producers of wealth in advanced information based societies, that working from home will be commonplace and a foundation for the other shifts taking place in 21st century society.

Self Discipline

The ultimate mass migration of knowledge workers in society to telecommuting will not occur without challenges and obstacles. Looking at telecommuting from the perspective of the Industrial Age that is still dominant in the early part of the 21st century, these obstacles seem insurmountable. Much as the lack of paved roads seemed insurmountable to our great grandparents 100 years ago.

A central challenge will be the self-discipline required of telecommuting knowledge workers. Self-discipline and motivation are touchy subjects. We generally attribute them to ourselves, and less so to others. If we are correct in our recollection, as far back as the sixteenth century the French educator Montaigne jokingly advised unmotivated students be whipped and then apprenticed to a pastry chef.

In the 20th century, workers did not require much self-discipline because there was external discipline. Organizations hired people full time to supervise and manage. They had no other work to do other than provide external discipline for other workers.

Schools provided external discipline as well. Thus, we are at a peculiar point in history when we as adults are supposed to teach something — self-discipline — of which we really know little about and have not had to practice in our own work lives. Our response has been to administer external discipline in the hope that eventually it would lead to self-discipline. We have also established the somewhat arbitrary ages of 18 and 21 and declared, "Wha-la!" you young persons are now required to be self-disciplined. Neither practice has worked very well. The process of learning self-discipline starts early in life. Some elementary school teachers are beginning to explore ways in which to teach self-discipline to their students, so that by the time today's young people reach working age they will be sufficiently self-motivated.

This issue is a far greater challenge for adults already in the work place than it will be for those born in the 21st century.

Somehow, a child born today will have the required traits of self-discipline. Our agrarian ancestors had to plant, plow and harvest all on their own with little external discipline, and they did fine.

Social Interaction

Another of the central issues with working at home is the supposed lack of social interaction with others. Some economic thinkers regard this issue as another insurmountable barrier to the growth of working from home and telecommuting.

John Seely Brown and Paul Drugid, in *The Social Life of Information*, call the home office an "isolated social setting." And they call their chapter arguing against working at home "Home Alone."[13]

The home, of course, is not an isolated social setting, and never has been. After the September 11 attacks, Americans did not find comfort and security in their offices, but in their homes. Home improvement purchases rose significantly after that event, as people spent even more time in their homes.

In Shift 5: Communities Become Dense, we explore further the role of neighborhoods in providing social interaction for people in this century.

How Telework Differs

What knowledge workers do, and how they work, will shape the entire society. As Drucker writes, "Knowledge workers will not be the majority in the knowledge society. But in many countries, if not most developed countries, they will be the largest single group in the population and the workforce.

"And even if outnumbered by other groups, knowledge workers will be the group that gives the emerging knowledge society its character, its leadership, its social profile. They may not be the ruling class of the knowledge society, but they already are its leading class. And in their characteristics, their social position, their values and their expectations, they differ fundamentally from any group in history that has ever occupied the leading, let alone the dominant, position."[14] The requirements of teleworkers are significantly different from workers in a centralized office. As organizations respond to the workforce needs of knowledge workers, our work values change. Here are a few examples.

Work Flow

The more we work at home, the more we disregard the 9-5 or 8-5 work day.

There is a time when each of us is more productive. For Bill it is from 9 am to 2 pm. Julie is much more productive later in the day than Bill is. For one of our staff, Danita, it is from midnight to 3 am. And there are external circumstances as well. If one is on the phone selling from the West Coast of the U.S. trying to talk to someone on the East Coast, there are only so many hours when one can make contact.

There are also spontaneous moments or hours, when you just rush to your home office, inspired, and start working. For example, one night neither our son nor Bill could get to sleep, so they started working on a web site at 2 am.

And there is the flow of nature. Memorial Day is a holiday in the United States and the traditional start of summer when Americans en masse head to the beach, woods, mountains, or lakes. One year we were working on Memorial Day and Bill got an e-mail from someone. "I knew you would be working today," she wrote. Bill e-mailed something trite back. But what we did not tell her was that it was raining where we were. And two days later, when everyone else was back in their offices, it was sunny and we headed north to our lake cabin.

Taken all together, each telecommuter has his or her own work flow. Your daily work flow, weekly work flow, and seasonal work flow. And, as they say, go with the flow.

There are times when projects and work simply have to get done. And we stoke up on our favorite caffeine delivery mechanism. And there are times when pushing on does pay off. But there are many times when forcing work into a more artificial or less productive schedule does not yield maximum productivity.

Time becomes more valuable

Time is very different for telecommuters than it is for central office workers.

For central office workers, time gets wasted. Time is something one complains about, and there does not seem to be enough of it, and yet it gets used in the most unproductive ways. There are time obligations, when people do not have control of their own time. And there is time as fuel, just throwing a few more hours at a project. In a strange way, time is not valued very much. And if one is working 12 hours a day, one is presumed automatically to be productive.

But as soon as one starts to work at home, time becomes much more valuable. Because one is not judged by the length of time input, time assumes a whole different quality. Time is more precious.

If one uses time well, one can either: a) produce more or make more money; or b) have more time for family, leisure or community. Either way, time is too valuable to be wasted.

This leads to a changing behavior.

Here's an example. We live six blocks from downtown in a small town, with independently owned shops and stores that must necessarily charge much more than chain stores for the same item. Yet, we will spend $5 or $10 more for stationery supplies (or any other item) and purchase them locally, rather than driving 15 minutes each way to Wal-Mart.

We do this because that half hour of drive time to save $5 or $10 is simply not worth it to our organization.

As the average worker makes between $200 and $500 an hour for her or his organization, that half hour drive to save $10 costs $100. And since time is now our time as well as our organization's time, we are going to use it in the most productive manner possible.

In the old view, we might just say save the $10 and work an extra half hour later. But that doesn't produce more for either the worker or the organization. If one wanted to work another half hour more, why not spend it producing another $100 for the organization.

Travel time reconsidered

Travel time is another area where one's concept of time, now more valuable, changes. The drive time to our state's capital, where we occasionally do business or meet with people, is four hours one way. To meet with someone there takes eight hours of driving time. Eight hours of wasted time. But one time we were able to schedule a meeting so that we could take a train to the city and back. The day before someone asked us for a report in two days, and we replied we couldn't get it done, because we were "on the road" the next day. Then we remembered we were to be on the train. So we took our computers, worked all the way down and back, and had the report done on time.

Now here's the question: what is the travel time to that city if one is working all the way there and back?

It still took eight hours, and probably closer to 10 hours, by train. But since we were working for eight of those hours, one could easily make the case that it only an hour to get to that city by train, instead of four driving. Because it did take four hours of our time driving, but only one hour of our time via the train.

If one can work and travel at the same time, getting someplace literally takes "no time at all."

Right now it takes ten hours to drive to our vacation cabin on a lake up north. If we were able to take the train there, we would be able to spend another day at the cabin and still maintain our existing productivity.

Workaholism and the Next Generation

An interesting issue is whether telecommuting is subject to workaholism and measured by the same standards (long hours) that centralized office work is subject to, or whether telecommuting can lead workers into a situation where people are able to work fewer hours.

Americans now work more hours a year than workers in any other country in the world. It is more than 2,000 hours a year. Just a decade ago, American newspapers would run stories about the workaholic Japanese, then the most overworked nation in the world, and poke fun at them and point out the liabilities. No more poking fun at the Japanese. And no more stories about working too long.

Europeans average about six weeks of vacation a year, at least double what Americans get.

Worse, long hours are valued.

- If one works 12-14 hours a day, one is automatically presumed to be effective and productive, to be doing one's job. No one says they are so ineffective they have to work 12-14 hours.

- At a recent college reunion, Bill confessed that he takes two months off in the summer. The others at the table regarded that as heresy. I couldn't do that, each one countered, and then cited some reason why their particular situation would not allow so much time off.
- At a Rotary Club meeting, one member reported he just took his first vacation in three years, and then proceeded to tell us he had no idea what to do with all that wasted time, and was eager to get back to work.

As we have noted elsewhere in this book, telecommuting should be favored because of its increased productivity. And noting that the average telecommuter works longer hours than a similar person in a central office certainly helps justify this new work situation, and ease the minds of senior managers.

But the longer hours may very well not be the cause of the increased productivity. It may very well be that the longer hours come from more time spent in "work engagement," and that telecommuting might allow workers to work fewer hours and still produce a middle-class standard of living.

All this might have to wait for the next couple of generations to take over the workplace. The baby boomers are helplessly workaholic, and their up-and-down precarious retirement situation may keep them working even if some would prefer to be retired. Regardless, baby boomers are not likely to lead, or favor (this is an ethic and value of that generation), the charge to fewer work hours.

Generation X, however, has a distinctively different value system, which holds that a "balance" between work and non-work (family, leisure, hobbies, education) is far more preferable to workaholism.

It is usually elegantly and succinctly phrased as "Get a life."

And since baby boomers are likely to tie up and hold down the best jobs in the economy for awhile, there is an economic necessity (and resentment) for Gen X's view.

Thus, a trend toward, and value of, stay-at-home moms in Gen X, while baby boomer women sought the workplace. Which brings up a question we would like to ask, if Gen X stay-at-home moms could get telecommuting jobs that were of a more professional nature than stuffing envelopes, would stay-at-home moms take a part-time telecommuting job? Our guess is yes. Our guess is that the trend toward stay-at-home moms is not motivated primarily by a desire not to work, but by a desire to spend time with their children. And that if both conditions could be fulfilled (work and children), more women than not would prefer to work.

Here's an illustration of the generational differences about work and how they relate to telecommuting:

Our nephew Jeff used to work fixing X-ray machines, a job that required graduate university work, in one of the top ten hospitals in the country. But after awhile, he decided he wanted to also play in a band, even though this was a purely avocational activity and was not intended to lead to stardom or a career in music.

He approached the hospital about working half- or three-quarters time. They hesitated. So an outside company that fixes X-ray machines for hospitals offered Jeff a job meeting his conditions. The hospital soon agreed to his conditions as well, but it was too late. The hospital's initial coolness to the idea raised the prospect of future bureaucratic and foot-dragging behavior.

Soon Jeff was not only working less than full time, but he moved out of state to another city altogether and continued working for the company, fixing X-ray machines for hospitals, and playing music.

The initial reaction among his relatives in the baby boom and World War II generations was, of course, much horror. A promising career, judged by these two generations' standards of full to overtime work, was being cut short. But for Jeff, and millions of other Generation Xers making similar decisions in the workplace, balance was being restored, a life was being fulfilled.

The next generation coming into the workplace, variously called Gen Y, the Net Generation, Baby Boomlet, or the Next Generation, will have a different work value system than Gen Xers. So there are many reasons why the Net Generation may not just prefer but demand telecommuting as a means to preserving and enhancing their non-work time.

Office workers will continue to be replaced by, and/or become, knowledge workers.[15] Knowledge workers will continue to become the most valued employee sector for advanced nations. They will continue to require a different resource and support base that includes telework or working from home. Moving work out of a central office and dispersing it is creating a second major shift in our lives, the transition from a physical office to a virtual office.

Chapter 7
Intranets Replace Offices: Shift Two

"I think I could, if I only knew how to begin.
For, you see, so many out-of-the-way things had
happened lately that Alice had begun to think that
very few things indeed were really impossible."
— *Lewis Carroll*

Shift Number Two is that a form of intranets, called virtual offices, will replace physical centralized offices.

Once people begin working from home, they need to be connected with each other in their organizations.

Quite simply, intranet offices will improve productivity, supervision, communication and results for organizations, including companies, businesses, government, education and nonprofits.

Intranet offices can do these essential organizational functions better than a physical office. And there will probably be some business functions that you cannot even do except by using an intranet office.

Even if you are with a small office, even a one person office, your intranet will become indispensable. Even if all your staff are in one location, even one building, an intranet will be indispensable.

An intranet is an area on the Internet, usually on your own web site, that is password protected so that only authorized individuals can have access to the area. The Internet is available and open and intended for everyone. An intranet is closed and intended for only a few.

"An intranet is separated from the rest of the Internet by a firewall — a hardware and software combination that prohibits unauthorized access to the intranet," writes technology author Preston Gralla. "People who work in the company can access the Internet and use its resources, but intruders are kept out by the firewalls."[1]

Intranets have many uses. An online classroom is an intranet. An online club is an intranet. Here we refer to the use of an intranet as a virtual, online or web-based office that replaces the physical office as the place where people in a company or organization do business, communicate and do work.

The organization running its intranet can specify who can have access. Gralla says three types of business groups typically use a corporate intranet. The first group is employees of the corporation. A second group is subcontractors or vendors who interact with the corporation, and might have access to limited and selected areas of the corporation's intranet. And then Gralla says that customers are a third group for whom it is possible to have an intranet, as customers access a company's catalog or inventory and make purchases.

Here are just a few things you can do with an intranet office right now:

- Have individual staff reports.
- Do a calendar of upcoming events and activities.
- Assign tasks, priorities and projects.
- Report on when tasks and projects are accomplished.
- Create an information database for use in customer service, policies and procedures, and other business functions.
- Maintain a database on customer interaction.
- Maintain financial records and expenditures records.
- Create an approval system for expenditures or purchase orders.
- Hold meetings and discussions.
- Do information-based work.
- and much more.

We could go on. There are many more variations and uses of an intranet office, and more uses that have not even been invented yet. What we know is that the hierarchical organizational structure of the Industrial Age and 20th century will not work efficiently in the Information Age and the 21st century. Replacing the hierarchical organizational structure will be a more flattened networked structure.

"Businesses will increasingly use Internet technology to create private corporate networks called intranets that will replace current local area networks and will be the prime computing resources of corporations,"

Gralla states. "In the long term, companies will make the most use of intranets in workgroup applications — software that allows people to work cooperatively with their computers."[2]

That networked organization will be managed and run more efficiently and effectively using an intranet, because an intranet can respond to the needs of the 21st century organization in ways that traditional ways of doing business cannot.

Once an organization's workers are located in more than one place, then the issues of communication, supervision, and collaborative work become visible and apparent.

There are many reasons why the intranet will become standard in almost all successful information-based organizations in the 21st century, and why your organization will benefit from having an intranet replace your physical office. Here are a few of them:

1. Get the best people.

To recruit and then manage the best people, regardless of the location of your best people.

2. Work any place.

Not only are workers in different locations, but an individual worker travels as well, and needs to be connected with the organization from a variety of locations, whether it be the airport, a hotel in another country, or visiting customers.

3. Work any time.

The office of the 21st century needs to be open 24 hours a day, seven days a week.

4. Instant communication required.

No longer can workers and teams afford to wait days or even hours for the latest information. Collaborative communication needs to be instantaneous.

5. Supervision is reduced.

Organizations cannot afford to spend time and money on high levels of supervision. Supervision time and cost must be reduced.

6. Accountability needs to increase.

Accountability of all workers and team players needs to increase.

7. Temporary workers need access.

Part-time, temporary, contract and short-term workers need access and faster integration into the organization.

8. Outcomes have to be measured.

Input, or time, or even activity no longer is the measure by which organizations succeed. Outcomes and results have to be recorded, and measured.

9. Accuracy must increase.

The accuracy of communication must increase.

10. Vendors and supplier communication.

There are adjunct players in your organization, such as vendors and suppliers. They need limited access, and you want to be able to communicate with them.

11. Speed.

Things have to happen faster.

In all of these aspects, the intranet or virtual office is superior to the physical office. But the most important, most fundamental reason, why intranets will replace offices is that only intranets foster and allow universal access to information.

The value of intranets for running a business was perceived almost immediately after the invention of the World Wide Web and first appearance of e-commerce around 1996[3]. Actual implementation of intranets by business has been growing cautiously but steadily. The fear of air travel following 9-11 helped move business online, as did the recession in the succeeding few years.

And technological advances have been helping. For example, virtual office web sites, given the acronym VOW (virtual office web site), are aided by the increasing access to broadband. "For teleworkers working from home one day per week, those with a broadband connection compared with those using dial-up, saved their employers more than $5,000 every year," says a 2003 report on telecommuting.

"'At AT&T, where 33% of the company's managers work from home at least one day per week and 7,500 employees are full-time teleworkers, that number can be significantly higher,' said Joseph Roitz, AT&T's telework director and ITAC research committee member.

"'When we set up a person with a virtual office we receive better than a one-year return on investment,' Roitz said. AT&T's program nets the company more than $150 million in increased worker productivity output and savings every year and that number is expected to rise as more and more employees have access to broadband either in their homes or at a remote location."[4]

At Xerox Corporation, telecommuting was tried several years ago but abandoned. "The technology of the time wasn't advanced enough to make it work," a company manager told the *Buffalo* (New York) *News*. "That is not an issue now, with personal digital assistants, e-mail and high-speed Internet connections plentiful," the manager said. "Even product demonstrations can be performed using a computer," he adds. Thus, with the software for a virtual office, Xerox is again promoting working from home.[5]

Of course, intranets used as virtual offices can also be mismanaged, just like physical offices can be mismanaged. Some intranets are used merely as information dumping grounds[6] with obviously unsatisfactory outcomes. Like the early automobile that sputtered, broke down, and got a flat tire every hundred miles or so, the intranet as virtual office is being created and corrected at the same time.

Universal Access

For organizational success in the 21st century, universal, total and complete access to information is essential. In the old physical office, information is limited. Knowledge cannot be given to all employees and staff in the obsolete framework of the pyramid and physical office. Limiting information and knowledge is now dysfunctional and counterproductive.

Today all staff or persons in an organization need to know just about everything about the organization.

All workers or people in an organization are needed to make the organization successful. Answers and solutions may come from any quarter in the organization.

It is impossible for a manager or director to know exactly what information each person in the organization needs to know to do his or her job, to help solve the organization's problems, and create opportunities.

Instead of you telling me what I need to know, I determine what I need to know to do my job. Only when communication is put online in a permanent record accessible to all persons in the organization can information be successfully shared, collaborative ideas generated, individual contributions be made, and those closest to the action be able to make decisions (regardless of their relative status or position on the hierarchical scale). This is the fundamental reason why intranets will replace offices.

It is this radically different approach, organization and delivery of communication in the 21st century that marks the underlying difference between the work environment of the Industrial Age and that of the Internet Age. The requirements for communication are so dramatically changed, the difference in their characteristics so significant, that it is worth exploring how communication is rapidly transitioning in our work, our lives and in our education.

Death of Verbal Instructions

Verbal communication was one of the two hallmarks of communication in the Industrial Age office of the 20th century, as well as for our 10,000 year human history before that. The other hallmark of communication was paper communication, both handwritten and typed.

Verbal communication is simply obsolete today for information purposes. There are a whole host of uses for which verbal communication is superior to written online communication. There is verbal communication in building trust, in building personal and professional relationships, solving relationship problems, judgment, measuring gut instinct, in engaging in a long term partnership, in using humor in the workplace, and more.

But for informational communication, such as supervision, instructions, reporting, and regular business communication, verbal communication is no longer viable.

- **Verbal instructions are too imprecise.** The single biggest reason why verbal communication is obsolete today is that it is too imprecise for the 21st century. Verbal instructions are often not detailed enough. There is little ability to have footnotes, explanations, definitions, or references to additional material providing a background or explanation.

    For example, our son in high school was given the instruction to include "citations" in his term paper. But he was unclear whether a citation meant a bibliography, footnotes, references embedded in the body of the paper, or any combination thereof.

    When those instructions were put online, they were much more precise, with a link that explains what a citation is and what is expected.

- **Verbal instructions are subject to interpretation.** Different people can receive and interpret those verbal instructions differently.
- **Verbal instructions vaporize.** They disappear after they have been said. The person giving the instructions can then alter the instructions afterward ("I didn't say that").
- **Verbal instructions do not hold either party accountable.** The norm is that the person with the superior position in the organization places accountability on the other person/s for correctly interpreting the verbal instructions. The instruction giver is not held accountable, and there are few verifiable independent ways to confirm what the instructions were.
- **Verbal instructions are not universally known.** Others with a need to know are not privy to verbal instructions and communication.
- **Verbal instructions can be non-contextual.** The workplace is a very complicated organizational setting today, where there are hundreds of previous instructions already existing, dozens of variables to be taken into consideration, and often a need for input from more than one person in the organization. A verbal instruction can be given from one person to another, without others knowing about that instruction, that has little to do with the matrix of instructions that already exist. And it is difficult for others in the organization to have input on a verbal instruction that may not be consistent with the matrix of instructions that already exist.
- **Things can and do go wrong with verbal instructions.** In most instances, the consequences of verbal instructions are correctable mistakes. Or they might involve minor consequences in terms of a few dollars lost. But big things can go wrong with verbal instructions. And people can and do lose their lives because of the inadequacy of verbal communication.

The End of Handwriting

We first became aware of the beginning of the end of handwriting when our son was in seventh grade. He came home from school one day and told us about Jenny Frederickson. Jenny was the last person our son knew who could write in cursive.

hello willie how are you doing here's your cursive that you wanted!

Handwriting is now in steep decline. And the pencil, soon to be followed by the pen, is in its final 20 glorious years before it joins the cartridge pen and quill pen in obscurity.

The futurists once predicted a paperless society. They were looking at the wrong end of the process. Led by the obsolescence of handwriting, it is the pencil and pen that are going into steep decline.

Consider:

- Fewer and fewer students and young people can read cursive handwriting. It is fading from use.
- Many students cannot read the teacher's handwriting on the blackboard anymore. A number of teachers have stopped using cursive.
- Penmanship stopped being taught a while ago. Now cursive is being taught less and less.
- The post office doesn't even rely on letters anymore for income.

The modern-day pencil was perfected in 1795 and was sophisticated new technology in the early part of the 19th century. Henry David Thoreau, author of *Walden*, was on the cutting edge of new technology, owning a pencil factory. After two centuries of a rise in sales, sales peaked in 1997 at 130 million gross and declined by 10% in the next four years, according to an official of a major pencil manufacturing association.[7]

In an e-mail message, the official told us most pencils were now made in China, noted that future sales in advanced societies would likely decline, and noted that future sales would be dependent on such newly industrialized societies as China.

Handwriting is falling into disuse in our society because it is becoming useless. Handwriting cannot be:

- Stored.
- Edited.
- Saved.
- Sent.
- Shared.

Handwriting can also be fatal. More than 7,000 people die every year because of handwriting, according to an Institute of Medicine report. Physicians' handwriting is misread by pharmacists and nurses, resulting in the wrong medicines being given to patients.

One health care provider reported that 50,000 medication errors had been eliminated in less than two years since a physician computer entry system was begun at its clinics.[8]

Electronic writing, soon to be called "writing," can be stored, edited, saved, sent, and shared. And for many of us who did not pass penmanship, electronic writing can be read by others.

The final blow to handwriting, pencils and pens will come when laptops and PDAs make keyboards portable for the majority of workers.

It is interesting to speculate when "Signature" will disappear from forms. Handwriting is already disappearing from our schools and colleges. As Generation Y moves into the workplace, it will disappear there as well.

Push Versus Pull

Part of what is going on here with the demise of verbal, handwritten and paper communication is what is known in the communication business as "push versus pull." We are going through a transition right now from "push" communication to "pull" communication.

"Push" communication is information determined and sent by the author or sender. "Pull" communication is information retrieved and determined by the recipient.

A memo is push communication. A staff meeting is push communication. Verbal and paper communication is "push" communication. Even e-mail is "push" communication.

There are several problems with push communication. They include:

- Too much information. We do not know what everyone needs to know, so we send all the information out. People receive more than they need to know.
- Not the right information. We guess wrong on what an individual needs to know.
- Not the right time. We send information out before, and sometimes after, someone needs to know it, and thus that information is not readily available when the person needs to know it and wants to retrieve it.

Not all push communication is unwanted, of course. If something mailed is desired, we call it a letter or a bill. If it is not desired, we call it junk mail. If a phone call is desired, we call it a call. If it is not desired, we call it telemarketing. If an e-mail is desired, we call it a message. If it is not desired, we call it spam.

With too much information being sent out, attempts are being made at making push communication workable. Having grown up with direct mail, most people tolerate junk mail. In phone calls, however, "do not call" lists have recently been installed in many states and a national registry is in the works. And in e-mail, people are very sensitive to spam. Even if we have yet to devise ways to reduce or eliminate it, people hate unwanted e-mails and support ways to minimize them.

Within an organization, we would not refer to any communication as junk mail, spam or telemarketing. Yet even within an organization, there is too much information, there is the problem of an individual getting the right information, and there is the issue of getting that information "just in time," when someone needs it.

Consequently, we spend hours in staff meetings listening to reports that may or may not be relevant. We read memos from the boss whether they are meant for us or not. People attend meetings just in case an issue is raised or a decision is made that may affect them.

Push communication is no longer efficient or effective.

What is slowly replacing push communication is pull communication. In pull communication, a person pulls the information in (or down) according to what the person needs to know, and when the person needs to know it.

Pull communication is accomplished using an intranet. A series of message boards are created with all the information anyone in the organization could possibly want to know. Each person then retrieves whatever information that person needs to know, at the appropriate time.

The information is always there, so someone can come back and get that information later, even years later.

The information is organized in a variety of ways, including by topic or subject matter; by date, so someone could review all the new messages or information posted; and even by person, as some information is posted with a list of names of people for whom it is of particular relevance or interest, like a CC: in an e-mail. (For posterity, we will note for our younger readers that CC: stands for "carbon copy," which in the last century was a sheet of paper in a typewriter with a copy of the original letter on it, usually in dull blue or purple ink that often smudged.)

Moving from a push mode of communication to a pull mode of

communication is a difficult transition, one with which adults raised in the last century have a good deal of difficulty. At the time of this writing, there is also the fact that the software developed for pull communication on an intranet is still in its infancy and not perfected yet. Nevertheless, pull communication will eventually replace push communication as the only way individuals can deal with the exponential and permanent growth in information.

Changing Role of Paper

As of this writing, it is unlikely that paper will disappear, despite the forecasts of the paperless office made by so many. Indeed, it not only appears unlikely, but undesirable. Yet the role of paper in our work, leisure and learning is changing.

It is clear that paper files, stored in one place and costing money to store, are inefficient and expensive. Paper files also limit access to only those in close physical proximity. Information in the files can be removed, usually for legitimate purposes, but nevertheless posing the risk that someone else might not gain access to that information in a timely manner, and certainly that more than one person cannot have access at the same time. Putting paper files online and having them stored electronically on a server with access via one's intranet only makes sense.

Reports and other information are also better shared, retrieved, and edited when put online. Education offers an excellent example. In the case of our son's student worksheets, we have had the experience of taking days to get worksheets from teachers. Sometimes our son lost the worksheets. Other times the teachers ran out of copies.

When the worksheets were turned in, it was usually unclear whether or not the teacher had received the worksheets, and when they were turned in. After turning in the worksheets or paper, our student had no access to the work. Finally, it takes longer for a teacher to grade physical worksheets and papers than it does online work, with the added disadvantage that when the teacher returns the work to the student, she or he does not then have a copy of the graded work.

Online worksheets and papers solve all of these problems.

On the other hand, paper itself is unlikely to disappear. Our experience with online courses has demonstrated over and over again that the hard copy textbook is a fundamental ingredient in successful online learning. Likewise, whether at work, or in our leisure time, we need and want the ability to print out copies of information. There are times when paper is easier to handle, absorb, or carry.

In terms of the essential functions of communication, the intranet is a wide open book that anyone in your intranet office can read. It enables everyone in the organization to know whatever types of knowledge and information they deem appropriate and useful.

From how we communicate in the 21st century, we move to another essential difference in the way organizations are run in the two centuries, management and accountability.

Supervision in the 21st Century

In today's world, supervision time must be minimized, outcomes must be maximized. More organizations are finding that it is simply not a good use of time and money to have their best people engaged in the supervision of other people. Indeed, over the past several decades the numbers of middle management personnel engaged full time in supervision have declined significantly. Instead, the best people are having their time redirected into producing income or cutting costs.

With an intranet, supervisors can more quickly and easily communicate with their employees and monitor their activities.

- Responsibilities and duties can be assigned quickly.
- Reports can be posted so that supervisors can see what has been done.
- Problems can be posted so that they can be addressed.

Supervision using an intranet is more effective than in-person supervision. For example, the often heard off-hand — "The project is coming along pretty well, boss" — comment at the water cooler is vague and lacks specificity in outcomes.

It is also not able to be communicated to others in the organization who may be depending on that project or activity. And often times a supervisor will not want to jeopardize a relationship, cause a scene, or hinder morale in verbal conversation. With an intranet, you can be a nice boss.

The record on the intranet will show what has been done, and what has not.

Another aspect of any organization is decision making. This involves not only the CEO and senior management, but people at all levels of the organization. At least one study done on decisions indicates that while the decisions supervisors make during a typical workday have increased, the amount of time they have to make decisions has not.

In the survey, some 77% of supervisors say that the number of decisions they have to make has increased, yet 42% say the amount of time they have to make those decisions has stayed the same, while another 43% say the amount of decision making time has actually decreased.[9]

An intranet facilitates decision making in at least two ways. First, the intranet provides much more data and facts upon which someone can make a decision, thus speeding the process considerably. And second, the intranet allows decisions to be pushed down in the organization so that the lowest possible person in the organization makes the decision. This allows top managers to spend their time on the high dollar decisions that only they can make.

Greater Accountability

The virtual office actually offers greater accountability than the physical office. Here's how it works.

A supervisor posts instructions online. If the supervisor does not post the instructions online, they do not exist. Verbal, paper or e-mail communication do not trump online postings.

The person doing the activity requested does a regular status update, say weekly. When the activity is complete, it is posted. The activity has not been done unless the person posts that it has been done.

In this way, instructions are visible and complete. And completion of the job is reported immediately, and fully (what is done, what is not done).

Supervisors become more accountable, because their instructions are visible to all. It is not possible for a supervisor to say, "I thought I told you to…"

And workers are more accountable, because their actions are visible to all. The likelihood of cheating becomes significantly reduced. If a person posted that something was done and it was not, there would be evidence in writing (the person's own report) for discipline or firing.

CEOs also become more accountable. CEOs need to be as accountable in organizations as are their employees and staff.

In our organization, for example, Bill not only initiates projects, but also usually is responsible for writing copy for them. Not long ago, our desktopper Danita posted this very diplomatic update for one of our projects:

"Still waiting on copy from Bill. ☺ — Danita."

The smiley face indicated she was writing a friendly reminder. But the message was clear, and had to be stated. The project was waiting on copy from Bill.

Here are some other aspects of accountability in the work place of the 21st century that are enhanced by virtual offices.

Performance outcomes must be results oriented, and measurable.

Staff performance has to move from "activities" to "outcomes." The test of whether someone is doing the job can no longer be measured by the time clock or whether someone was at her or his desk for eight hours.

Instead a person's performance needs to be measured by the outcomes, by whether something was accomplished.

With an intranet, performance objectives can be stated in black and white, and they are much more clear. If they are not clear, the specificity of the intranet demands that they be clearly stated in writing. Likewise, when an objective is accomplished, when a result is achieved, when something is done it can be reported accomplished by the person using the intranet. If it is done, it is reported.

Thus, what a given person has accomplished is measurable. It is also recorded. And it can be seen by all.

The gray areas of performance are considerably reduced, and the ability to improve productivity considerably enhanced.

Communication needs to become synchronized for greater efficiency.

A recent *New Yorker* cartoon shows a secretary with a note for her boss and she says, "You promised you would play phone tag with your daughter today."

Phone tag is no longer play. It is hard work, and not very rewarding. We all have busy schedules, and we all have different schedules.

With an intranet, you can communicate with a hundred different individuals more effectively, because they can log on and get the information at their convenience, reply at their convenience, and this "convenience" can result in faster communications, with things getting done faster.

"Fill out this form and return it to me" no longer needs to take weeks or even days. Now it can be done immediately.

Organizations need specialists on contract for limited times and high-quality specialty work.

Welcome to the era of specialization. Welcome to the era of contract workers and consultants, part-time workers, temporary project oriented specialists. It is now more productive to hire outside of your organization for a growing variety of specialized tasks than it is for a generalist on your staff to do the task. Outside specialists can do the job better, and in less time.

You get better results. And you only pay for a limited time or even activity outcome, so your actual costs are lower.
The way these outside specialists and consultants can participate most effectively in your organization is by including them in your intranet.

Vendors can be monitored, timetables set, communication facilitated.
For years, every week we would have to walk over to our printers and inquire about a certain brochure or publication. Several times a year we would hear, "Oh, it was printed a couple of days ago. Didn't you get the message?"

With an intranet, the vendor can keep you posted on a daily basis about the status of your order or service. Any vendor or supplier with whom you work closely can be included in your intranet, a separate intranet can be built, or the vendor can gain access to only certain aspects of your intranet.

How We Started to Go Virtual

We first learned about the Internet in 1995. And within a year it had changed our entire organizational outlook and plans.

Begun in 1974, LERN had grown by 1995 to become the largest association in the world in lifelong learning, with more than 4,000 members in 16 countries.

We had grown from a volunteer staff to 30 paid employees. We even had an evening second shift to process orders and ship publications.

We had built up our corporate headquarters from a file cabinet and borrowed space to 10,000 square feet of office space. This would have cost a third of a million dollars a year in rent if we were headquartered in Washington, D.C., where most associations are located. We had plans for a museum, video theatre, expansive entranceway with fountain, and conference center. Members would fly in from all over the country to visit our headquarters. Or so we planned.

And then three events occurred in short succession that changed everything. The first one was modest enough. Bill went to Oneonta, New York, for an executive retreat for the officers of our board of directors. The chair of the board, Hugh Hammett, met him at the Albany airport and drove through the beautiful New York countryside. At a particularly nice overlook, he talked about the emerging World Wide Web, then called simply the Internet, and told us we had to get involved with it.

Second, we began to study up on the Internet and gained just enough knowledge to be dangerous and over confident. Our printer had a going-away party for a long-time worker, and we were confidently expounding on the Internet to a woman. She responded, "Yes, and the intranet is amazing." We replied that the word was Internet, not intranet, to which she said, "Yes, I know all about the Internet, but the intranet will be even more powerful." This sent us in a rapid retreat to the punch bowl. And we spent another six months and several hundreds of dollars buying books about the intranet.

Third, like every organization, we had staff turnover. So when a couple of full-time professionals left, we started recruiting the best people we could find. We called Paul Franklin in Portland, Oregon, and said, "Paul, come work with LERN." "Great," he replied. "Move to Manhattan, Kansas," we said. "No," he replied. "Denver? Chicago? Minneapolis?" Paul wanted to stay in Portland.

We called Greg Marsello in Providence, Rhode Island. Greg is a co-founder of LERN. He had been president of the organization for twelve years. Greg was in the process of selling his family-owned jewelry company, a business that employed 500 people, but as a manufacturing company was finding it increasingly difficult to compete with overseas-based jewelry companies with lower wage scales.

"Greg, come work with LERN." "Great," he replied. "Come move to Manhattan, Kansas," we said. "No," he replied. "Denver? Chicago? Minneapolis?" Greg wanted to stay in Providence.

We wanted the best experts. They were willing to work with LERN. But they wanted to live where they wanted. With the Internet, that would be possible.

The impact and implications of these three events were reinforced by the intellectual fervor of the mid 1990s. Several times a year we would meet in Washington, D.C., with other associations engaged in adult education. The organization was called the Coalition of Lifelong Learning Organizations. We had a brilliant elderly gentleman named Sam Brightman who wrote a newsletter for us. He said of the coalition, "They meet, they talk, they do no harm."

At these meetings we talked, and more often listened, to Ed Schroer, the Vice President for New Products at the American Society for Training and Development, a large association serving trainers in the private sector.

Every meeting, it seemed, Ed would talk about another book that had just come out, another startling new perspective or concept. "The priesthood is dead," he noted at one meeting. We knew he wasn't talking about the church or religion, but it took us a few years to figure out what he was saying. Schroer introduced us to *Net Gain* and the concept of virtual community. He mentioned The Centerless Corporation, introducing us to business units as the fundamental structure of business in the Internet Age.

Within one year we designed a plan to destroy our headquarters office and become a virtual organization.

We decided we would:

1. Destroy our central corporate headquarters building.
2. De-emphasize or even eliminate offices and office space.
3. Contract, hire or otherwise engage the best people we could find wherever they are.
4. Let current employees, with some guidelines, move.
5. Communicate and operate our organization using an intranet.

For us two, this meant we could move to Wisconsin. While we loved living in Kansas for 22 years, it was time to leave. We wanted to be close to a major hub airport. We wanted to be closer to our cabin in northern Wisconsin. We wanted to be closer to more technology resources.

Our initial plan was to have an office in downtown Minneapolis, with a great address, a nice view, close to everything.

But we wanted to live in a small college town about 45 minutes away — River Falls, Wisconsin. And we also realized that no matter where we relocated the office, only a small fraction of our members would actually come visit us. Did it really matter where the office was, or if we even had an office?

Then we thought about driving two hours a day to a downtown office. Then we thought about driving two hours a day in snow and sleet. Then we thought about a home office in River Falls.

Sometime in 1996 we planned to move to River Falls, Wisconsin, in the spring of 1998.

How this transition to a virtual organization would happen, we did not know. By then Greg Marsello was on staff, living and working near Providence. The three of us began meeting four times a year to plan the first stage of the transition.

We began discussing and planning the many issues involved:

- Would employees be transferred, given a choice, exited through natural attrition, or let go?

- What employees had jobs that could be done at a distance?
- What employees had the work characteristics and/or personality to function independently at a distance?
- Could we rewrite some job descriptions from activities that have to be supervised and measured hourly to outcomes that do not require supervision and can be measured from a distance?
- How do we form business units?
- Who supervises whom?
- What people need to be in the same office or physical proximity?
- What functions should stay in Manhattan; what functions and jobs should go to Providence; what functions and jobs should go to River Falls?
- What jobs and functions should be contracted out and not done by current employees?
- How do we physically communicate?
- How do we connect to our business software, which was not Internet based. Phone lines, ISDN lines, modems, costs.

We discussed what we should do one week out, one month out, and made plans for six months out and nine months out. One fascinating conclusion was reached after much debate. All three of us agreed on what we should do one week out and one month out. And we all disagreed on what should happen in six to nine months. After a while, we concentrated on the immediate tasks of what should happen in one to four weeks, on which we had remarkable consensus throughout.

Other than we two moving to Wisconsin, the first full-time employee to move was Danita Dickinson. She was moving to Ann Arbor, Michigan. Before transitioning to a virtual office, we would be sorry to see good staff members leave and would hold a good-bye party for each one. Some only moved sixty miles. Now, we begged Danita just to take our computer with her when she moved and to continue her job of desktopping our newsletters, publications and promotions. She would e-mail the files to the printer. We would e-mail our stories and copy to Danita. The printer worked with her to make the process run smoothly.

Actually, Bill privately estimated she would only last about six months, working in isolation in her apartment all day with no one with whom to socialize. And businesses in Ann Arbor would offer her a job working in an office with other people. Bill was wrong and Danita is still working for us full time.

Later, Danita moved to Nebraska, and then to Colorado. Within two years, she lived and worked in four states, all while keeping the same job.

At one point she told us she wanted to be the first employee whose boss did not know where she was. While her physical address kept changing, her e-mail address remained *danita@lern.org*.

It is a new work environment. Now younger workers without family responsibilities can move anywhere in the world, as often as they want, as long as they take the computer and keep an Internet connection. What freedom to be able to move to a new city without the economic uncertainty of having to find a new job, and with the social security of enjoying one's job.

Our Text-based Tour of the Virtual Office

The best way to understand a virtual or intranet office is to experience it. Our text-based tour of our virtual office will be inadequate, but a start.

Someone in our organization goes to our web site. The person enters their username and password and is given access to our virtual office.

In our newest version, a person has his or her own customized web site. The person can automatically bypass the username/password access if they are using their own computer.

In our first virtual office, we constructed a floor plan like an architectural floor plan of a building. It gave the impression that one was actually in a building. Though our current version no longer uses a floor plan design to navigate our virtual office, that impression, that image, that feeling is still important to us.

The first page that appears in our virtual office is the main page. It has links on the left hand side. The rest of the page is devoted to staff news. This is where anyone in the organization can post a news comment. The effect is dual. First, one immediately sees what is new and stays in touch with the latest happenings. And second, there is a feeling of being in touch with others in the organization, of being connected, of staying current, of being a part of the organization.

From there, a person has many options. We have these sections to our current virtual office:

A. Communications.
1. **Staff Reports.** Each week everyone on staff makes a weekly report on their week and what they did.
2. **Product information.** This is where we post information about new products, new services, new activities.
3. **E-mail access.** Each person can gain access to their e-mail via the

Internet. For instance, if a staff member is traveling and using another computer, the staff person can log on to e-mail here.

4. **Calendar.** There is an online calendar, so people can find out who is traveling that particular week, who is on vacation, what events are being held, and what deadlines are coming up.

B. Project Management.

Supervisors post instructions on what is to be done. Staff involved in various aspects of the project add specifications. The status of the projects is updated or reported on weekly, so everyone knows what has been done and where the project is at.

For example, if we are sending out a brochure, one staff person will report the number of people on the mailing list to whom the brochure is sent. Another person will post the copy for the brochure. A third person will layout or desktop the brochure and report whether there is too much copy, too little copy, or whether other changes need to be made. A fourth person works with the printer and reports when the brochure is printed and mailed. Another person reports the cost of the brochure.

C. Gateways or links.

These are access to other password protected areas. In our organization, for example, we have a number of online classrooms where we offer online courses. And we have an online club or member service area for our 4,000 members. So staff have access to those areas from our Staff Offices or virtual office.

D. Information.

We have a section with information of importance to people in the organization. For example, we have a database of policies and procedures. And we have a listing of the voluntary leadership in our organization.

E. Web applications.

This is where work actually happens online. That work will differ by organization. To give you some illustrations, here are some of the web applications or work we do online.

1. **Brochure critiques.** An online form that cuts the time it takes us to critique a brochure from more than a half hour down to about 15 minutes. The form also improves the quality of the critique.

2. **Story writer.** An online form that automatically posts a news story or article to our web site so our customers can get the information. Anyone writing a story can post it.
3. **Customer database.** Our customer database is now online, so any staff person can view the database and get information from it, anywhere from a customer's e-mail address to finding out who attended our last conference.
4. **Transaction database.** If someone orders a publication, it is posted online. The person invoicing the order does that work online in our virtual office. Then another staff person, in another location, processes the order and ships the publication ordered. Finally, the financial staff person sends the invoice and records the payment when it is received.

That's a quick and text-based tour of our virtual office. In the future, we will be adding voice, pictures, live web shots, and other features to the virtual office.

Transition Issues

To be sure, during the time period of 2005 and 2015 there are enormous obstacles to transitioning to a virtual or intranet office. They essentially are the same enormous obstacles that faced organizations 100 years ago: pre-existing infrastructure; and existing culture and traditional behavior.

For example, many horse drawn delivery companies were not able to make the transition to truck delivery in the early part of the twentieth century. Some of them were so encumbered by their infrastructure that they could not financially manage the transition. They had hay barns, drivers who only knew how to drive horses, blacksmiths (people who molded horse shoes and other iron materials to specification), farriers (people who put the horse shoes on the horses and maintained their hooves in good condition), and so on.

Some of them were enamored of the culture of the horse-driven vehicle, the smell of the hay, the friendly manner of the horses, the fresh air, the circle of friendships among the workers. They so valued that culture that they preferred to retire, stay with a declining business, or even go out of business than to switch to motor-driven delivery trucks.

And thirdly, like today, they knew that the new technology was not superior in all forms or ways. With a horse-drawn delivery vehicle, for instance, the horse was so trained it would automatically move from one delivery home or building to another while the driver was taking the package or material to the house. Without the driver at the reins, or even giving a command, the horse knew to proceed to the next stop. Something no truck would ever master.

Today, people and organizations face those same three challenges.

The Culture of the Physical Office

For most adults who are used to the physical centralized office, the office culture is almost overwhelming as long as one is in a physical office setting. It is very difficult to adopt the behavior of the virtual office while working in a physical office with other people in the same organization. This may be different for Generation Y and young people coming into the workplace. They may be able to move easily between an individual working space and a collective centralize office and still retain all the behaviors required in a virtual or intranet office organization. But our experience, at this time, is that it is very difficult for adults to remain in the physical office with other workers and acquire the online or intranet behaviors required for a successful web-based organization.

- People who are not in the same physical office, are left out. They are "left out" emotionally as well as being kept "out of the loop" information-wise.

    Sitting on a plane overhearing a conversation, we heard a man tell his colleague that he used to telecommute from home. But all the good sales leads for his division were kept in the office and only by being in the office could he hear about and have access to those leads. So he gave up telecommuting and returned to the office.

- Internal communication within the physical office gravitates toward being verbal, two way, and push communication.
- Online communication using the intranet then tends to be ignored, used less often, or used inadequately. It is often seen as duplication of effort, since everyone in the office has been informed.

These are the main detriments or obstacles to moving people still gathered together in a physical office into a virtual or intranet office.

Then there are other industrial-age behaviors which are simply inefficient. They include:

- The time it takes to say hello to everyone in the office in the morning. Especially as a boss, we had to make sure we included everyone in our office hello, otherwise someone might think they were on the "outs" with the boss.

- Getting permission, delegating and other needless "passing off" of activities. In a physical office, there is a perceived or actual hierarchy. Thus, sometimes a person will need to get permission to do a certain duty (like use the fax machine). Or someone will perceive her or himself to be above doing a certain duty (like using the fax machine) and then delegate or pass-off the activity to another person. And there may be discussion involving two or more people before such passing-off is accomplished. All this takes time.
- Staff meetings. We have no objections to staff meetings. We love staff meetings. But when staff meetings are purely or mainly informational, they are a waste of time.
- Deciding things. Who takes care of the phone over lunchtime, when people take breaks,
- Social conversation. Some activities, apparently, must be accomplished with a minimum of social conversation.

Then there are attitudes and office politics related to the move to the virtual or intranet office.

People in a physical office often resent or, more likely, are fearful of those working in a virtual or intranet setting. This stems mostly from not knowing what it is like to work virtually, but also a fear that they will be forced to work virtually as well.

And people in a physical office, even while moving to a virtual or intranet office, continue to be subject to the office politics of the Industrial Age.

For those working virtually, one of the unforeseen but beneficial consequences is the reduction in "office politics."

We have been pleasantly surprised that people working at a distance are likely to have fewer personal problems with others in the organization, fewer cliques form, there is less of a hidden or invisible power structure. There are fewer power fights, possibly because there are fewer tangible things over which to fight, such as a corner office, access to management, and so on. There is less rumor and gossip, probably because most all information related to the organization is visible and made available to all. Now these things do not disappear altogether. But our experience has been that there is a significant reduction in office politics without the office.

Stop Building Buildings

As we have stated, some organizations may not be able to make the transition to the Internet Age because they have continued to invest too heavily in the infrastructure of the old age, the Industrial Age.

Buildings are the albatross, the burden, the biggest threat to organizations in the 21st century. In the Industrial Age, the age of factories and offices, buildings were a sign of success. But the Internet turns so many things upside down. It is clear that in this century buildings are a sign of weakness, not strength.

We first became aware of the need to reduce the attention given to buildings, the so called "edifice complex," in 1991. We were in an airplane on the runway of the Philadelphia airport, reading the Wall Street Journal. The paper that day had a story about the new boss of Scott Paper Company, and how he was about to sell the corporate headquarters building. As we looked out the window, we saw the Scott headquarters building, built in the shape of a paper towel, the product it made. If such a symbol of corporate identity was being discarded, we thought at the time, it must be a major shift.

Many other corporations followed suit, and continue to this day to reduce their financial and spiritual allegiance to their buildings. In Silicon valley, many software and other dot com businesses have very plain and unadorned buildings.

In this instance, business may be ahead of the government, education and nonprofit sector. For the nonprofit sector has yet to relinquish its adoration and worship of the building.

Peter Drucker first told universities to reduce their buildings back in 1996.

The reasons are becoming increasingly clear and painful: institutions have to devote huge investments into technology and intellectual capital (their people) to remain successful in the Internet Age.

In the period between 2000-2005, the period which we thought could sustain both the costs of the Industrial Age and the costs of the Internet Age, organizations continued to build buildings unabated.

Between 2005 and 2010, organizations will realize they have to choose between building buildings and investing in technology and people. By 2010 organizations will realize that the only viable course of action is to invest in technology and people. But by then it may be too late for some organizations.

Just as some companies 100 years ago had too much invested in hay barns, blacksmiths and horse farms, some organizations may wind up with such a huge burden of debt and maintenance of buildings, they might not survive.

With these imperative financial demands costing millions of dollars, the building and maintenance of buildings is an increasing burden that institutions can no longer afford.

While this dictum holds true for all organizations, it is particularly relevant for government and education, those institutions in which we all as taxpayers have an investment.

Buildings will decline in terms of importance and value for several reasons.

1. Some space is obsolete.

Lecture halls, meeting rooms and other space no longer serve a valuable function, as meetings can be done better online.

2. Offices are wasted space.

Millions of dollars could be saved by eliminating offices.

3. Existing space must be refitted.

Not all space needs to be destroyed. But classrooms need to be turned into discussion rooms. That means refitting existing classrooms into spaces where chairs can be set up in a circle, with carpeting and good lighting. Meeting rooms also need to have wireless Internet connections.

4. Building maintenance eats up too much money.

It is an estimated that a typical institution spends almost 10% of its annual budget on facilities and staff to run those facilities. In business 10% is often the difference between success and failure.

Certainly we will have buildings in the 21st century. But the criteria for whether or not those buildings are cost effective is likely to be the 18 hour rule. Just about the only companies for whom buildings are "profitable" in and of themselves are hotels. If you analyze the space usage of a hotel, almost all of the space is in use for 18 hours a day. Sleeping rooms are in use for around 18 hours a day, from 3 pm (check-in time) to noon the next day (check-out time). Meetings are scheduled in meeting rooms from 6 am breakfasts for local clubs to midnight, when ballroom, dance and social gatherings usually end. The restaurants are often open from morning to night.

If space in a building is used 18 hours a day, it is likely to be of value to the community. For instance, if a swimming pool can be used by the community for 18 hours, it is likely that it will receive support to continue it. A gym or a swimming pool used only a few hours a day is unsustainable for most communities.

By continuing to build new buildings, institutions almost certainly will be jeopardizing their future as quality and competitive organizations. In the worst of scenarios, the edifice complex could create such huge burdens the institution may not survive past 2020.

The mandate is clear: stop building buildings.

Our organization is not alone in creating and building a virtual office using an intranet. Thousands of businesses and organizations are putting more work information for their employees online every day. Virtual offices make communication more effective, work more accountable, and productivity more efficient. Virtual offices also help destroy the obsolete organizational structure of the last century, replacing the pyramid with a more flexible and adaptable structure called a network.

Chapter 8
Networks Replace the Pyramid: Shift Three

"We cannot solve problems with the same thinking that generated the problems."
— *Albert Einstein*

Our whole way of perceiving how we as individuals function in relationship to others is changing. In the 20th century, we functioned in terms of pyramids. The organizational chart pervaded life. It was not merely a way of structuring hierarchy in the workplace. Schools, churches, social organizations, clubs all were structured in terms of a pyramid.

"In fact, for the past hundred years, daily life in North America, Europe and Japan was based almost entirely on the operation and expansion of huge industrial bureaucracies," writes Dan Sullivan in his breakthrough book, *The Great Crossover*.[1]

"These organizations were built like pyramids, with many levels of managers and workers doing repetitive tasks," writes Sullivan. "Until recently, this was the only structure that allowed for the orderly flow of communication and information up to and down from the people in charge.

"Bureaucracies relied on conformity and loyalty. In return, they gave you a form of security. In most major corporations, you went to work, and if you were relatively competent you could be reasonably assured of a paycheck until you retired, and then a pension until death.

"In industrialized countries, you grew up playing by the rules of a bureaucracy. And they were the only set of rules you knew," notes Sullivan.

The pyramid structure is not limited to business and corporations. It is the structure all nonprofits use as well. And schools and colleges use it to prepare people for the workforce.

"Computers are wiping out layers upon layers of management and workers — the pyramids are breaking up," says Sullivan.

"Over the next thirty years, most of the jobs and dependencies based on huge bureaucracies will be eliminated. For people who have never learned any way of life other than life in a bureaucracy, it will be a slow and painful reckoning with a new reality."

The organizational structure of the pyramid is detrimental to organizational success in the 21st century. It is too costly, too limiting, and does not allow your organization to tap into the kinds of people you need to maintain your quality and improve your success.

As we move further into the Internet Age, the pyramid is being replaced by the network. We are starting to see relationships and even physical structure as being a network.

Computers, of course, are linked together in networks. And some scientists recently revealed a new diagram of the universe: a web of networked galaxies. Enemies are less apt to be countries (governmental pyramids) and more likely to be networks. Even the food pyramid is being dismantled. Pyramids are collapsing everywhere. The network is not only the technological underpinning of our age, but the conceptual framework as well.

"Restructuring the organization around information — something that will, of necessity, have to be done by all large businesses — invariably results in a drastic cut in the number of management levels and, with it, in the number of 'general' management jobs," writes Peter Drucker.[2]

"We need emphasis on assignments to task force teams, which will be the only way, in most cases, in which professional specialists can acquire a 'view of the whole' now that they will no longer be routinely promoted into managerial positions," he says.[3]

"But as advanced technology becomes more and more prevalent, we have to engage in analysis and diagnosis- that is, in 'information'- even more intensively or risk being swamped by the data we generate," Drucker explains. "So far most computer users still use the new technology only to do faster what they have always done before, crunch conventional numbers. But as soon as a company takes the first tentative steps from data to information, its decision processes, management structure, and even the way its work gets done begin to be transformed."[4]

In the pyramid organizational structure of the 20th century, information and knowledge resided with the people at the top of the pyramid. In the Information Age, the information and knowledge is primarily at the bottom, in the hands of specialists and frontline staff.

The information-based organization requires far more specialists overall than the command-and-control companies of the last century, notes Drucker. These specialists do different work, and direct themselves. They work with other specialists in task-focused teams.[5]

As far as supervision in the network, Drucker points to the British system of supervision in India for the two centuries the British ruled the country. With more than 100 district officers spread out over thousands of miles, these district officers were supervised by only one person. Each month the district officers would write down their four major tasks or goals, report on what actually did happen, and report on any discrepancies between what was expected to happen and what actually did happen. Then the district officer would write down what he expected would happen in the next month coming up. That was it, but Drucker says this is the essence of supervision in the Information Age. It is based on results. It is based on written documentation. And outcomes and accountability are very clear.

Drucker also has the insight to foresee that what we report on is very different from what we report on in the industrial organization and pyramid. In the industrial organization and pyramid, we report on what we did and what we want others to know. One way in which much time and staff energy is wasted in organizations is that managers and employees report on their activities, rather than results and outcomes. An even bigger waste of time is that managers and staff report on what they want others to know. Either they pass on information which may not be valuable to some or even all of the other staff, or — not knowing what information might be valuable — they pass on all the information they have. The end result is not only wasted time reading and receiving information which is not relevant to one's job. But an even worse consequence is not getting the information one does need, at the time one needs it.

Drucker understands this clearly and totally inverts the communication paradigm from what I want you to know to what you want me to tell you. He notes, "The key to such a system is that everyone asks, Who in this organization depends on me for what information? And on whom, in return, do I depend?"[6] Having gone through this transition in our organization, this is a huge and dramatic shift in how people communicate in an organization.

Life in this century is being reformulated around networks, with good reason. The network is superior to the pyramid for the 21st century. When we look at dysfunctional systems and approaches, it very well may be because the system or approach looks like a pyramid instead of a network.

The key ingredient to a network is information. Networks are all about information. With the right kind of information, resources can be properly allocated. As business guru Peter Leyden notes, "The fundamental principle of networks is that no one is as smart as everyone. So networks utilize everyone in the organization. And each individual brings more value than just one person. So the total of the network is greater than the sum of its parts."[7]

Why the Network is Superior to the Pyramid

Here are our top ten reasons why the network is superior to the pyramid:

1. More information is discovered.

In a pyramid organization, information normally flows downward. Sometimes it flows upward. Rarely if ever does it bypass 'normal channels.' Rarely does it go laterally. Thus, less information is discovered.

In a network, information flows in all directions. You never know when someone will be able to use the information. You never know who in the organization will discover something new or important.

The networked organization has the advantage in discovering more information.

2. More information is shared.

In a pyramid organization, information is not readily shared.

In a network, all information is shared. Everyone is given the information she or he needs to have.

3. The sum is greater than the parts.

Everyone together knows more than one person knows individually. In a network, the totality of the knowledge of everyone is tapped, says Leyden. More work is being done more efficiently by collaboration.

4. Greater access to people and resources.

In a network, time and place are irrelevant. That means a network can tap into people anywhere in the world. So a network can have superior human resources.

5. People bring networks with them.

Once an organization taps into an individual, that individual can also be a link to his or her set of relationships, or networks. So by connecting with an individual one can often gain access to a whole new set of human resources.[8]

6. More relevant information.

In a pyramid, I tell you what I think you need to know. Or I tell you what I want you to know. Or I tell you everything and waste a lot of your time.

In a network, you tell me what I need to tell you. And I tell you what you need to tell me. This means everyone gets more relevant information. Less time is wasted providing irrelevant information to people.

8. Individual talents are stressed.

In a pyramid, people often play a role. In a network, people are more likely to have their individual talents stressed. In a network, mass customization is possible. Thus, individuals are more likely to be able to contribute their unique talents, thus maximizing the success of the network.

9. Outcomes are measured.

Because pyramids normally function synchronously, the input of time is often a standard for success. A person in a pyramid will feel more successful, for instance, working 12 hours a day instead of eight hours a day. Time becomes a standard of measurement and success.

In a network, outcomes are measured. Whether something is achieved in eight hours or 12 hours does not matter. And because it does not matter, and because time is very valuable, something produced in less time actually has a higher value.

10. Decision making is better.

In a pyramid, the people at the top make the decisions. In a network, the people with the most information make the decision. One consequence is that often decision making moves "down," so that front line people are making more decisions.

As the number of decisions that have to be made has increased exponentially in the last several decades, it is no longer feasible nor cost effective for so-called decision makers to make all the decisions. In a network, everyone can participate in decision making, thus relieving decision makers of involvement in minor issues. And the chances of making the correct decision improve because the people with the most information now make the decisions.

Replacing the pyramid as the organizational structure of this century is the network, composed of business units.

What Business Units Are

A business unit is anywhere from 1 to 15 people who are focused on a single responsibility or set of activities.

The business unit is responsible for a given set of outcomes or results. The unit has all the resources it needs to do the job. If it does not have access to information in the computer, for example, or has no control over the printing of the brochure, for example, it is not a business unit. It is still part of the pyramid.

The business unit is not an isolated or totally independent unit. It takes certain resources from either outside the organization, or from another business unit. And it produces something of value and sends it to another business unit, or an entity outside of the organization.

To illustrate, promotion and marketing in our organization is a business unit. Copy for a brochure is written by one member of the business unit, and sent to the desktop person to layout. The desktopper sends the completed brochure to the printer. Another person works with the printer and tracks the progress of the brochure through delivery to the post office. All of the people in this business unit are located in different parts of the country. Yet they work together on a daily basis to produce something of value to our organization.

Another business unit in our organization is customer service. Three people are all located in one physical office, where they answer the toll free phones, get faxes, open the mail, respond to e-mail inquiries, process online orders, and do instant messaging with customers on our web site. The business unit is focused around handling customer orders and inquiries.

Before becoming a business unit, customer service and promotion were all part of a pyramid structure. In the pyramid, for example, a receptionist answered the phone and routed the phone calls. Later an automatic phone machine routed the calls. Either way, a customer was routed to someone in the organization, and the printer calling our promotion people also went through the same central system. That proved dysfunctional and costly, as customers received less service and immediate attention than they required.

Now only customers call the customer service business unit, where they receive immediate and personal assistance. The printer has no reasons to call the customer service business unit, and communicates with the promotion business unit. Better, faster, more personal customer service is only one of the benefits we have experienced with reorganizing our operations around business units.

A business unit can either be led by someone in the business unit, or by a director or manager outside of the business unit. People in the business unit can either be in the same physical location, or in different physical locations. Business units are also responsible to each other. In a pyramid, there is responsibility up in the hierarchy. In a network, the business units have to respond to other business units.

Your organization will need to undergo a massive transformation in order to remain successful, competitive and able to satisfy the needs of your participants. It is time now for CEOs and decision makers to begin thinking and planning about how to make that transformation.

What you will do is to replace your pyramid structure with networked business units. You will have different staff and people in different locations, drawn together not by geography or location but by the Internet and other networking technology. This will occur regardless of whether you are with a local organization with everyone working in the same town.

Just as distance has nothing to do with distance learning, networked business units have nothing to do with distance. Communication via technology is more efficient and productive than communication in-person for routine office work. Of course, meetings continue to occur, and some important work will be done in face-to-face meetings. But most office communication will occur more efficiently and productively via technology.

One of the first books to address the emergence of networked business units was *The Centerless Corporation* by Bruce A. Pasternack and Albert J. Viscio. "To thrive amid the formidable complexities of the new business environment, an entirely new type of corporation is called for, one that is distanced from the excessive levels of command that companies have become comfortable with," write Pasternack and Viscio.

"The traditional corporate model focuses on linear chains of command to govern independent and relatively isolated entities. The structure is hierarchical, with a large corporate and division staff, centralized functions, and self-sufficient divisions. It is multidimensional along major product lines.

"The Centerless Corporation is pancake flat with a network of interdependent business units and strategic alliances managed by group executives. It is not horizontal per se, but rather nonlinear, meaning that rather than everything flowing up and down it flows in whatever direction it is most effective for it to go."[9]

Here are the key concepts that Pasternack and Viscio say are making up the new networked office, and combining to replace the old organizational structure. With every skill and function becoming more sophisticated and competitive, your organization will need to focus on a few "key capabilities" that you can do better than anyone else. Your organization cannot do everything well. So it will have to choose.

Those key capabilities and functions are then organized into business units. A business unit could be one person, or several, but it is a small unit organized around a single activity, focus, operation or function.

By restructuring with business units, your organization gains accountability at the business unit level. You have the opportunity to simplify and streamline the business unit's operations to make them the most productive and most efficient possible. By structuring around business units, you reduce the potential for bringing in extraneous or miscellaneous tasks and activities which are not central to the mission of your organization.

At the center of the centerless corporation, argue Pasternack and Viscio, is the organization's leadership. The leadership has these functions which bring the organization together:

- Identity
- Mission
- Values
- Strategy
- Leadership
- Communication
- Training
- Evaluation

Supervision is not there. Attending lots of meetings is not there. Locking up the offices at night is not there. Leadership will have to be reorganized around those things that are productive for the organization. Everything else you simply cannot afford to do.

"The corporation must have a much stronger focus on the basics of what ultimately creates value — knowledge and people and coherence. It must evolve toward a new business model that fosters the creation of value and ensures that each piece of the business contributes to system-wide value." say Pasternack and Viscio.

"Never before has knowledge been as critical as it is today, and yet many companies are at a loss in knowing how to tap and manage this vital resource. In the Centerless Corporation, the management of knowledge is one of the highest priorities. Quite simply, knowledge enables growth and productivity."[10] The new centerless corporation, with networked business units, does just that.

Networks are Flexible

Pyramids were created in order to manufacture materials, goods and tangible products. Products were the principle business of advanced countries in the last century. But the manufacture of products also was inflexible.

"The purely economic advantage that mass production had over production by individual craftsmen (of previous centuries) was obviously very great," historian Kenneth Davis notes. "Craftsmen and industries dominated by craftsmen could quite easily turn their skills and relatively simple tools from one kind of production to another- a woodworker from the making of tables to the making of chairs, a blacksmith from the making of plowshares to the making of swords- but a modern mass-production line, with its huge jigs and conveyor belts and complicated machine tools, was geared to the making of certain specified items to the exclusion of all others and could not be converted piecemeal to new uses," he notes.[11]

In the 21st century, the primary resource and tool of most companies is not a manufactured product, but information. Even manufacturing companies understand that their critical edge in competitiveness and success lies in having the best information about their customers, costs, competition and so on.

While the pyramid was the best organizational structure for manufacturing goods, the network is the ideal structure for the information age.

One reason for the need for flexibility lies in the economic change from products to people. Companies and organizations now have to change their central focus from a product or service that is produced to the customer or audience served. As customers and audiences and market conditions change more rapidly, organizations have to revise their strategies and even products to meet the changing demands of their customers and audiences. The pyramid cannot react and respond this quickly. But the network can. The network has the unique ability to acquire or create business units immediately, and to release or redesign other business units just as quickly.

Meetings Decline

The majority of face-to-face (F2F) staff meetings are wasted time. Time is wasted convening, as not everyone arrives at the same time. Time is wasted getting acquainted. Time is wasted with verbal reports, as some people may already know what is being reported, while others may not need to know what is being reported. Time is wasted in decision making based on information. Most decision making involves items or issues where information is crucial. Information can be better shared, evaluated online than F2F. Any decision making and F2F meetings where information is shared and decisions are made based on information is wasted.

We were once invited to keynote a conference and as a result, we were invited to serve on a conference planning committee. Most of the meetings involved logistical details about the conference that did not involve us. Some of the meetings involved marketing, which is a particular skill of ours, only the discussion involved everyone on the committee, who then had to be included in the decision making process, even though they knew little or nothing about the marketing of conferences.

One meeting was spent deciding in what room and at what time each session would be held. One person could have done that in a half hour. With ten people, it was done in ten person hours. And then this really drove us up a wall. The next meeting was spent canceling the sessions that took all that time in the previous meeting to schedule. It seems that the brochure got out late and they had created a deadline for conference registration, one of the worst mistakes conference planners can make. So we were now meeting once again to undo everything we had done in the previous meeting. If the committee members had spent their meeting time promoting the conference and "working" on it instead of meeting, the conference would have had double the attendance.

In F2F meetings, only one person can speak at a time. In online meetings, everyone can 'speak' at the same time.

There is an important role for F2F meetings. F2F meetings should be spent doing those things that cannot be accomplished in an online environment. Bonding, incorporating new people into the group, addressing emotional issues, developing trust, getting acquainted again, sharing personal stories, and making major decisions based on judgment, intuition and those that involve consensus or group support, brainstorming.

Yes, we have F2F meetings, but they aren't daily or even weekly.

Electronic Versus Human Communication

Electronic information, that gained from the computer, has until now been subject to the validation by a human being. We have always trusted, in our most serious matters, a human over a computer.

One of the challenges for us in this century is to accept and trust electronic information.

Interestingly, we often trust electronic information over human information in minor matters. Recently, we both used an e-service check-in at the airport. We each checked one piece of luggage, and watched the other person use the e-service machine. When we proceeded to give our baggage to the airline agent, she informed us that there were four luggage tags. She assumed we both had made a mistake. The likelihood that the computer had messed up was not plausible to the agent.

On the other hand, when it comes to serious matters, we have a very difficult time trusting electronic information over that of a human.

An airliner was flying over Europe when it came on course to collide with another airplane. Both the air controller on the ground and the on-board computer informed the pilot of the possible collision.

But in what to do they differed. The air controller on the ground told the pilot to go to a higher altitude. The on-board computer, on the other hand, indicated that the pilot should take the plane to a lower altitude. With these mixed messages, the pilot hesitated and did nothing. Then the air controller on the ground issued a second, more demanding command to take the plane higher. The pilot did what almost all of us would have done, he obeyed the voice of another human. The pilot took the plane higher, and collided with the other airplane. Some 154 schoolchildren from Russia were killed.

An airline expert stated afterward that if the pilot had obeyed the on-board computer, he would have avoided the collision. The expert further noted the on-board computer detecting midair collisions had never been wrong, and that no one had died when the pilots had followed the instructions of the on-board computer.

Computers make errors as well. But they make them far less frequently than humans do. If a computer had the same error rate as humans, computers would have been outlawed many years ago. If computers had the same error rate as humans, they would probably break down every hour.

Electronic information is simply information. It is not judgment, emotion, spirit, wisdom or even experience. While a few people believe the computer will exceed human intelligence in several decades, virtual reality creator Jaron Lanier notes that we have yet to create a computer that can replicate a cockroach, much less a human.

But when it comes to simple information, storage, retrieval and display of facts and data, the computer is superior to the human most of the time. We now need to come to grips with that reality, and trust electronic information and communication.

Asynchronous Versus Synchronous

One of the major changes in communication that the World Wide Web has created is from synchronous work and communication to asynchronous work and communication.

The central office is not only location-specific, but synchronous, or time specific. You not only have to be in the central office in order to work, but you have to be there at the right time, at the same time as everyone else. This concept has its origin in the factory, where clearly everyone on the production line had to be in the same place at the same time.

Telecommuting makes work possible around the clock, 24 hours a day. Work can thus become asynchronous. What that means is that you can work, and communicate with me, at midnight. We can work, and communicate back to you, at 8 am. And work gets done, communication is accomplished successfully, and actually more work and productivity can occur.

The central office works on real time. If you arrive an hour late to the staff meeting, then you missed it. If you are on the third shift, and the meeting is during the first shift, you missed it. If you're working, but in another city, you missed the staff meeting. Any way you want to slice it, not only did you miss out on the staff meeting, but the staff meeting was not as productive and the organization missed out because you were not there. In an asynchronous world, everyone makes the staff meeting.

New Roles for Face-to-face

Meeting face-to-face (F2F) is not bad. It is good. And even as telecommuters, we need to meet F2F with others:
- our manager, supervisor, boss
- other telecommuters in the organization
- those still working at the central office
- customers, vendors and competitors
- other professionals for networking
- in training and education.

So we need to meet F2F with others. However, the nature of those F2F meetings might very well change. They might very well need to change to be more productive.

We do not need to engage in F2F staff meetings to hear reports, hear what other people are doing, or make the myriad of small decisions and those decisions that can best be made by analyzing the information. Those things can be done better online.

There are other things that can be better done F2F. Here's an example. During World War II, U.S. President Franklin D. Roosevelt and the Prime Minister of the United Kingdom, Winston Churchill, had yet to meet, even though their nations were allies. So a meeting was arranged at sea, where ships carrying both leaders would rendezvous in the North Atlantic.

During the ocean trip, aides and military people for both the Brits and the Americans were energetically preparing information for reports, trying to devise strategies, and coming up with proposals for the other side.

Roosevelt and Churchill, quite independently of each other, were both treating the voyages as personal and leisure time, not involved at all in the rush of meetings and preparation of reports.

Both Churchill and Roosevelt knew that the purpose of the meeting was for each of them to get acquainted, for a bond of trust to form, and to create a long term relationship.

The success of the meeting was not at all the exchange of information, or the decisions made, but the emotional "changes" that would take place.

During the on-board "meetings," there were:
- ceremony, and playing of each other's national anthem, creating respect and mutual loyalty to the other nation.
- dinners, where toasts were made, creating friendship and trust.
- informal discussions, where "gut level" trust could begin to be created.
- a church service and prayers, where emotional and spiritual energies and commitment could be established.

Each F2F encounter had a very clear purpose, one that could not be accomplished via distance or the exchange of visits of emissaries. The information, the strategy, even the decisions, could be done later, at a distance. But the things they accomplished on the ship helped win the war.

It is those very same things, for which we have few words and much less understanding, that should engage us F2F. Such inadequate terms as "bonding," and such unexplored areas as "trust building," are those things that should be done now F2F.

We actually know less about the role of F2F in business work and communication than we do about online work and communication, because we have focused almost entirely on information and information-based decisions, now the province of online interaction.

Centerless Organization
with Business Units

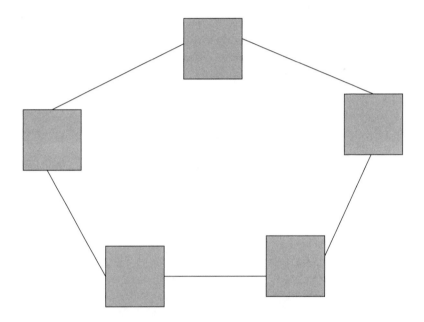

The likely organizational structure for the 21st century is a number of business units connected to each other in a network, what Pasternack and Viscio call a "centerless organization."

Here are some "new" things that F2F can do better than online interaction:
- Getting acquainted
- Creating long-term relationships
- Making gut-level (not information-based) decisions, based more on judgment, hunch, and commitment
- Gauging trust, confidence, commitment, and honesty levels of another person
- Enhancing emotional or even spiritual loyalty or commitment levels
- Sensing and sending physical cues and messages
- Reinforcing relationships
- Team building
- Conflict resolution
- Praise and recognition
- Celebrations

Work Engagement

We are told, and the studies confirm, that working at home is more productive because we work longer. That is a good thing for our bosses to believe. It is a good thing to tell them. And we do work longer. But we are not convinced that is the reason we are more productive. We think the real reason we are more productive is that we spend more time in "work engagement" than our counterparts in the central office.

This is a more threatening rationale to those still supporting the centralized office than the more acceptable "we work longer" rationale, yet it deserves some exploring.

In education there is a term called "student engagement." This is the time a student is actually engaged in learning, whether it be listening to the teacher, working with other classmates, discussing the subject matter, or even doing homework while in school. The average student spends six hours a day in school. The average student spends three hours, or only 50% of that time, actively engaged in learning.

The other half of the time is spent in a variety of other activities, such as taking attendance, rearranging desks, being interrupted by guests, time out for disciplining one or more students, setting up equipment, and so on.

The same concept can be applied to the work place. We call it "work engagement." Because telecommuters are not subject to the non-work engaging activities that regularly, continuously and universally occur in centralized offices, we are able to be more productive in the same or even less time.

Here are some examples of non-work engaged activities, which take central office workers away from the task at hand, lower productivity, and take up inordinate amounts of time:

- Staff meetings, with information sharing, reports, and decisions made
- Decision making based on consensus or conciliation rather than on information
- Saying hello every morning, re-establishing support and conviviality levels in the office
- Communicating with others who are not directly related to one's work
- Socializing
- Telling someone else what happened, what is to happen, or what did not happen.
- Repeating what happened, what is to happen, or what did not happen, to others in the office, sometimes including certain persons so they will not feel left out or not a part of the team, even though they may not need to know the information.
- Explaining why something did not happen
- Telling another person about what and how you did something, rather than simply the result or outcome
- Waiting for someone to show up
- Travel time between offices
- If 80% of verbal communication is miscommunication, then the communication required to correct the original miscommunication.

Loving Cyberspace

"I love being in cyberspace, and my students love being in cyberspace," says Dr. Rita-Marie Conrad of Florida State University, who teaches graduate courses for adults online.

Indeed, cyberspace is a wonderful place. One can:

- meet friends that one would not be able to meet otherwise.
- network with colleagues from around the country, or around the globe.
- find out just about anything using the best search engine. (Google, at the time of this writing.)
- listen to your favorite radio stations, no matter where they are, or where you are.
- renew friendships with an old pal or a relative.
  And so much more.

Cyberspace is a different reality. But it is no less human, no less interactive, no less emotional a place than physical reality. It is a wonderful gift. And it adds tremendously to life.

E-mail is not really cyberspace. E-mail is still a "push" rather than "pull" technology. Even its name, "electronic mail," is a transitional term, just like the "horseless carriage" and "talking pictures."

Cyberspace is the World Wide Web, file sharing, chats, and much more. It is the foundation not only for the future of telecommuting but of the workplace and business.

You have heard of telecommuting, but what about "tele-emersion." Jaron Lanier, who invented the term "virtual reality," is now working with scientists in universities using Internet II to create a meeting place in cyberspace. Your hologram (a virtual 3-D image of yourself) and one or more others will be able to virtually meet, share documents, work on projects. This will cut down on travel time, travel cost, and allow more people to meet and work together. Lanier says it will be viable and affordable in about ten years. Whether or not this particular project comes to pass, it is clear that we have just begun to utilize the Internet for doing business and work. And that there are more exciting things to come.

What is important for telecommuters is to enjoy being in cyberspace, to participate in cyberspace, and to utilize it in our work.

Networks and 9-11

In 1939, trying to ready American military forces for the upcoming fight against Nazism, President Franklin D. Roosevelt traveled to an Army base in Alabama, where he witnessed the last remaining cavalry division conducting exercises. Aware of the speed and ferocity of Nazi tank units and their blitzkrieg (lightning) strikes, FDR quickly dismantled this last vestige of 19th century combat. Roosevelt later won the war by outmanufacturing the Axis powers, turning auto factories into war materiel factories and outproducing Germany and Japan.

The tank and motorized combat had premiered much earlier, of course, in the first World War. The war was begun by the assassination of a duke in Sarajevo. Automobile historian Michael Frostick reminds us, "we must note that it was in a car that the killing took place." Frostick follows up by stating, "we cannot escape the fact that on the credit side it proved to be the greatest forcing ground for automobile development that could possibly have happened and the cars which came into being in the period

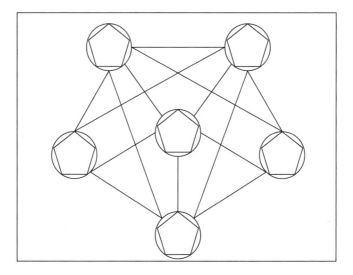

The likely structure for business and organizations in the 21ˢᵗ century is a network of business units. In the example above, the organizational boundaries are closed and clear. In the example below, the organization's boundaries may change as people and business units are brought into and exit the flexible organizational structure.

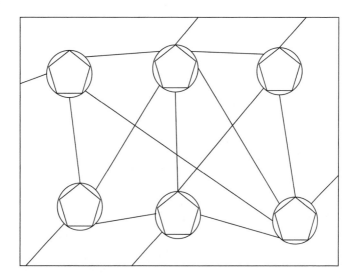

after the war were fundamentally those which we drive about today."[12]

War is often an experience where the latest technology is premiered, and wins out.

One of the more disconcerting initiations to the concept, operation, and superiority of networks over pyramids in the 21st century was introduced by the tragic events of 9-11. The organization sponsoring the attacks, Al Qaeda, was organized as a network rather than a pyramid. American news reports almost always referred to their members as being in a "cell" or a "network."

On the other hand, one of the main criticisms of the U.S. intelligence organization before and after 9-11 was that it lacked coordination in communication between the governmental agencies. These agencies were structured in the last century model of pyramids, where under the dubious belief that "knowledge is power," kept knowledge from other agencies.

In the years following 9-11, wherever there has been a U.S. victory against Al Qaeda, it has come about because of "intelligence." And where there have been weaknesses and vulnerabilities, there has been the presence of last century concepts like pyramids and geographic boundaries.

Even here, or especially here, we are painfully aware that the network is superior to the pyramid.

Who's on Staff?

In a networked organization, the terms "employee" and "staff" become vague and less helpful in defining those persons in your organization.

When our organization was a pyramid, we knew how many staff people we had: 30. There were 20 full-time employees, 10 part-time employees, and thus the equivalent of 25 full-time employees. They were all in one location. Using a 40-hour week as the definition of a full-time employee, we could define and measure employees.

As we transitioned to a networked organization, we began to contract out with more and more people. Instead of hiring people on an hourly basis, we wrote contracts that specified outcomes. Many of the people with whom we have contracts work only 20% of their time for our organization. A few even work for their own companies, such as our printer and the webmaster hosting our web site.

Soon it became impossible to design an organizational chart, and then even respond to the question how many employees or staff we had.

Replacing the term and concept of staff for our organization is the term "team." Everyone working for our organization, even those on a contract basis, consider themselves as part of our team. And we as senior management consider them as part of our team.

Networks Constantly Change

One of the fascinating new features of the networked organization is that the boundaries of the organization are frequently changing. What units are in the organization, what individuals are in the organization, keeps changing.

And one of the key new leadership skills of managers and CEOs is to find new team members, link business units to the organization, link business units together, and then at some time in the future unlink individuals and units that are no longer needed by the organization.

Organizations today have to be focused around audiences and markets and people served. This is very different from the last century, when organizations were focused around products, programs or services.

Today, in order to continue serving an audience, that may mean changing the products, programs and services delivered as the audience's needs and wants evolve and change.

That is one reason why it is estimated that workers born today will change jobs about once a year during their work careers. Jobs will be viewed more as "projects." When a project is completed, the person may very well move on to another organization requiring the individual's unique set of skills.

Peter Leyden says that one of the things leaders in the 21st century now have to do is to develop and foster networks. One of the skills involved with network building is what Leyden calls "connecting the dots." Connecting the dots is finding the people resources out there and knowing what is relevant and useful to one's organization at a particular given time. And it is not just finding one individual. "One of the key things individuals bring to an organization is access to that person's network," notes Leyden.[13]

In the last century, the organizational chart and pyramid as structures were not limited to the work place. The pyramid also shaped how the community, education and leisure aspects of our lives were shaped. So too will the network shape our personal, family and community life in this century. The economic forces that are creating new ways of working in the 21st century are also creating new ways of living. In the next chapter, we explore how our travel will change.

Chapter 9
Trains Replace Cars:
Shift Four

"Sometimes it's worse to win a fight than to lose."
— Billie Holiday

In just ten years, between 2010 and 2020, cars will go into decline, replaced as the predominant mode of transportation in the U.S. by light rail and trains.

"The very freedom that the motor-car first brought and for which it was so much in demand is beginning to be its own executioner," automobile historian Michael Frost has written. "It seems most unlikely that it can ever see even its 150th birthday in the form in which we presently know it. Its use must surely soon be totally restricted or the whole concept of its design changed. In terms of history it will be very short-lived."

In August 2001, Gray Davis, the governor of California, signaled the end of the age of automobiles. In that month he christened the last freeway in California and declared that no more freeways would be built in the state.[1]

At the same time, a train line was being developed between Los Angeles and San Francisco, and towns all along the California coast were lining up and fighting to have train stops on that line.[2] The towns knew that to have a stop on that line meant middle to upper-class professional people could live in their town, and travel to either big city easily. To not have a train stop on the line is likely to lead to the decline of the town, just like towns not located on an Interstate declined over the past fifty years, and towns not having a train stop before that were passed over.

Not coincidentally, California in 2002 passed laws to reduce automobile pollution of the environment, becoming less car-friendly.

In the last half of the 20th century, and into the 21st century, California has often been the trend setting state in America. With regard to transportation, it is likely to continue its leadership role.

Trains will replace cars, but not because of environmental concerns. Environmental concerns are legitimate, but have rarely trumped economic concerns. The extent to which cars pollute the air is a concern, but not a sufficient mandate for action.

Trains will replace cars, but not because of the price of gasoline. The price of gasoline may actually decline in the next two decades, as the number of cars in the advanced countries declines. Worries about oil reserves are based on another hundred years of driving, and the auto in advanced societies has but twenty years to go. On a consulting visit we made to the United Arab Emirates, the sheikh who was the head of the ministry of higher education implied that the future of his country rested more on Internet technology than on relying on oil production.[3]

And trains will replace cars, but not because of public policy or Congressional legislation. Rail advocates point hopelessly to a change in heart from Congress as the key to the future of trains.

Economics rules, and trains will replace cars because of a fundamental economic need to replace cars. Public policy will change, Congress will have a change in heart, but it will follow the economic need, not precede it.

Here are the top reasons why trains will replace cars:

1. Cars are too slow.

As early as 1900, automobiles were reported to have reached speeds of 70 miles per hour (mph). Some 100 years later, it is not safe for the majority of drivers to go much faster.

Trains, on the other hand, can go up to 150 mph, almost twice as fast. Speed wins.

2. Cars take too long.

In 1990, the average car went 30 mph. In 2000, the average car went 20 mph. And by 2010, the average car is predicted to go just 11 mph.[4] Cars obviously can go faster than that, but these are the average speeds of automobiles today. They keep going lower because more and more time is spent stuck in traffic.

3. The next generation won't commute.

The next generation coming into the workplace, Generation Y, will refuse to commute. They understand the value of time, and they are unlikely to spend two to three hours a day driving to something — a computer and access to the Internet — that they already have in their own apartments and homes.

4. It is becoming too dangerous.

Since it was created, the automobile has annually caused thousands of lives to be lost. Currently around 50,000 people in the United States are killed by cars every year. As a society, we have long ago accepted this tragic loss of talent, friends and loved ones as just an inevitable 'fact of life.'

In the list of fears, most Americans have a much higher fear of such unlikely events as anthrax, an Al Qaeda attack, a plane crash, or getting attacked by a black bear or a wolf. Try to find out when the last person was killed by a black bear. We live in a state with lots of black bears, and it has been over 50 years since someone in the state has died from a black bear. These unlikely events pale by the thousands to the risk of getting killed in a car.

Furthermore, the level of fatalities is likely to rise. Some car pile ups on the Interstate now involve 50 or 75 cars. Cell phones and other distractions are contributing.

But here's one demographic trend that cannot be beat. The aging of the baby boom generation means that by 2020 there will be around 60 million people aged 80 or over driving around on the freeways. They will be driving down the on-ramp at 25 mph, causing an unacceptable level of fatalities. In states with retirement communities, the increased risk has already been documented.

5. No answers to congestion.

There are simply no workable answers to solving the problems of traffic congestion. The auto industry, states, the federal government have all tried to come up with solutions. We saw a bumper sticker recently that said: "More lanes, not trains."

That pretty well sums up the costly and unworkable plan to date. More lanes mean only more of the same: more time spent driving, more congestion as the population continues to grow and we get more drivers, more deaths.

In responding to California Governor Davis' announcement about the last California freeway, *The New York Times* editorialized, "It means that the cost of adding more freeway miles — measured in political will, environmental and social sacrifice, as well as real dollars — has grown unacceptable."[5]

6. One cannot work and drive at the same time.

Here is the crux of it all. Here is an indisputable and irresolvable problem with the horseless carriage. You simply cannot work and drive at the same time.

People have tried to work and drive at the same time. And auto manufacturers will continue to add "features" (Internet access being the big one) that suggest maybe you can. But we, as humans, cannot work and drive at the same time.

Not that we aren't trying. The increase in cell phone usage among drivers is significant. It is so significant, it is causing traffic accidents and death.

In fact, talking on a mobile phone while driving is more dangerous than being over the legal alcohol limit, according to the research.[6] Reaction times are nearly 50% slower when talking on the phone. Hand-free phones were almost as dangerous as hand-held ones, and still more dangerous than being drunk.

Using a hand-held mobile phone while driving is illegal in more than 30 countries. In the U.S., New York State was the first state to ban hand-held cell phones while driving. But the problem isn't our hands. The problem is our heads. "The problem is you actually get sucked into the telephone conversation, and the conversation starts to take precedence over the driving task," Roger Vincent of the Royal Society for the Prevention of Accidents told the BBC.

"When you get into a phone conversation, it's different from the normal way we evolved to interact," David Strayer, a professor of psychology at the University of Utah, says. "Normally conversation is face to face. There are all kinds of cues. But when you are on the phone you strip that away. It's virtual reality. You attend to that virtual reality, and shut down processing of the here and now," he notes.[7]

Strayer has done tests of people who were driving and talking on phones, and found that they remember far fewer things than those driving without phones, auto writer Malcolm Gladwell concludes.[8]

So no matter what gadgets and devices are invented or installed, this is not going to change.

Humans simply cannot drive and do something else at the same time. Mistakes happen. Notes Gladwell, "Every two miles, the average driver makes four hundred observations, forty decisions, and one mistake. Once every five hundred miles, one of those mistakes leads to a near collision, and once every sixty-one thousand miles one of those mistakes leads to a crash."[9]

Gladwell offers this astonishing report, "one of the many peculiarities of car crashes is that they happen more often under ideal road conditions than in bad weather."

On the other hand, work and a host of other activities can be done on a train equipped with Internet connections. The first airplane flight to have broadband connections was from Frankfort, Germany, to the U.S. in January 2003. Internet connections will be universal on trains.

In his book *New Departures*, Anthony Perl notes that the decline of the train in the last century came about because of a lack of speed and flexibility.[10] Those are the very advantages that trains have today over cars. Trains can go faster than cars, and with the ability to work on trains, they offer more flexibility for the traveler. "If the train does not offer faster, cheaper and technologically superior travel opportunities compared with autos or planes, there is little evidence that the public will beat a path to Amtrak's or VIA's [Canada's passenger rail system] operations," notes Perl.[11]

And therein lies the irresolvable problem. Because, as we have noted, time is too valuable. And traveling continues to be important in both our work and personal lives. A typical American spends about three hours a day driving, some two hours a day on average commuting to work, and another hour or so a day getting groceries, going to the movies, going shopping, going to church, and getting the car's oil changed. We may well still have some form of auto for the next fifty years. And we may continue to use the auto where trains and light rail are not in service, such as rural areas.

But for 80% of the population, and for 80% of their transportation needs, they will need and want to take light rail and trains. Once one becomes a telecommuter working from home, the world no longer revolves around the central office and the route between work and home. Now the work world revolves around time. From the perspective of the telecommuter, time is too valuable to be wasted in travel. Travel itself will not cease once one starts working at home. In fact, some may even travel more. But spending time simply traveling is a waste.

If one can travel and work at the same time, then travel is not wasted time. In fact, travel can take "no time at all" as long as one is working at the same time. Here's the comparison.

- One person drives a car four hours to a business meeting, getting there tired, late and not having done anything productive for the past half a day.
- A second person takes a train to the business meeting, getting there rested, earlier, and having worked for several hours along the way.

The second person has utilized her or his time well. Regardless of whether that person has chosen to use that time as work or play, or some of each, the person who travels by train has not wasted time. And this is precisely what we, as people who work from home, want and need.

One of the arguments against light rail is that not enough people use the trains. This is currently the case. Light rail will never be sustainable financially, nor take over the commuting job from the car, as long as people commute to centralized offices. As long as people commute to offices, they will live in suburbs. As long as they live in suburbs, they will drive, because suburbs are by nature spread out. Light rail lines are, unalterably it would seem, tied to stations. Light rail stations thrive in dense communities where riders are within 3-6 blocks from the train station. That cannot happen in a suburb. And certainly not in a metropolitan area composed of suburbs.

It is only when people begin to work from home that they value their time so much they want to:

- travel by train so they can work.
- travel by train because it is faster.
- live in a dense community served by a light rail station.

The dominance of light rail will come only when a sufficient number of people work from home and live in a dense community. Those trends are gaining, and the confluence works more or less in tandem with the others.

The other chief argument of those against light rail is the infrastructure and public sector cost. Mass transit is simply too expensive. Let's look at that.

First, this country once supported light rail (trolleys) and a massive train system in this country. If it could be supported in an earlier, less prosperous era, it can be supported now.

Secondly, building an infrastructure for light rail and trains will be expensive, massively expensive. But the return on investment, the payback, will far exceed the costs. Having a nation's workforce spending 25% of its time, energy and resources stuck in traffic is a far heavier burden to bear. Infrastructure costs are likely to be borne by 30-year bonds that will spread out the costs over time.

Thirdly, the existing public subsidies, support and costs of our automobile, air and highway systems of travel is staggering. Auto and plane travel are supported by a "public-private partnership," according to Perl. Of the existing auto-plane public support he notes, "This public-private partnership is so successful that most travelers (and taxpayers) do not pause to think about the essential public contributions that enable 'private' driving and flying.

"And when the very significant taxes collected and expended on air and road transportation are brought to the public's attention, most citizens pronounce themselves quite satisfied with the use of the money."[12]

The public support of auto travel is massive, including:

- Low gasoline taxes, which subsidize inexpensive gasoline, about half the cost of gas in other countries such as European nations.
- Subsidies for the steel industry.
- The cost to cities, counties, states and the federal government for our highways.
- The cost to plow roads in the winter.
- The cost of automobile insurance.
- The cost of medical insurance for automobile accidents.
- The cost of state patrol officers, whose valuable resources could be diverted to more important health and safety activities.
- The cost of police and sheriff departments, where probably over a majority of their time and work goes into auto-related activities.
- Hospitals, where auto accidents are a significant patient cost, and ambulance services.

And on and on.

We have yet to mention the intangible costs of polluting the environment and the change in climate due to increased temperatures from concrete and asphalt roads, streets, and parking lots.

And how do you measure the 50,000 or so lives lost every year? A staggering total that far exceeds the number of men lost in all the wars the United States has ever fought. All the talent lost when a gifted person dies in a car crash, all the young potential lost by teen accidents, the crime committed using cars.

If one adds up the existing costs at all levels of society of maintaining our automobile infrastructure and way of life, that cost can be transferred to a superior, and safer, system of light rail and trains. "If expectations are that train travelers would eventually pay a roughly equivalent share of their travel costs as people who fly or drive, then short term transition costs are acceptable," Perl concludes.[13]

The general public is certainly behind mass transit. For example, a survey in the Minneapolis-St. Paul metro area showed that 85% of respondents agreed with the idea that neighborhoods should be walkable and transit oriented. More than 47% chose adding rail and bus transit as their preferred solution to dealing with traffic congestion, as opposed to 18% who preferred building more roads.[14]

And a national survey on growth by Belden, Russonello & Stewart Research and Communications polled 1,007 Americans 18 or older, finding that 47% identified public transport as the solution for reducing traffic, while only 21% chose road building.[15]

What's Good for General Motors

If the decline of the carriage is a guide, the automobile will not suddenly collapse. As the making of horse-drawn vehicles between 1900 and 1910 declined by only 10%, it is likely that new auto sales may only decline by a similar percentage between 2000 and 2010. It is in the decade beginning in 2010 where the steep decline will be seen, around the same time that light rail systems are more functional and train routes are being rebuilt.

One of the most famous misquotes in the 20th century occurred sometime around the 1950s when the president of General Motors (GM) said, "What is good for the nation is good for General Motors." This was somehow misquoted and reported as, "What is good for General Motors is good for the nation."[16] True to the tenor and belief-system of the 20th century, the public approved of the latter version, and generally sought to insure what was good for General Motors.

It was only until the dawn of the 21st century that General Motors ceased to be the biggest company in the United States. Taken together, GM, Ford and Chrysler represented a huge portion of the nation's economy, employment, and of course federal lobby.

While U.S. automobile companies are having their problems and losing market share in the first decade of the century,[17] they are unlikely to simply surrender the highways to the rail advocates.

We can already see what counter measures Detroit is taking. And by looking back 100 years to the time when carriages were being replaced by the motor-car, we can also see what Detroit will be doing over the next decade.

The auto companies are already engaged in two of the three main strategies carriage, buggy and wagon companies tried one hundred years ago. First, auto companies are opposing any change in the existing highway status quo. Like carriage companies and horse-drawn vehicle proponents of yesteryear, auto companies and the champions of driving will fight hard and long to preserve the roadways. In Minnesota, for example, auto advocates in the state legislature have rallied around the slogan, "Freedom to drive." The freedom to drive campaign includes proposing (as yet unsuccessful) to raise the speed limits. They wish to get rid of the diamond or carpooling driving lanes. They successfully got a short term experiment to turn off the on-ramp meters that regulated how many vehicles could enter the metropolitan Twin Cities freeways at any given time. That experiment was inconclusive and did not result in permanent shut down of the on-ramp meters. Similar positions, activities and proposals are likely to come in all states from the pro-driving advocates.

Second, auto companies are attempting to adapt to the Internet. They have installed Global Positioning Systems (GPS). They have put televisions in cars. They have put hot plates in cars. They have put hands-free cell phones in cars. They will put in Internet connections as soon as possible. They have tried "talking cars" that provide verbal instructions and/or reports. They have cars that automatically lock, and unlock, from a distance. When an unauthorized person comes too close to a parked car, they can beep.

None of these adaptations have gained sufficient popularity. The only really popular innovation since 1985 has been the cup holder. If this is the best new idea in 20 years, the automobile is in trouble.

Carriage companies adopted as many automobile features as they could 100 years ago, and advertised these new features to the horse-driving public. To no avail, of course. Likewise, while auto companies will modify their cars as much as possible, they will be unable to reverse the primary reason for the auto's downfall: one cannot drive and work at the same time. A secondary contributing factor is that 80% of cars on the highway at any given time have no passengers, only the driver in them.

That leaves the third strategy that carriage, buggy and wagon companies tried 100 years ago. This was the strategy that worked. Companies that did not employ this strategy did not survive.

The strategy was to begin producing the new technology.

You know Studebaker as an automobile company. Studebaker origi-

A page from General Motors web site, circa 2001.

nally made carriages. Studebaker started making autos around 1910 and made both carriages and autos between around 1910 and 1916, when it stopped making carriages. Studebaker made only carriages before it started making autos around 1910.

J.I. Case is a tractor company today. J.I. Case made both tractors and wagons sometime between 1910 and 1920. And J.I. Case made only wagons before it started making tractors.

This strategy — to make trains — would not be General Motors' first or even second strategy. But a good company would want to hedge its bets. A good company would want to have a Plan B and Plan C. So we went to General Motors' web site. What we found was locomotives. It turns out that General Motors is the largest producer of locomotive engines in the country.[18]

Whether GM would say so or not, the company is already positioned for success in the new era of trains. Business school professors are often fond of telling the story of the decline of trains in the last century by noting that railroad executives thought they were in the railroad business and did not realize they were in the transportation business. This time around, it will be interesting to see if automobile executives understand they are not in the auto business, but the transportation business. Once again, what is good for the nation could very well be good for General Motors.

The whole scenario that trains will replace cars seems unlikely halfway through the first decade of the new century. That is because we are just half-way through the first decade of the new century.

The transition from cars to trains will happen because of economic forces, not political, attitudinal or public opinion forces. Yet unlike working from home, redesigning organizational structures as networks, or even replacing physical offices with intranets, this Shift will take enormous societal consensus, commitment and financial investment. Thus, it is likely to take a little longer, involve quite a lot of debate before the trains movement gathers steam, which should come about sometime between 2010 and 2020, roughly midway into the second decade of the century.

The conversion from cars to trains is a consequence of our first two Shifts. People will not gravitate toward trains in any huge numbers until they begin working from home, using an intranet as their office. As long as someone lives in a suburb and commutes to a physical office, cars are the option of choice for most, as dysfunctional, frustrating and dangerous as that option is. As long as someone works by the clock, whether hourly or salaried, time cannot be saved, time cannot be valued. And so time is wasted.

But as soon as someone starts to telecommute, time not only becomes more valuable, it can also be saved and used more wisely. Telecommuters will demand light rail and then trains, because only trains conserve time.

Already light rail systems are operational in 17 of the 50 largest cities in the United States. And light rail systems are being planned or under construction in another 20 metropolitan areas. It is likely that by the next decade more than half of the nation's population will be within twenty miles of a light rail station.

The move to light rail is taking place in other countries as well. A new system is being built in Delhi, India, described for the BBC by one Indian as "a dream come true" for Delhi commuters. The three busiest light rail systems in the world are not in the U.S. Moscow is the busiest, followed by Tokyo and Seoul. New York City is tied with Mexico City for fourth busiest. [19]

Now, light rail systems are being built under the misguided notion that people will take them to work. This is not happening now. This will not be happening in any significant or dominant way. As long as people are commuting to work, "commuter trains" will be underutilized. The simple fact is that most commuters live in suburbs or in suburban-type communities. These low-density communities are much too spread out to provide convenient and easy access to a light rail line. Trains and light rail require high-density neighborhoods in order to be the predominant mode of transportation. Which is why New Yorkers in Manhattan can live without a car, and New Yorkers in Westchester cannot live without a car. As long as the dwellings where people live are so spread out, and the dwellings where people work are also spread out, trains provide a positive but modest transportation system.

This is why the "lanes versus trains" debates on public radio stations around the country are indecisive, a stand-off between a dysfunctional collapsing auto system and a rising, but not popular, mass transit system.

The middle ground in mass transit — bus transit — satisfies neither the Industrial Age of suburbs and offices, nor the Internet Age of telecommuters and wireless laptops.

Buses are not the solution for a variety of reasons. Buses are:
- Subject to highway congestion and traffic. Buses do not eliminate cars, and thus they do not eliminate congestion and traffic.
- Not nearly safe and secure enough. Few business people would be willing to take a $3,000 computer on a bus where people can hop

on and off at every other street corner. Few parents in the United States would send a child on a bus downtown.

• Not nearly fast enough, even without traffic. With stops and transfers, it takes even longer to travel on a bus than in a car. Their route systems are much more difficult to decipher for visitors and out of town business people. Their frequent stops and less than smooth ride make it much more difficult to work on a bus.

The light rail systems are being built now. When they are built, more and more riders will demand wireless Internet connections on them. A telecommuting Internet expert already reports the light rail system in Portland, Oregon, has Internet connections.

The vast majority of telecommuters will prefer trains to cars because trains conserve the only resource telecommuters have, their own time. As long as someone can work on a train, it takes no time to travel by rail, no matter how far the physical distance.

It is difficult for commuters to understand this. But telecommuters understand this intensely, deeply, in-the-gut. Telecommuters are not workaholics. When we indicate that one can "work" on a train, we mean productive or enjoyable activity. One has the choice of whether to work, or to play. With a wireless Internet connection, one can talk to friends and relatives, listen to music; read, listen or watch the news; watch a movie; go shopping; eat; sleep; or go offline and read. But either way, one is not wasting time on a train unless one is really trying to waste time.

Aside from remembering his name, one of the more memorable radio interviews we have heard in the last few years involved an American journalist living in Tokyo, Japan, with his wife and nine-year-old daughter. One day his daughter and a Japanese girl friend of the same age wanted to go to the newly opened Disney theme park in Japan. The park was about a three-hour train ride away. The journalist assumed the other girl's mother would be chaperoning the girls on the trip. He was astounded to learn the other girl's parents had no intention of going, and no concerns whatsoever about two nine-year-old girls being on a six-hour round-trip train ride unaccompanied.

Much of that security can be ascribed to the Japanese culture. But some measure of it needs to be ascribed to the safety of the rail system as well.

With light rail, it is likely that even in the United States parents will feel comfortable about allowing their middle school-age and high school-age children to travel on a train to school, after school activities, movies, concerts and parties on their own. They may be met at either end of the train ride by an adult, but this chauffeur-saving alone will save parents weeks of time every year.

With light rail systems in a majority of the major cities in the country, it will be a logical and much easier step to connect the cities by intercity rail.

Some sort of national rail system will be built and carry the majority of intercity passengers. Here is why, and how, that is likely to happen.

Trains Between Cities

Trains will not replace airplanes for long trips, such as Chicago to Seattle, or New York to Los Angeles, or any other trip that can be done in significantly less time via air than train. The airline mode of travel is not broke. It requires tweaks and changes, but it is not broke.

Where airplanes have overstretched their usefulness is in short haul routes. The only alternative to driving even two to five hours, airlines have sent too many small planes into the air, taking too few people a short distance for too much money. Continuing to use air travel for short trips is too expensive, too congestive of the skies, and too inconvenient. And one has to drive when one lands. For example, *USA Today* reported in the months after the September 11, 2001, tragedy, "In the Northeast, Delta (airlines) also is dueling with an unlikely foe: the train."[20] Trains will not replace airplanes for long trips, but trains will replace airplanes for short air trips.

The real forte of trains is replacing the one- to six-hour auto trip, from 50 to 500 miles. For travel between 50 and 500 miles, trains are faster, more convenient, safer, and reasonably priced. Longer than that, take a plane. Shorter than that, take light rail.

A model plan for fast train service based on this concept is taking place in California. The California High-Speed Rail Authority plans hourly service between and among the state's major cities, with travel between San Francisco and Los Angeles taking only two and one-half hours.[21]

Since California has often led the nation in new directions, this one state initiative could mean the end of the automobile as the dominant transportation for Americans.

Current analysis of both ridership and profitability on various Amtrak routes illustrates this. The routes where Amtrak loses the most money are the long-haul cross-country routes, such as Chicago to Seattle. And the routes where there is the most ridership, and where Amtrak actually makes money, are the 100- to 500-mile trips in between two major cities.

It is not just on the eastern corridor where these profitable routes are. One of the most profitable routes, according to an Amtrak report, is between Oklahoma City and Dallas. This is in the heart of no-nonsense, freeway loving, truck hugging country.

The two key variables: mid-range distance of 100-500 miles; and connecting two major cities.

Another of Amtrak's troubles is that a number of long routes are not only too long, but they don't go through any cities of any great size. The Chicago to Los Angeles route, for example, starts in Chicago, but does not go through St. Louis. It does not go through Des Moines. It does not even go through the Quad Cities. It goes through corn fields all the way to Kansas City, where the scheduling ace has it arrive at the unpopular hour of around 2 am.

Here's how to make that route profitable. Have it go from Chicago to St. Louis. Then St. Louis to Kansas City.

One positive step has been Amtrak's introduction of the Acela train on the east coast, a high speed train that can travel up to 150 mph. Its initial runs gained praise.

USA Today reported, "Despite early glitches, the high-speed Acela Express train had a successful first month in drawing riders and operating on time, Amtrak said. The train's daily round trip between Washington and Boston earned more than $1.25 million in ticket sales, beating projections by 12%, Amtrak said. The train was on time — defined as within 15 minutes of its schedule — 94% of the time."[22].

But route length and destinations are not the only hurdles facing Amtrak, or any national rail service. Here are some more challenges.

Building new track.

Critics will point to the billions upon billions of dollars that will be needed to build new track between cities that have no rail service. The critics are right. It will take billions upon billions of dollars. And government, sensing a growing public consensus (business leaders will be far more influential and a determining factor than other sectors of the public), will come up with the investment needed.

We know this because our nation did this once before. Between 1880 and 1920 the nation had thousands of trains running at the same time. There were more than 300 trains arriving and departing Chicago's 4-5 train stations on any given day. There were trains going to towns of 1,000 people located in the mountains, in the hills, in the woods, out on the prairies.

In fact there is still a lot of unused track around. In some areas of the country new track will need to be laid, but there is a good deal of former railroad land currently idle. An interesting subplot: the "rails to trails" movement may be reversed, taking away idyllic bike trails and returning them to rail service. Another subplot will be whether to decommission Interstates to two way highways and use half the land for rail lines. The shortest line between two points is often an Interstate.

Track ownership and maintenance.
The railroad track in the United States is pitifully out of date. It is inadequate even for 80 mph service, and needs a total reconstruction to be able to run trains at 150 mph, which is what is necessary.

There is no profit in maintaining railroad track. Just as there is no profit in maintaining highways. As the historian Kenneth Davis once said, corporations are very socialistic. Anytime there is a loss, they are willing to socialize it.[23] Private companies will graciously allow, and then demand, that government maintain the track, even if that means government owning the track.

Passenger rail service ownership.
Passenger rail service can be very profitable. Passenger rail service will be very profitable. Passenger rail service may benefit from competition.

There will be enormous pressure on Amtrak to become privatized, and then dissolved as a monopoly. Companies will want to get back into the passenger rail business. Every bureaucratic procedure, every inefficiency, every customer service boo-boo will be highlighted and attributed to government inefficiency. Every efficiency and profit statement will be criticized as unfairly competing with the private sector.

We shouldn't be surprised if passenger rail service becomes privatized.

These issues will consume much public debate, governmental indecision followed by decision, and court battles between 2010 and 2020. The bottom line: rail service will be the primary means of transportation between cities 50 to 500 miles apart.

The Future of Amtrak

Amtrak is a mess. Regardless of one's position on mass transit, regardless of whether one is employed by Amtrak or employed by the auto industry lobbying association, just about everyone agrees that Amtrak is a mess.

That is where the agreement ends. Some people believe Amtrak should be abolished. Some believe Amtrak should be privatized. Some believe Congress should not mandate the impossible tasks that Amtrak serve rural areas and make a profit. Some believe the problem is with the track. Some believe the problem is with management. Some believe the problem is with the public's lack of interest. Some believe the problem is with the organization of Amtrak. Some believe the problem is insufficient funding.

And some point to state initiatives, such as the California High Speed Rail Authority, as leading the way regardless of Amtrak's situation.

Regardless of Amtrak's future, Amtrak as an organizational structure is not central to the future of passenger train service. Some sort of national rail system will be built and carry the majority of intercity passengers.

The New Role of Cars

Cars are unlikely to disappear. But they will go into steep decline.

Some 80% of people live in metropolitan areas. They will use light rail and trains 80% of the time to meet their daily and weekly travel needs.

People will still fly in airplanes, still ride bikes, still walk (walk more actually), still travel by boat. And they will still drive. But not very often.

Changes in society begin in urban cities, move to smaller cities, and then to rural areas. So it will be a long while until rural areas have rail service. Even then, there will be an end of the line somewhere. So cars will be used by rural residents many decades beyond that of urban residents.

Cars are likely to be used in small cities and semi-rural areas as well. But it will be much more economical to take a train and then rent a car. Rental car agencies may grow.

For urban residents who do have cars, the cars are likely to be much smaller. This is not because of any gas savings, or parking requirements. It will be because large cars take up more space, and one will not need a large car. A small car takes up much less space in a garage. Space is money. Less space is less money.

And people will not need large cars. Four people can sit in a small car adequately. As for transporting things, there will be hourly delivery services to do that, no matter what size or weight the item.

Delivery trucks might grow, as more people have goods and purchases delivered to their homes, or anywhere else their "stuff" needs to go. Except for neighborhood deliveries, however, trucks are likely to be confined to "the last mile" for transport. For greater distances, rail freight service is one-third the cost of trucks.[24] Look for convenient standardized shipping boxes of various sizes to be become popular, so that delivery companies can move your stuff easily, tracked by the Internet of course.

Once more people begin to work from home, their wants and needs for transportation become very different. They (we) want to be able to utilize our time while traveling. With light rail and trains, travel is no longer wasted time.

Weeks of time every year are added to one's work and personal life, enriching and enhancing both our work and our leisure time. When one adds the added benefits of greater physical safety, much lower fatality and accident incidents, and less pollution, light rail and trains will predominate and cars will go into decline.

Chapter 10
Communities Become Dense: Shift Five

"We are unsettled to the very roots of our being.
We have changed our environment more quickly than
we know how to change ourselves."
— Walter Lippman, 1914

A friend tells us of the time he was in Japan. Seeing some nice homes on the mountainside overlooking the city, he remarked to his guide that the home owners must be fairly well to do. Oh no, his Japanese guide replied, those homes are much too far from the train station to be of any value. The well-to-do live near the station.

Between 2010 and 2020 we will see suburban sprawl halt. By 2020 we will start to see a significant shift away from living in spread out suburbs as people begin to live in more densely populated communities.

These communities will certainly be in the cities, but they will also be in smaller towns. Even suburbs may have neighborhoods that become more densely populated and grow while the outlying half acre plots decline in value, increase in supply, and fall in demand.

We do not have to wait that long to see the first signs of that movement, as it is happening already. Recently *Crane's Weekly* reported that in downtown Chicago some 4 million square feet of office space had been converted to apartments and condominiums. The trend is reportedly happening in Boston as well.

"Sprawl-weary Los Angeles Builds Up and In," proclaimed a recent

New York Times headline, noting "the nation's second-biggest city is growing inward and upward in an attempt to free itself from the automobile." The story indicated that Los Angeles issued more new housing unit permits inside the city — more than 8,500 units — than at any time in at least a decade, the kind of housing planners praise as the antithesis of sprawl.[1]

In another ten years the two largest generations in society, the Baby Boomers and Generation Y, will be fighting over apartments, townhouses, and condominiums in downtown urban areas.

The Baby Boomers, their children grown, will not need their large suburban houses, will not want to spend long hours mowing the lawn and vacuuming. They have already shifted their wants from things to experiences. They will find experiences, including restaurants, markets, museums, art galleries, lectures, concerts, and movies, downtown.

Says Robert Gibbs, a retail consultant, "They're coming onto the market looking for smaller multifamily luxury housing in town. They spent their lives in suburbs, driving their kids to soccer. They want to be able to walk to shops and restaurants. Their tax advisors are telling them they don't have to own a home."[2]

The children of the Baby Boomers, Generation Y, will be moving into the workplace around the same time. Generation Y will want to live downtown as well. Generation Y does not want to spend 2-3 hours a day commuting. They will want to be downtown, near different restaurants than Baby Boomers, near different art galleries, concerts and movies.

Big downtown office buildings, which used to provide offices for people between 8 and 5, will be converted into apartment buildings.

In Cleveland, for example, a department store was converted into 36 loft-style apartments with 12-foot-high ceilings, hardwood floors, and oversized windows. Cities that are economically healthy depend on "bringing back residents from the suburbs by offering them unique new housing options in lively, walkable communities," says Laura Noble, assistant director of Cleveland's Ohio City Near West Development Corp.[3]

Living in more densely populated communities and working at home bring changes in interaction as well. In New York, for instance, more restaurants are serving breakfast. As chef and restaurant owner Scott Campbell told a newspaper reporter, "Breakfast has changed, especially in this neighborhood. People are no longer tied to offices, they're working at home, and this is a better option than meeting someone at Starbucks."[4]

Not everyone will want to live downtown in a big city. Many will want to live in small towns and small cities, some very far away from the city. But they too will live in densely populated communities. The reason, once again, is that knowledge workers value their time. It is their only resource. Knowledge workers will work from home in order to save time. And once one is working from home, one needs and wants to save time.

Within about 5-10 minutes travel time, or around 6-12 blocks, a knowledge worker will want just about everything she or he needs on a regular basis. This includes shops and stores, and a central feature to every neighborhood in the 21st century — the train station.

For those neighborhoods in urban areas, it is a light rail train station. For those living in a small town or city, it may be a train station. Either way, transportation will be critical in this century, just like it has been in every other century.

When America was first moving beyond the original thirteen colonies, the most efficient inland travel was by river. So major cities sprang up along the rivers, especially the confluence of two rivers.

When trains came along, citizens fought legally and illegally to get the trains to stop in their town. If the train stopped in your town, it meant your land value went up, business would thrive and new business would arrive.

If the train by-passed your town, it meant your village would remain a small village, no growth, no riches. When three villages in southcentral Kansas competed for the train station in the late nineteenth century, Haysville and Derby lost out, and the rejoicing went to the businessmen from Wichita, which then grew to be the nation's 50th largest city.

When the Interstate highway system was announced, the whole process began all over again. Towns located on the Interstate, or that could persuade the highway authorities to run the Interstate by their towns, prospered from the 1950s into the 21st century. And those towns left off the Interstate system declined in prosperity, business, and population.

So when a passenger rail line between Los Angeles and San Francisco was announced, California cities and towns all along the proposed route lobbied and argued to have a train stop, and station, in their town. They know that once again, towns with access to transportation will prosper, those without access will not.

It is likely that these communities, whether in a large urban area or a small town, will be a wireless community. People will have access to the Internet anywhere in the community, including out of doors. The first city to be reported to be wireless was Hamburg, Germany, which in 2003 activated some 250 "hot spots" or wireless connectivity areas.[5] Wireless connections will not be limited to families of sufficient financial means. The first low-income housing project to go wireless was Camfield Estates, a rebuilt 102 unit public housing development in Boston.[6]

Another feature of community life beginning in a decade or so will be home deliveries. When an online home delivery service went broke a few years ago, one commentator noted that the idea would be reborn sometime around 2010. People will not want everything delivered to their home. They may well want to go to the store to inspect the leg of lamb or the fresh vegetables. But for canned vegetables, toothpaste and a hundred other ordinary items which we do not need to squeeze, an online ordering service combined with home delivery will save extraordinary amounts of time.

When people work in the same community in which they live, the amount of time they devote to community organizations, church/synagogue/mosque, and supporting local activities goes up.

One of the new trends moving communities in this direction is a new hybrid of retail development and housing, reports living arts writer William L. Hamilton. These new malls have shops and stores on the first and street level, with apartments and living quarters above them. More than a dozen such malls are breaking ground nationally.[7]

Some of the reasons Hamilton includes:

- A PricewaterhouseCoopers report on shopping malls estimates that 18% of the nation's 2,800 malls are dead or dying as commercial ventures.
- Increasing dissatisfaction among suburban shoppers tired of highway traffic.
- More social interaction. "There is city life and there is some life, and there is no life — the suburbs," says Dr. Keoni Udarbe, who lives in an apartment above one of these new stores.

A Return to Community

Neighborhoods today all too often lack a sense of community, of social interaction. It has not always been this way. In fact, until fairly recently, neighborhoods were the primary source of social interaction.

As we noted in Shift One, a major concern about telecommuting and working from home is that workers lose social interaction.

Neighborhoods will again regain their social vitality as places where people who work from home can establish and maintain professional and personal relationships.

The office and factory at one time was not a center of social interaction, and was not seen as a place for social interaction. It was merely a place where work got done. Home, church and community was where social interaction took place.

When Bill worked for his father in a newspaper office in the 1960s, there were almost no parties or social functions in the office. Work might be interrupted for two or three minutes for an important announcement, congratulations, or the passing out of cigars. But that was it. People in the office did socialize with each other, on a weekly if not daily basis. But the "office party" took place after work hours, and in a nearby tavern or restaurant. And people in the office would socialize in the evening and on weekends, but not in the office.

To "humanize" the work place, companies gradually included various social functions. The motivation may have been to make the work place more pleasurable and enjoyable, resulting in more productive and customer friendly workers. Late in the Industrial Age, another effect also was achieved. The social interactivity at the work place made increasingly longer work hours more palatable.

At the same time, perhaps unconsciously and maybe even unintentionally, there was a decline in social interactivity in the community. The switch to socializing in the office came with a simultaneous decline in the social infrastructure in the community and in our neighborhoods.

A farm wife and friend of ours, Glenna Wilson, once told us that it used to be common knowledge that "the Kiwanians ran the town, and the Rotarians owned it." Yet even in Rotary, the most robust civic organization today, time-out from the workday to participate in community functions became squeezed. In the last several years, Rotary officials have reported more clubs meeting in the morning before members go to the office, and a decline in clubs meeting at noon, taking time out of the work day.

By the 1990s the work place had entirely taken over many of the social functions that were previously fulfilled by neighbors, family, church, and civic organizations. They include: birthday parties, lunch dates, holiday office parties, gossip, friendships, after hours drinks, betting pools, and much more. The increasing dominance of the workplace in people's lives — a combined result of more people being employed, longer work hours, and more social activities at work — led to the gutting of community life.

Volunteerism declined so much that charities and nonprofits had to restructure their work. Membership in civic organizations went into steep decline. Work with nonprofit organizations was valued less than before. Community and civic work, once seen as an integral part of a manager's job, enhancing the business' image in the community, is no longer rewarded by companies. Some people did not know their neighbors, something that would have been unheard of just fifty years earlier.

The decline in community in our neighborhoods has very recently become "built-in," architecturally reinforced to discourage (once again, unintentionally or not), communication with our neighbors.

We lived for twenty years on a block where, unlike the nearby suburbs in our area, everyone knew everyone else on the block. We did not have block parties, but we said hello to others, caught up on the news, and offered congratulations and sympathies when those occasions arise. And on Flag Day, almost everyone on the block would put out a big American flag in front. Looking down the street, one would see two rows of American flags waving in the breeze.

There were several reasons why we, otherwise disparate demographical entities of old, young, working-class, middle-class people, would get to know each other. One is that most of us did not have garages, so we would park our car on the street and often have the opportunity to say hello to a neighbor doing the same. Another reason was that we all had porches, and at one time or another, all used them. Also, there was a sidewalk on both sides of the street, something we took for granted at the time, but no longer a universal feature in neighborhoods. Sidewalks allow mothers to stroll with their baby carriages, men to walk their dogs, young people to help older ones shovel the snow off the walk, and much more. And just in these casual comings-and-goings we all would engage in conversation with others on the block. The suburban homes, by contrast, all had garages, almost none had porches.

Now we drive through a nearby suburb and find another kind of neighborhood. Our newest suburbs have two, even three, large garage doors. Folks can drive up the driveway, automatically open the garage doors with their garage door openers, and not even see the neighbors. The garages have doors leading right into the house. Some of the houses do not even have a front door, so unusual is the occurrence of a friend or neighbor coming to call. With no sidewalks, there is little pedestrian traffic passing by. If one is lucky, location on a cul-de-sac will insulate one even more. People in these newest suburbs may indeed have social relationships in the neighborhood, but the barriers to overcome are enormously high.

Perhaps the best treatment of the decline in community in America over the last thirty years is Robert D. Putnam's book, *Bowling Alone: The Collapse and Revival of American Community.*

Putnam looks at just about every indicator of community life and finds that community involvement has declined steeply in the last thirty to forty years. The peak of community involvement was around 1960, when Parent Teacher Association (PTA) meetings were crowded, youth enrolled in scouting and 4-H, and neighbors knew each other.

Since then every civic and social club has seen its membership decline or even dwindle. Church attendance has declined. The list of decline (with statistical references and sources) goes on, including charitable giving, work on community projects, trust between generations, informal socializing, family dinners and social visiting. While the number of people bowling has increased, the number of people bowling together in leagues has dwindled, thus people are now 'bowling alone.'

Putnam analyzes the causes for community decline and finds:

"It is difficult to overstate the symbiosis between the automobile and the suburb. We went from a society of one car per household in 1969 to nearly two cars per household in 1995, even though the size of the average household was shrinking over this period. Between 1973 and 1996 the fraction of Americans describing a second automobile as 'a necessity,' not 'a luxury,' nearly doubled from 20% to 37%. By 1990 America had more cars than drivers. Much of this change has occurred quite recently. As late as 1985 only 55% of all new single-family homes included space for two or more cars, but by 1998 that index of automotive dominance was 79% and rising."[8]

Adding to the commuting problem the car creates is the shopping problem.

"Between 1969 and 1995, according to government surveys of vehicle usage, the length of the average trip to work increased by 26%, while the average shopping trip increased by 29%. While the number of commuting trips per household rose 24% over this quarter century, the number of shopping trips per household almost doubled, and the number of other trips for personal or family business more than doubled." And each trip was much more likely to be made alone, for the average vehicle occupancy fell from 1.9 in 1977 to 1.6 in 1995; for trips to and from work, the average occupancy fell from 1.3 to 1.15. (Since vehicle occupancy cannot fall below 1.0, these figures represent a decline of a third in passenger occupancy for all trips and a decline of 50% in passenger commuting).[9]

Taking the mystique out of the ride, Putnam hits it right:

"One inevitable consequence of how we have come to organize our lives spatially is that we spend measurably more of every day shuttling alone in metal boxes among the vertices of our private triangles."[10]

Putnam concludes:

"The car and the commute, however, are demonstrably bad for community life. In round numbers the evidence suggests that each additional ten minutes in daily commuting time cuts involvement in community affairs by 10% — fewer public meetings attended, fewer committees chaired, fewer petitions signed, fewer church services attended, less volunteering, and so on."[11]

"In fact, although commuting time is not quite as powerful an influence on civic involvement as education, it is more important than almost any other demographic factor. And time diary studies suggest that there is a similarly strong negative effect of commuting time on informal social interaction."[12]

Interestingly enough, Putnam also sees the parallels between our time and that of 100 years ago. He says, "Just as did our predecessors in the Progressive Era, we need to create new structures and policies (public and private) to facilitate renewed civic engagement."[13]

Yet this is hardly an irreversible trend. Just as community has been destroyed in the last thirty years, community can be restored by reversing the processes. Putnam writes, "So our challenge is to restore American community for the twenty-first century... I am optimistic that, working together, Americans today can once again be as civically creative as our Progressive forebears."[14]

As for the solution to the return of community, Putnam and we do part company. He sees some sort of voluntary collective will power, and a return to the values of the last century, as the hoped-for answer.

We see a more underlying economic force driving society toward a different but equally vibrant sense of community. And we may measure community by different yardsticks than twentieth century community was measured. Putnam hopes the younger generation will return to reading newspapers. We suggest that newspaper readership in the age of online resources may be an outmoded benchmark, and that virtual communities will complement and even enhance face-to-face communities.

From our perspective, when there are significant number of telecommuters, they will start to reform the community. When business sends its workers home, it will begin to support community building activities, aware that the social context of its workers is important for morale, nay, productivity and profits.

Community for Teleworkers

In the meantime, however, one of the significant issues facing people who work at home today is finding social and community connections. While the numbers continue to grow, we are still isolated from each other. And there are not enough of us to gather in groups, clubs and engage in social interaction that we left in the office or factory.

So how do telecommuters and those of us who work at home get the human interaction and socializing experiences we all need? To find out, we asked Bill's mother. She, along with millions of other women, worked at home fifty years ago. They were called housewives.

It turns out that before large numbers of women entered the workplace, and before the workplace took over social interaction from the community, there were a number of healthy, positive and fulfilling ways in which women who worked at home found social interaction.

What immediately comes to mind of course are coffee klatsches. Two to four women would get together several times a week in the morning to have coffee. Another form of social experience was afternoon teas. These were more formal affairs, and women wore gloves and a hat to them.

Then there were activities with their husbands and other men. Bridge clubs were immensely popular. There could be anywhere from four to sixteen people playing bridge at someone's house. Saturday night was a popular bridge night, and bridge clubs often met twice a month.

There were also cocktail parties, which occurred six to eight times a year. They involved anywhere from ten to thirty people. Some parties were so large that printed invitations were mailed. Sometimes they were so frequent that people would go to two or even three cocktail parties in a single evening. And some of them had so many people that there were two shifts, one from five to seven, and another from seven to nine.

All these social activities, plus volunteering, church, and civic groups, made for a wide variety of positive healthy social experiences that kept housewives in touch with both men and women in the community.

By looking back, we can see how social experiences will be rebuilt in the community for the growing number of telecommuters and those of us who work from home. A turning point will come when corporate executives understand the value to the corporation of having people work from home and telecommute. At that point in time, companies and businesses themselves will actively support the rebuilding of community organizations to bolster this support network in the community.

Here is our top ten list of some of the ways in which telecommuters will find social interaction in their communities.

1. Civic and social clubs.

Long in decline, civic and social clubs will experience a rebound in membership and activity. They offer networking, a chance to meet people outside of one's profession, an opportunity for local civic activity, and a nice meal together.

2. Profession-specific clubs.

These clubs may not be as local in nature as civic clubs, but will provide a more specialized networking within one's profession. Here one can associate with others engaged in the same type of work.

3. Coffeeshops, bookstores, and bars.

Local places to hang out offer an unstructured atmosphere, something to drink, and interesting people and topics to talk about.

4. Neighbors.

People will get to know their neighbors again. Casual conversations, neighborhood security, occasional help with mundane and household matters, and sometime party partners are all functions that good neighbors play. The neighbors also provide an age diversity that is refreshing for everyone.

5. Hobby clubs.

Avocational and hobby clubs are another source of social interaction and experience. They are focused on non-work related topics. They often have local or regional events, fairs and conferences.

6. Churches.

Churches may well experience increased membership. Churches offer another source of community, adding a unique spiritual dimension not found in other social settings.

7. Fitness centers.

Local fitness centers also provide a social network for members.

8. Downtowns.

As shopping and business centers become more condensed, a visit downtown becomes a more social experience.

9. Classes and courses.

Classes and courses have become a popular social experience, and are likely to continue to be a way to meet people and enjoy contact with others in a stimulating environment.

10. Community centers.

As physical space becomes more costly, sharing a physical space becomes more desirable and feasible. Community centers have the opportunity to provide shared meeting space for people for a range of activities.

You may have already thought of other ways to socialize, network and find community locally. These, coupled with virtual communities, will provide a support network for telecommuters and those working at home.

Neighborhood Travel

In a dense community concentrated around shops, stores and a light rail station, there is still the question of how one gets to the light rail station. And as dense as the typical community will be, how does one get around the community, traveling six blocks or twelve blocks for groceries, supplies, seeing a movie or going to church. Not everyone is a big walker, not everyone is equally pedestrian.

The answer came in 2001, provided by world-renowned inventor Dean Kamen. Kamen had earlier invented a wheelchair that could go over sand, go up stairs, and even stand up on two wheels using a gyroscope to maintain balance. The next great invention was hyped in the media for almost a year as pundits tried to guess what it would be. It was known only by its code name, Ginger, for Ginger Rogers of the Fred Astaire and Ginger Rogers dance team of the 1930s, a favorite duo of Kamen's.

When it was finally released and made known to the public, there was a huge deflation. It was not the incredible new rocket-age whiz-bang gizmo anyone had expected. It was the Segway Human Transport, a scooter that would go about 10 miles per hour. It is steered almost intuitively, by slight motions in the body. And it is very very hard for a rider to fall off.

By the reaction in the scientific and media sectors, it was clear few people understand what the Segway is all about. Most people thought it a toy that someone else might use, but not themselves. Taken in the context of the car, it does not make sense. But taken in the context of light rail and trains, it provides a local method of transportation that almost everyone can use.

The Segway:
- Gets you there quickly.
- Gets you there safely.
- Does not pollute.
- Does not take up much space.
- Can be parked easily, and taken onto a train.

It is the perfect 21st century transportation.

Small Towns

Not all knowledge workers will want to live in metropolitan areas. The majority of people will continue to live in metropolitan areas, where access to education, cultural activities, and airports continue to be attractions.

But small and medium sized towns can also flourish, provided they are located on high-speed train lines and have a train station in town.

The town of Chatham, in Ontario, Canada, population 43,547, is an old industrial town currently on the decline. It is a wonderful place to live. It even boasts of an early automobile inventor and company. But the automobile-related factories are quickly downsizing or even leaving town.

Yet Chatham is perfectly positioned to be a thriving small or medium sized town of the 21st century. Chatham has two aspects of location that are valued in this century. It is close to water, located just minutes away from both Lake Erie, one of the Great Lakes between the U.S. and Canada, and from Lake St. Clair, a large lake from which one can access either Lake Erie or Lake Huron. Chatham is also already on a train line from Toronto, Canada's largest city, to Windsor. Windsor is located on the Canadian side of the border with Detroit. Today one cannot take a high speed train from Detroit to Toronto, but soon that connection will be made, to the economic benefit of both Americans and Canadians. And that train will stop in Chatham. With easy access to both Toronto and Detroit for business, Chatham becomes a preferred place to live for many knowledge workers.

Best positioned for prosperity are towns located on train lines between two major cities, major cities located roughly 4-6 hours apart from each other in today's auto driving terms.

In the Midwest, an area with which we are familiar, lines are likely between cities like St. Louis-Kansas City; Oklahoma City-Dallas; Minneapolis-Madison; Des Moines-Chicago; Des Moines-Minneapolis; Des Moines-Kansas City, and so on.

Thus towns located on train lines between two major cities will be well positioned for prosperity in the Internet Age — provided they also have top notch education. Schools, colleges and continuing education are an essential requirement in the choice of residence for knowledge workers.

eGovernment

eGovernment is practically a given in the 21st century. The decline in citizens willing to run for local office, the debacle in Florida and other places over voting, the potential for increasing the cost-effectiveness of government services, and the increased need for information from government all point in the direction of eGovernment.

In our town of 12,000, there was an election recently for township supervisors. Hardly anyone ran for office. Three people wrote in the name of someone for township supervisor. He won handily. The morning after the election, the man was very surprised he had won, because he wasn't running for the post and had no idea a couple of people voted for him. After a couple of days of indecision and consideration, he decided to take the unpaid role in government. Most people would have declined the time-consuming service.

About the same time, we attended a hearing in the state capitol. Since the capital is a four-hour drive away, we drove down the night before and stayed in a hotel. The hearing got underway around 10 am and was not nearly complete by 2 pm when we had to leave for the long drive home. A day and a half was all the time we could afford to listen to the proceedings. An important legislative hearing about virtual schools in the state, we estimate about a quarter of the state's population would have had to spend more than a day's time attending the hearing, provided they could have taken time out of work.

In late 2002, the mid-term elections in Minnesota pitted Senator Paul Wellstone against St. Paul mayor Norm Coleman. A week before the election, Senator Wellstone died in a plane crash. Absentee ballots had already been distributed. People could pick up new ballots, but if they were already out of the state there was not enough time to print new ballots.

The solution to all of these issues, and many more, is eGovernment, or making government web based.

eGovernment is not simply putting up a web site with government information on it. It also involves these key components:

1) sending government employees home to work,
2) providing interactive web sites for each individual citizen, and
3) conducting the people's business asynchronously and online.

Elections

Let's start with elections. Quite simply, elections should and will be conducted online, with citizens voting via computer. The first test of online elections in the U.S. was held in Arizona in 2000. Our friend and colleague, software guru Cem Erdem participated from the technical side of things, reporting all went smoothly.

Elections via the Internet need not be a chaotic everyone-log-on a dozen times and vote, with half of the population without computers being left out of the process.

Online elections can be conducted at the same polling places as elections are now held, using the same procedures and checks and balances. These aspects would be different:

- Instead of a manual or machine ballot, a person would vote online using a computer. Like making an online purchase, the computer would confirm with you your votes before you hit the final 'submit' key.
- A copy of each vote can be instantaneously sent to an independent election audit center to prevent any local officials from tampering with the vote counts.
- People voting via absentee ballot would be able to go to any election polling place and vote online.

Eventually the vast majority of people will have computers, and software safeguards will be in place that will allow people to vote anytime, anyplace, from any computer.

This will allow people with varying work schedules, travel schedules, those affected by bad weather, and those unable to travel, to still participate in elections.

Those still without Internet access can vote in libraries, schools, government buildings, churches, friends' homes, at work or anywhere else there is a computer.

Online elections provide a much higher level of assurance that more citizens can vote, that one's vote will not be misinterpreted, that votes will be counted fairly, and that minorities or other groups of citizens will not experience discrimination in exercising their voting rights.

Citizen Web Sites

Another feature of eGovernment that is coming is an individual web site for every citizen and taxpayer. On your web site, you will have:

- **Your taxpayer record.** You will be able to see what you have paid in taxes, what municipal services you are receiving, who is running for office in your ward and precinct in the next election, and what local issues are being debated.
- **Citizen input.** You will be able to contribute your thoughts to the discussions. The city council can take weekly or even daily polls to get citizen input. You can listen live online, or you can pull up a recorded debate. Some debates will be online, with elected officials logging on from their homes and offices.
- **Municipal business.** You will be able to apply for permits and licenses, rent a picnic table and volleyball net, pay fees, and engage in other work or family related municipal business and activities.
- **What if.** You will be able to play "what if…" games and explore possible scenarios online. What if you want to build a garage on your house, how much would that add in taxes and what building permits would be required. What if you want to dig a hole for a pole in your backyard, are there any lines underground you might hit. What if your civic group wanted to have a parade through the city park, what hours and days are available?

This aspect of eGovernment is already beginning to happen. "Officials are transforming government web sites from tedious electronic brochures into virtual service counters where the form to report potholes is only a few windows away from the vehicle registration page," reports Rebecca Fairley Raney in *The New York Times*.[15] Raney also reports that a study released by the Pew Internet and American Life Project found that 60% of those who had used such sites said that the process improved the way they interacted with government.

Government Goes Virtual

We have too many government buildings. They are used for less than half of the day. Taxpayers spend money on mowing the lawns of these government buildings, paying for heat 24 hours a day.

And when we want information, services, or to voice our opinions, we have to go there. We have to spend time to get to someplace, a government building.

We can generate cost savings and improve government service by sending most government employees home to work. We will still need some buildings, and some in-person services available, but government is an information business and government employees are or should be knowledge workers. And knowledge workers can produce more, and save their employer (the government) more by working from home.

Initiatives are already underway to encourage more telecommuting in government. Just as private sector knowledge workers will go home, so too will increasing numbers of government employees.

eGovernment is coming, but governments also face massive internal reorganization.

This will be difficult for government to do. "The technology supports it and makes it easy," says Avi Duvdevani, first deputy commissioner of the Department of Information Technology and Telecommunications for the city of New York. "The hard part is the human part, he says."[16]

The 'human part' as Duvdevani calls it also involves a new perception and conception of how government information is organized. One eGovernment inquiry in Ireland reported, "Our research finds that most Irish County Councils have mirrored the physical structure of their organisation on to their Web sites rather than create a virtual office structure that focuses on the needs of the user."[17]

The Nature of Nature

One of the trends we observe is the increased value and concern over the environment, and especially the interest in preserving and extending parks and wilderness areas. This is also a trend in which we participate.

We do not completely understand why this is so, that knowledge workers engaged in an even more "urban" pursuit than office and factory work, should have this urge to spend more time in nature.

The author and futurist John Naisbitt has said that for every high tech development, there is an equal and opposite high touch response. This is definitely the case for those who work online. In far greater numbers, those who work online have a need to spend time in nature.

Telecommuter Tom Steinert-Threlkeld says being in nature has some mental benefits, noting, "My favorite is to cycle with my son. You get the joy of watching him in action, while he climbs hills, and you get the beauty of the outdoors and the endorphins of exercise. Plenty to get the creative juices flowing."[18]

Nature re-energizes the spirit, enriches the soul, replenishes sapped intellectual energies, and prompts creative thoughts to emerge. And spending time in nature is fun.

In the first decade of this century, we are admittedly experiencing the potential for widespread devastation of our natural resources due to human-made accidents. We are seeing species of flora and fauna disappear. Forests are being depleted. At the same time, the environmental efforts of the last half century are seeing benefits as previously endangered species make a comeback. The eagle is now less endangered. The wolf and elk are being reintroduced into more states. Bear are now numerous enough to be hunted again.

Knowledge workers will look near and far for second homes, vacation lands, and places in and near nature. One hundred years after conservative Republican president Theodore Roosevelt set aside massive amounts of land for preservation, knowledge workers support governmental regulation and preservation. Their support for nature is less an attribute of liberal thinking, more of an internal need for their own work and business lives.

Our favorite bartender up north is Jeff. Jeff is an industrial-age man. He worked for an industrial distribution company for many years. One of his customers was the large Fortune 500 company Bill's great grandfather helped found. Jeff rides a snowmobile and motorcycle. But Jeff's children are different. He calls his daughter a "tree hugger" because she will not go on the lake in his motorboat, and loves nature. Jeff is not a luddite, as he goes online regularly to communicate with his son in college.

Yet in trying to explain the "wayward" direction of his daughter, Jeff told us, "I blame the Internet."

It is unclear at the time of this writing whether environmental preservation efforts will succeed or not, whether additional areas of the earth will be conserved, or whether economic development will trump nature. It is clear that this will continue to be an area of concern on both sides of the argument.

And it is apparent that a large number of knowledge workers balance living in dense communities, whether in metropolitan areas or small towns, with time spent in nature and out of doors.

Community life in society is an extension of our economic life. The neighborhood is dependent on the work place. As knowledge workers become more predominant, they will want and need to live in dense communities with local community life providing a very different support system. While the local environment changes, the larger societal environment also changes as new social infrastructures evolve to respond to the needs of the majority of citizens in society.

Chapter 11
New Societal Infrastructures Evolve: Shift Six

"Issues which really make the life of a society
do not spring spontaneously out of the mass. They exist
in it — a thousand potential currents and cross-currents;
but they have to be discovered like principles of science,
they have almost to be created like works of art."
— Van Wyck Brooks, 1915 [1]

The new technology creates inequalities in wealth in a time of economic transition.[2] And the infrastructure of society becomes immediately obsolete and unable to address the issues of health, safety, education, and justice in the new economic era.

Over time society and governments adjust to the new society, and create a new framework of protection and service that benefits the majority of citizens. At least that is what has happened before in our nation's history, and in other nations as well. The will is there to follow in the same path in our current era. The Internet provides the means to reshape our social interactions in ways that will enhance them and lead to a rebirth of social connection. Just as new structures evolved in the early 20th century to replace the loss of community that many felt, the potential is there for a similar course in today's world.

As we have noted earlier, this is one shift that is not inevitable, not solely dependent on the unassailable economic forces resulting from the power of the Internet. This is a shift dependent on volition, on communities and societies making a conscious choice. This is not automatic.

The two most likely scenarios:

A. Governments install new rules, new legislation, that provide benefits to the majority of citizens. The majority of people participate in the benefits of the Internet Age. The gap between the rich and the rest of the population narrows. OR

B. Corporations look globally for knowledge workers and do not support society-wide benefits that raise the standard of living for everyone in society. Instead, within any given society the huge gap remains between an increasingly smaller rich elite and a majority of people with a stagnant or declining standard of living.

Plan A is the preferred scenario, and the one that occurred in the last century.

There is pressure for corporations to look globally for knowledge workers, and that process has already begun.

In mid 2003, a too-frank report by an IBM executive brought the issue to the surface.

"By 2015, we're going to see over 3 million U.S. jobs move off-shore," noted Tom Lynch, director for global employee relations for IBM in a leaked IBM teleconference. "We're looking for an emerging trend to move services abroad. Some of those services include engineering, financial services, accounting, places like India can do bookkeeping for a fraction of the cost in the U.S.," he said.[3]

"White collar jobs, those requiring a college degree, can be outsourced overseas as well," notes Jim Zarroli, National Public Radio business reporter. He reports that India alone receives some $13 billion in income from outsourcing jobs from other countries.[4]

"The U.S. is the world's most prolific outsourcer, with companies such as IBM and General Electric running huge operations in countries such as India where their software development or transaction processing activities are carried out for third world wages," writes reporter Lesley Stones in the Johannesburg (South Africa) Business Day.[5]

While companies say the move is a reaction to competition, others disagree. "I think it has more to do with greed, plain and simple," union organizer Lee Conrad told the Kingston, New York, *Freeman*. "Companies like IBM are going where the lowest costs and wages are."[6]

Companies will not be able to move a significant number of knowledge worker jobs overseas without a reaction from unions, nonprofits, the education sector and government. Former U.S. Secretary of State Henry Kissinger is an outspoken critic, invoking fears that outsourcing will undermine the economic might of the nation.[7] The trend is not inevitable, things can be done, and government, people, nonprofits and education will take action, maintains Marcus Courtney, President of the Washington Alliance of Technology Workers. His group is organizing technology workers to prevent more job loss to overseas outsourcing. Zarroli concludes, "We have always thought of these (technology, knowledge work) as the backbone of American jobs. Washington will want to take action. It's inevitable."[8]

It is also in the best interests of business that there be new social infrastructures built and less inequality in income. Business can sell more and make more by bringing back a large middle class. Olivier Zunz, a social historian, suggests that the relative prosperity Americans enjoyed in the 20th century had its foundations in the far reaching social-engineering strategies at the beginning of the last century. He argues that the expansion of the middle class in the last century, which formed a conforming consumer center, has been the source of American domestic prosperity for the last century.[9] We are making a pro-business argument by suggesting that society address the inequality of wealth situation by creating new societal infrastructures.

The business sector also benefits from a more relevant social infrastructure for knowledge workers, the primary creator of wealth and profits for business in this century. Many of the new social policies proposed will be in response to the knowledge work sector.[10]

The Slovenian intellectual Slovoj Zizek notes, "Now we talk all the time about the end of the world, but is much easier for us to imagine the end of the world than a small change in the political system. Life on earth maybe will end, but somehow capitalism will go on."[11]

We are not prescient enough to forecast all of the new policies and structures that will be put in place to re-establish an economic and social balance in society. It is clear that we need a square deal, and then a New Deal for the new century. Here are a few issues and possible solutions likely to be discussed.

Intellectual Property

One of the great equality-inequality struggles will be over intellectual property, over the right to own and use information. At the time of this writing, the intellectual property war is being fought on at least two fronts.

The most visible front is that regarding music. The kids are downloading millions of music files and sharing them with other friends, to the

187

economic and legal consternation of the recording industry. The recording industry maintains that the sharing of music files is a form of stealing, and that no sharing should take place. The kids maintain that the information is not being sold, that they are not making any money out of the transfer, and that music is merely being shared.

The first legal case involved Napster, and while the record industry won that battle, they continued to lose the war as more Napsters appeared to take its place and music sharing went on quite undisturbed. At this time, there does not appear to be any mutually beneficial solution to the issue. It also appears that the kids are currently winning this fight, with almost no curtailment of music sharing being accomplished. Reporter Jonathan Seabrook quotes estimates that fifty million Americans have downloaded music illegally. He notes, "A hundred years ago, music publishers were trying to sue player-piano makers out of existence, fearing that no one would ever buy sheet music again." Seabrook concludes, "Whether or not the record business figures out how to make money from MP3s, the format is here to stay. Just as CDs replaced vinyl, so will MP3s replace CDs."[12]

While the kids are fighting on one intellectual property front, teachers and other adults are fighting on the educational front. Adults may not believe that sounds can be shared, but they definitely believe that words should be able to be shared.

Companies and those who own the words beg to differ. Thus companies are trying to capture information, concepts and ideas online, create proprietary content objects. They then would charge others for access to this information. Each proprietary content object would have security provisions so that the owner can receive financial compensation in return.

Teachers and educators are not too happy about proprietary information. Teachers and educators would rather see knowledge available for free on the Internet. Indeed, at least at the time of this writing, it has been very difficult to provide words on a web site for a fee. News sites, online magazines, and other information sites often lose out to competitors when they try to charge for their information.

If companies have their way, words and concepts will also be owned with access restricted. This applies not only to creative property such as poetry, plays and fiction. It could also extend to concepts, formulas, facts, data and other information. At the time of this writing, no resolution or legal direction could be discerned by copyright and intellectual property experts, including Stephen Downes, Senior Researcher, Canadian Research Council, eLearning Group.[13]

Once again, companies are having trouble preserving and charging for their claim to intellectual property. In one incident, a secure system for Acrobat Adobe files was developed, and within days the security was cracked by a Russian technologist. When he presented his findings in the United States, he was arrested and charged with a crime. The charge was later dropped.

Whether information on the Internet will be all privately owned, or whether it will be available and shared, is a major issue right now.

Privacy

Another great struggle is over the right to access and use personal information about an individual. A host of privacy issues have been raised and more are likely to appear.

From just one month's news postings on the web site of the Electronic Privacy Information Center (EPIC), one could find in mid-2003 the following headlines, which illustrate the variety and emotional nature of the issues:
- New Report Criticizes Electronic Voting Systems
- Senate Nixes Domestic Spy Plan
- Groups Announce Spam Policy Framework
- Wal-Mart Cancels "Smart Shelf" Plans
- US Park Police Releases Video Surveillance Policy
- EPIC Urges Protections for the SSN
- Credit Agencies Perpetuate Inaccurate Consumer Reports
- EPIC Testifies on Credit Reporting Privacy
- Consumers Against Supermarket Privacy Invasion and Numbering Meet
- FCC Approves Telemarketing No Call Registry [14]

The privacy issue is not only about an invasion of privacy and the rights of the individual. It is also about society's right to know, and about what people can and cannot do with one's personal information.

Because privacy is really about personal information privacy, it is also fundamental and a prerequisite to other issues in the 21st century. For example, it is impossible to talk about health issues without involving privacy issues.

The most advantageous prospect for privacy issues is this:
- Most information about you, and me, will be made available to hundreds, maybe thousands of other people. However —
- It will be against the law for them to use that information in any way harmful to you.

Here's why this scenario is likely, and beneficial.

First, you want others to have personal information about yourself. You really want the hospital to know your allergies, your reactions to drugs, your medical history, your next of kin, and so on. You want the hospital, any hospital anywhere in the world, and any doctor anywhere in the world, and especially any emergency medical technician, to know this information so that they can save your life.

You also want your bank to know your financial situation so you can get money anytime you need it; you want your online grocery store to have your food purchasing history on file so you can have certain items automatically ordered in advance so you don't have to worry about running out of toothpaste every month and milk every week.

Second, it is beneficial for society to have personal information about yourself. You and others in society really have a "right" to know whether another person has a disease, because the combined data on that person and many others will stem an epidemic before it reaches you and your family, and also eventually lead to a cure when researchers are able to analyze the data on people with this disease.[15]

We really need to know whether the multinational corporation which supplies our electric power or our water is financially sound or on the verge of collapse, leaving us in the lurch.

Thus, it is beneficial both to the individual, and to society, for our "private" information to be available to those who need it.

What is not beneficial, what is not desirable, is for anyone to do anything harmful with that information. Thus, it should be against the law to use any medical information about a person to deny them service, insurance, employment or any other activity. It should be against the law to use any financial information to deny someone a home loan. And so on. It should be against the law for someone to belittle, ridicule, or verbally cause harm to one because of access to such information.

This all can be legislated.[16] We have done it before.

One hundred years ago it was legal to have your own private army, or militia. Rich people such as John D. Rockefeller had their own armed militia, that actually shot at and killed workers, with the blessing of the state (in one particular case, the State of Colorado). Today, you can have a gun, but you cannot have your own army. Yesterday one could discriminate against someone based on their sexuality, sex, age, and so on. Today one cannot discriminate on these criteria and many others.

This is the best answer to the issue of privacy. Society needs access to this "private" or personal information. We cannot have people walking around with diseases that are left unnoticed. We cannot have corporations providing vital services about to declare insolvency or leave thousands of their workers without retirement benefits.

What makes privacy such an issue is not what a person knows, but what one can do with that information. As long as one cannot do any harm to an individual resulting from information possession, no harm is done.

Privacy may also be, in and of itself, a negative, a barrier to progress, both for the individual and for society. Here's an example.

Right now, grades for students are posted online in a password protected or private manner so that only the teacher, the student, and the student's parents have access to that information.

Grades, as of this writing, are unfortunately calculated on the old Industrial Age method of grading, which compares one person to another, thus A, B, C, D, and F. This is the wrong way to display grades, as it offers absolutely no clue to anyone what the student knows and what the student does not know.

So let's assume grades are revised, as they will be, into a couple of thousand units and subunits about what the student knows. What if an educator discovers a great new way to teach multiplication to 8-year-old boys with a certain learning disorder.

Would not you, as a parent, want your 8 year old boy to be able to quickly learn multiplication and then be able to move on in his math studies? Would not you, as a student, want to study with this educator who can help you. And would it not benefit society to have this educator move thousands of boys with this certain learning disorder over this hurdle.

With an open access to one's educational record, this would be possible. With privacy, this is prevented.

The Car and Social Policy

While new social policy issues emerge in the 21st century, others will start to fade. There are numerous issues which can be substantially resolved as the automobile is replaced by light rail and trains.

Recently one public radio station aired programs about a number of policy issues. Those issues included water run-off polluting lakes, global warming, licensing of elderly drivers, and the lowering the alcohol limit for drinking while driving.[17] All of those issues, and many more, have a primary root cause in the automobile. As the automobile declines, these issues will fade as well.

Pay Doubles

When Henry Ford wanted to sell more automobiles, he did something that caused other businessmen and corporate executives to label him a traitor to the business class. He doubled his workers wages, to a whopping $5 a day.

Ford reasoned that if his own workers were unable to buy his product, that other people could not afford it either. And that if his workers could afford to buy his car, then he would get the money back as a purchase, and his workers increased standard of living would eventually spread to other people, increasing their likelihood of being able to purchase a Ford. He was right.

In this century, not everyone's wages will be doubled. But knowledge workers are likely to see their pay go up. The income of knowledge workers is driving the economy of the post-industrial society. Clearly the income of knowledge workers will increase, distributing more wealth and re-creating a middle class.

Wages in the last part of the 20th century stagnated for most workers. Kevin Phillips notes, "Pretense that the non-wealthy were gaining at any comparable rate was as hollow in the 1990s as it had been in the 1890s."[18]

College presidents today are fond of telling graduating seniors that they will make 80% more than a high school graduate over the course of their work lives. What college presidents do not tell their graduating seniors is that the income gap is largely due to the decline in wages of high school graduates, not the increased earning power of those with a college education.

The incomes of those with only a high school degree — those working in factories, those working at unskilled or semiskilled jobs in retail trade and services — are not likely to increase.

But when knowledge workers' pay goes up, that income is distributed to others in the community. National Chamber of Commerce statistics indicate that when a business generates most all of its income from outside the community, that each job creates another four jobs locally. That was true of manufacturing in the last century, and it is true of many information based companies and knowledge workers today.

Taxes Go Up

In order for the gap between the rich and the rest of society to lessen, money has to be redistributed from the rich to the benefit of the rest of people in society. It's that simple.

This is done with progressive tax rates.

And when knowledge workers see their pay going up, reforming a sizable middle class, then they will be able to afford to pay more taxes.

"Taxes go up" is not an exciting prospect for anyone. But in other nations, such as Canada, Europe and Japan, it is not equated with the apocalypse as it is in the United States.

In the United States, no politician can run for office, no government official can retain her job, no citizen initiative can be considered, no service rendered, if it means taxes will go up.

And so politicians, government and citizens in the United States create elaborate devices, terms, euphemisms and code words, to describe what sometimes is necessary and prudent. This process of taxes beginning to go up in the U.S. has already begun, starting in 2003.

Universal Health Insurance

Since Eleanor Roosevelt was in the White House, universal health insurance has been proposed, and rejected.

It might be rejected once again. While we do not have an indepth knowledge of medicine and health care, there are a couple of reasons why universal health insurance may stand a chance to be passed in the next couple of decades.

We know why workers want portable health insurance. A recent cartoon portrayed the personnel director welcoming the new employee, saying, "You can choose between our excellent company health plan, or a salary."

At our organization, staff consistently rank the maintenance of our excellent health plan not only the top benefit to preserve, but also are willing in tough times to trade a pay increase to keep all the medical coverage and benefits.

There is a good reason business might want to endorse universal health insurance. The primary reason is that it gives companies better access to recruiting new knowledge workers to the company, and equally importantly, releasing existing knowledge workers from the company.

If a typical "job" lasts as little as one year, approximating more of a "project" than a long-term job, then business will want and need the flexibility to release knowledge workers after their "project" is completed and there is no further need for their skills at the company. If an employee cannot move to another company for risk of losing health insurance, as is the case now, employees will be reluctant to leave companies regardless of their job happiness.

And on the recruiting end, the pool of available knowledge workers will remain small for businesses and companies if knowledge workers in transition are unable to retain their health insurance.

Another possible reason why the insured may want to make the sacrifice to bring the uninsured into the health care fold is the overall risk to all in society posed by huge numbers of uninsured people. We know it is moral and ethical to provide health insurance to all. Yet it may also be in the self-interest of those with insurance coverage to make it universal. If there is the possibility of an epidemic spreading faster in an uninsured population, or a contagious disease being more readily contained, it might make health sense to have universal health insurance for all.

Universal Higher Education

To get a job in the manufacturing sector in the last century, a high school degree was key. Thus the percentage of the population with a high school degree rose from around 7% in 1900 to 90% in 1998. High school education was made "universal."

At the beginning of the 21st century, only around 29% of the population in the United States possessed a four year college degree.[19]

In order to get a middle-class job, one in which one can support a family, a four year college degree is a prerequisite. In 1992, before the invention of the World Wide Web, President Bill Clinton announced that a two-year college degree was the minimum for a good job. Today, it is clear that a four-year degree is required.

Thus, a four-year college degree will need to become "universal," just like society unanimously created the resources necessary for all young people to achieve a high school degree in the early part of the 20th century.

The move towards universal higher education has already begun in Great Britain, where the Tony Blair government in 2002 set a ten-year goal of having 50% of its people achieve a college education.

During the 20th century, we only needed about 25% of the population to have a four-year college degree. Higher education performed its societal role well. Part of that role was to exclude 75% of the population from gaining a four year degree. Higher education performed this role well also. Today many institutions of higher education pride themselves on how many students are turned away. This obsolete measurement often is used to indicate how prestigious the institution is.

Too many leaders still see higher education as a privilege for the few, not the gateway to good employment for the vast majority of our citizens. In a recent New York Supreme Court ruling about education, even some justices feel that preparing children for the lowest-level, lowest-paying jobs is just fine, says *New York Times* columnist Bob Herbert. He notes that Justice Alred D. Lerner, writing for the three of the four justices in the majority, said, "Society needs workers in all levels of jobs, the majority of which may very well be low level."[20] This kind of resistance to expanding educational levels of society occurred 100 years ago as well. Education columnist Richard Rothstein notes the opposition to universal high school education back then, "The dean of Teachers College in 1906, James Russell, argued that schools should preserve civic order, not stimulate ambitions for mobility that 'cannot possibly be fulfilled.' President Theodore Roosevelt denounced academic programs that 'train the boy away from the farm and the workshop.'"[21]

But preparing less than half of the nation's youth for the workforce of the 21st century is no longer sufficient for higher education to meet its obligations to society.

Today higher education must provide a four year college degree to a majority of the nation's population.[22] As British Telecom technology expert Peter Cochrane writes, "If you want to contemplate and judge the implications of such technologies, it requires a larger percentage of society with a greater depth of understanding. Information technology and online education can go a long way to realising holistic cultures, but we need a greater change in our learning."[23]

We can already see the results of what will continue to happen if this goal is not achieved. First, a majority of citizens will not have sufficient education to get gainful employment, employment which can provide a middle-class living. "We're seeing low-income students priced out of a higher education," says Jornah Taylor, president of the United Council of University of Wisconsin Student Governments.[24]

Second, not enough knowledge workers will be available. In the year 2000, for example, the U.S. Congress authorized more than a half million well-educated workers from other countries be allowed to work in the United States. This in response to the fact that U.S. higher education in 2000 was able to produce only one college-educated worker for every seven technical jobs in the economy.

Thus, in order to recreate a middle class in society, higher education will need to provide a four-year college degree to a majority of the nation's population.

College enrollments will need to quadruple. They will need to rise well beyond the current estimates for 2010 and 2020.

Beginning in 2005, the Net Generation (or Next Generation) turns 18 and creates a huge demand on higher education. At the same time, a greater percentage of young people than ever before will need to gain a college degree. And the growth of enrollment in college among adults will not abate, as increasing numbers of adults return to school to gain promotions, pay increases, and fill knowledge sector jobs in our changing economy.

Individual Learning Accounts

"We're losing our customers — the middle class," noted Mary Bruning, former dean of the College of Continuing Studies at the University of Omaha, after seeing some statistics on the state of lifelong learning.

Indeed, as we enter the Information Age, a century when lifelong learning will be the necessary ingredient for any business to succeed, more and more Americans are not able to upgrade their skills and education levels in order to remain competitive as workers—and keep their companies competitive.

A likely answer is — Individual Learning Accounts, or ILAs.

First developed in England as Individual Lifelong Learning Accounts, the idea has crossed the Atlantic and was briefly mentioned in the Nation of Lifelong Learners report recently.

Some 80% of Americans view continued education and training as important to their careers, overwhelming support for lifelong learning. The support comes across the board, regardless of age, income, ethnicity or level of formal education.

A Washington State University research report explored what Americans want in lifelong learning. Here are some of the results.

- A large majority of adults (81%) think that getting additional training or education is important for them to be successful in their work.
- A similarly large majority (80%) have received some kind of job-related training or education in the last three years.
- The most important finding of this study is that regardless of age, income, race, and ethnicity, the great majority of Americans want to continue their education and training well past early adulthood.
- As the U.S. makes its transition to a knowledge-based economy, it is by no means a foregone conclusion that everyone is achieving

their educational goals.

The national sample of U.S. households in the 48 mainland states was surveyed by telephone in early 1995. The questionnaire included roughly 110 questions. The average interview time was 22 minutes. A total of 1,124 interviews were conducted, yielding a cooperation rate of 60%. National samples of this size have an approximate sample error of plus or minus three percent, the authors say.

The survey leaders say that the survey data closely approximate data from the U.S. Bureau of the Census on such characteristics as income, age, gender, race and ethnicity. Yet some 20% of all adults in the sample had less than a high school degree or its equivalent — roughly the same proportion as in the U.S. population overall.

"Perhaps more than any other piece of background information, that statistic should frame the findings we discuss," write the researchers.

The attitudes and behavior of people from all age groups, income levels, and backgrounds indicate that a large majority of adults recognize the value of lifelong education and training.

In fact, more than four of five adults say that getting additional training or education is important for them to be successful in their work. The proportion is highest for younger adults but, even among those ages 50-64, 59% say that more training or education is important.

The personal significance that people attribute to acquiring more knowledge does not vary with income. Those with annual household incomes under $20,000 are just as likely to value education and training as are those with annual household incomes of $60,000 and over.[25]

The Individual Learning Account addresses this need. In fact, the ILA is being called "a 21st Century tool" by one government agency. "This 21st Century ILA tool addresses the changing nature of learning and employee development," notes the web site of the United States Office of Personnel Management. "The use of ILAs moves agencies' focus from a one-time learning event to continuous learning; from required training to strategic workforce development; and integrates resources for training with balancing work and learning time."[26]

The initial British attempt to implement ILAs in 2001 did not succeed, but education officials report an interest in trying it again.[27]

Here's why business and society need Individual Learning Accounts:

- Continued learning is primarily a function of a) proclivity, or the active desire to keep learning; and b) the ability to pay for continued learning. Only those with the most education and highest incomes have both the proclivity and ability to continue their learning.

- Business requires increased skills levels from its workers, primarily those technical and office workers with more modest educations and income levels.
- In an age of continual change, learning has to be constant and continual.
- With employment being more short term, even temporary or on a contractual basis, business does not have the long term self-interest to invest heavily in worker learning.
- With income and wealth concentrating more on the upper 20% of workers, the rest of the workforce have fewer resources to invest in their own continued learning.

A study we did of the American workforce in the late 1990s showed 112 million people in the workforce. We analyzed both the income of these workers and their educational attainment.[28] Those with the highest education levels, and those with the highest income, together accounting for about 20% of the workforce, are not in need of assistance for their continuing education.

And those with the least amount of education and income, again around 20% of the workforce, are highly dependent on government training and education programs to enhance their work prospects.

That leaves some 59 million workers somewhere in the middle, neither dependent on government education and training programs, nor able to totally undertake their own continuing education and training in a highly changing economy.

While ILAs should be available to all workers, it is the middle half of workers who will benefit the most, need it the most, and for whom business needs to worry about upgrading the most.

Here's what an Individual Learning Account is:

- An account or amount of money in an individual's name for the express purpose of continued learning.
- The ILAs are held and administered by a national body.
- The ILA is portable, so that regardless of employment changes, the individual maintains the same ILA and does not lose any benefits in the ILA.
- The ILA funds are used for continued learning.

A background report done by the United States Office of Personnel Management noted, "These ILAs differ from traditional tuition assistance and reimbursement programs in which the employer pays, or reimburses an employee, for the expenses of education, in whole or in part. In an ILA program, the employee uses the account as he or she wishes for learning and education, within the parameters for which the account is established."[(29)]

Why Businesses Will Want to Establish ILAs

There are a number of reasons why businesses will want to establish ILAs. They are:

- A great recruiting device. Smarter workers will be attracted to businesses with ILAs.
- Studies show that workers who are learning are better and more productive workers.
- Good workers will be less likely to leave a company with an ILA.
- No administration. Employers, especially small business owners, do not have to administer the program or try to become educational administrators.
- No risk. A company's contribution is determined annually by the company. In an unprofitable year, the company does not have to contribute.
- Good investment. As a benefit, it will be far more productive for a business than other employee benefits.

The British Model

The concept and term Individual Learning Account (ILA) was first introduced in Great Britain. An early model was called the Bamford Taggs Model. It consisted of the following:

- Individuals, families, employers and the State could make payments into the accounts.
- Contributions are voluntary.
- "Promises to pay" are allowed.
- All forms of accredited learning courses qualify for ILA disbursements.
- Individual, but not business, ILA contributions and interest are not taxable.
- National Learning Bank administers the funds.

Our Proposed Model for ILAs

- Businesses set up ILA accounts for their employees and contract workers.
- The system is voluntary, no business is required to participate.
- The ILA account stays with the individual upon leaving a particular job.

- Contributions from the business are done annually. The amount is determined by the company.
- The amount is a set equal dollar amount per worker, not a percentage of salary or pay.
- A national nonprofit agency administers the funds, funding itself from a portion of the interest earned on the contributions.
- A wide variety of educational courses from any provider are eligible to be qualified.
- The individual determines when and which courses from which to use ILA funds.
- Local, state and federal governments have the option of contributing to ILAs if they wish.

Individual learning accounts help business as well as individual workers. And properly constructed and administered, they help workers at all income levels equally, thus helping to redistribute benefits and opportunity throughout society.

The social infrastructures of the 20th century, imperfect as they may seem, were successful in transitioning society from the Agrarian Age to the Industrial Age. They also made life better for a majority of citizens. In transitioning to the Internet Age, current social infrastructures are obsolete and inadequate, and new ones will evolve. In good measure, those social infrastructures will both be influenced by, and lead to, a new set of values and attitudes.

Chapter 12
Cheating Becomes Collaboration: Shift Seven

"The kids today are engaged in collaborative learning.
When I was in school, it was called cheating."
— *Richard Thieme, futurist and technology guru.*

Bill's mother, Alice, in her 80s, is now the matriarch of the family. Every year she hosts Christmas dinner, and her sons and daughter and grandchildren come from around the state for the family occasion.

One year our son Willie was in confirmation class at church, studying the Old Testament, and, during this Christmas season, Leviticus in particular. Seated around the dinner table, Alice tried to engage a reluctant teenager in conversation by asking Willie what his favorite passage in Leviticus was. Willie quickly replied, "Thou shalt not seize thy neighbor's ass." The whole table broke up in laughter, while Alice protested "That's not what it means."

Willie and Alice, while sharing the same moral and ethical foundation, are almost three centuries apart in attitude and values. Alice remembers when donkeys and mules did farm work and pulled carts. Willie has never even seen an "ass" and obviously does not associate the word with an animal. For Alice, a wireless is a radio, not an Internet connection, and a file is a manila folder, not an electronic song or document that can be downloaded from outer space at the rate of megabytes per second.

The core notion of speed and travel for Alice is miles per hour (mph). For Willie the most important speed and travel figure is kilobytes per second (kbps). Alice and Willie share, through heritage and genetics, the same fundamental outlook on life and possess the same ethics and moral beliefs. Nevertheless they live in different worlds in terms of attitudes and values.

The changing of the economic eras, from the Industrial Era to the Internet Era, also causes a necessary and inevitable change in attitudes, behaviors and consequently values.

This value change is one of the more visible, emotional and accentuated aspects of the shift as the culture moves from the Industrial Age to the Internet Age. It is here where the confrontation of the past century meets the present one; where the generational divide is most keenly felt. It is these internalized values that those centered in the previous century are most apt to defend.

There are timeless attitudes, behaviors and values of course. But much of what we "believe" stems from our current economic situation. It is of "our time." So when society transitioned from the Agrarian Age to the Industrial Age, a similarly gut-wrenching, family-dividing, upsetting and chaotic confrontation of values also took place.

The Death of Character

Our understanding of the change in values taking place is considerably enhanced by studying the work of James Davison Hunter, author of *Culture Wars* and *The Death of Character*.

Values are not timeless truths or moral imperatives, such as not lying or not stealing. There are ethics and morals that do not change over time and have been embraced throughout human history. Instead, Hunter sees values as utilitarian and changeable.

It is these values, especially those related to work and learning, that is our greatest focus in understanding the transition to the Internet Age of the 21st century.

Hunter also states that children are inevitably the centerpiece for discussions about values. "Children are indeed a symbol of the nation's uncertain future,"[1] and reflect adults' own anxieties. They also represent us as adults. "One need not listen very long to realize that children have become a code for speaking about ourselves," he notes.[2]

He then tells the story of how the values of the 20th century replaced character in the 19th century.

"The term 'character,' as Warren Susman has argued, achieved its greatest currency in America in the nineteenth century. It was frequently associated with words like 'honor,' 'reputation,' 'integrity,' 'manners,' 'golden deeds,' 'duty,' 'citizenship,' and not least, 'manhood.' Character was always related to an explicitly moral standard of conduct, oriented toward work, building, expanding, achieving, and sacrifice on behalf of a larger good — all those 'producer values' embraced within Max Weber's famous phrase, 'the Protestant ethic.'

"But as the American economy began to shift from a focus on industrial production to one of mass consumption in the early decades of the twentieth century, the psychological and ethical requirements placed upon an individual began to change as well.

"With growing abundance, more emphasis could be placed upon accumulation, leisure, and the cultivation of personal preferences. While the word 'character' did not disappear, an alternative vision of the self emerged. This vision was captured by the word 'personality' — a word that first appeared in the late eighteenth century but only gained wide currency in the early twentieth. The concept of personality reflected a self no longer defined by austerity but by emancipation for the purposes of expression, fulfillment, and gratification.[3]

Sunday Schools were created early in the Industrial Revolution to school children who worked in factories all week and thus had no schooling. They also had Sunday as a day off, and Sunday School served the dual role of teaching these working children basic education, as well as trying to prevent them from a day of idleness and bedlam.

Sunday Schools later involved middle-class children, according to Hunter, and by the early 20th century the Sunday School movement was well established.

The wealthy department store owner, John Wannamaker, believed that both his business and the Bethany Sunday School he supervised could gain from the principles of efficiency, mass production and advertisement. Due to his efforts, the Bethany Sunday School became the largest in North America.

Similarly, the Boy Scouts, Girl Scouts, Girl Guides, and YMCA movement all held to 19th century values, but organized their missions and disseminated their messages in the industrial factory-like way of the 20th century.

Lord Baden-Powell, who founded the Boy Scouts in 1908, patterned the organization after the military, the model of the pyramid and organization chart. He even heralded the Boy Scouts as "a character factory."

While they permutated over the course of the century, especially changing in response to new views on womanhood, the Girl Scouts still maintain many founding characteristics rooted in the character factory.

The YMCA was very similar, with a concern for behavioral norms of the 20th century. When our son came home from a rock concert at the local YMCA recently, we asked him what he liked about the YMCA. "I'll tell you what I don't like," he replied, "all those Christian ladies sitting behind desks telling you not to do stuff."

But perhaps the greatest influence on the change in values from the Agrarian Age to the Industrial Age was science and the scientific method challenging the concept of revealed religion, supernaturalism and the literal interpretation of God creating the world in seven days.

The first nationally publicized confrontation between these two clashing values came in the 1920s and was known as the Scopes Monkey Trial, in which the famous attorney Clarence Darrow defended a Kentucky school teacher who taught evolution in the classroom.

Over the course of the century, science and the scientific method won out over the belief that a personal God was responsible for acts of nature, illness and human events. Today few people blame God for global warming, and only a few football players attribute the game's outcome to divine intervention.

Hunter appropriately points to the work of the famous educator John Dewey for much of the early promotion of science and the scientific method in our public schools. In the 19th century, morality was imposed on a child. In the 20th century, children have the capacity to determine their own moral standards.

Habits define character and democracy was inherently moral in the last century. Moving from Hunter's work, the values of the 20th century were all within the context of the pyramid and the organization chart. It is not just that moving up on the hierarchy of the organization chart required these 20th century values, but merely existing within the organization chart and pyramid required adhering to these same values.

Thus self-confidence, integration and social adjustment became values as well as tools for working in the pyramid. "Works and plays well with others" became part of a child's grade card.

Behavior became inseparable from knowledge. We remember visiting our son's public school science teacher who noted that our son would do a lot better in science class if he only stood for the Pledge of Allegiance like the other kids.

Individualism was acknowledged, but along with individual privileges of being an individual came the responsibilities of being responsible for one's own position within the pyramid. "Take responsibility for yourself" became a latter 20th century teacher's admonishment to their students.

One had individual freedom, but the goal and objective for all people was the same: moving up in the pyramid.

To exist in the pyramid, one had to believe that moving up was possible. In the political pyramid, the concept that "anyone can become President" was embraced, looking at the historical evidence in the faces of the white men in the presidency notwithstanding.

For much the same reason, a survey of poor people revealed why they support lower taxes, because on the money pyramid, many believe they can, or will, one day be rich themselves.

There was a brief effort to retreat into 19th century values during the presidency of Dwight David Eisenhower, who grew up in the Agrarian Age. Eisenhower criticized Dewey's scientific method and it was during this time that "under God" was placed in the Pledge of Allegiance.

Then on October 4, 1957, at "22 hours 28 minutes Moscow time, the Earth's first artificial satellite was launched from Baikonur space port" in the Soviet Union.[4] The satellite was called Sputnik.

The Americans tried to launch a similar satellite just several weeks later. The rocket got only four feet above ground before it crashed, causing American journalists to name the American satellite "kaputnik" or "stay-putnik."[5]

Eisenhower's criticism of science abruptly ceased as the United States sought frantically to catch up to the Soviet Union in space exploration. The school system briefly attempted to circumvent or crack the pyramid, and Julie was a part of that first crack in the pyramid.

Then in the seventh grade, she was asked to skip eighth grade in order to move her math and science knowledge along at a quicker pace. After skipping eighth grade and completing ninth grade with straight As, the schools recovered from their lapse in adhering to the immutable and all-knowing pyramid. They realized that they would have a 13-year-old in tenth grade, where only 14-year-olds were and should be. Having a 13-year-old in tenth grade being totally anathema to the lock-step factory-like production system of education, the school made Julie repeat ninth grade. She thus became one of the few people in American history to be made to repeat a grade level after achieving straight As.

It would be several decades later that the pyramid would crack, and then crumble. Concurrently the values of the pyramid would then lose functionality, and then credence. Among the first casualties after the invention of the World Wide Web was that of the gatekeeper.

The Gatekeepers are Gone

One of the functions of the pyramid was to structure and verify knowledge, and limit the number of people with access to that knowledge. So committees, boards, associations, panels, agencies and scholars higher up on the pyramid served as the "gatekeepers" of knowledge, telling us what is true and what is not true.

In 1997, Edward Schroer, Vice President of the American Society for Training and Development, observed that "the priesthood is dead" in a meeting we attended.[6] Schroer was not talking about the church or priests. He was talking about the decline in the role of gatekeeper in society.

No longer would we have authorities to tell us what is true. Throughout the last century, we had gatekeepers. In news, the great American journalist Walter Cronkite could end his television news broadcasts by stating, "And that's the way it is." And everyone watching agreed.

Similarly, there were gatekeepers in just about every other endeavor in life, including science, music, publishing, diet, religion, and medicine.

In medicine, we remember our Uncle Bob, who was a family doctor. When we were young, he would bring his black doctor's bag to family gatherings in case someone got sick. Inside his black magic bag was everything needed to cure disease, including a stethoscope, tongue depressor and medicine.

Years later, as an adult moving into a new community and visiting the doctor for the first time, we waited for him to bring out his black magic bag. Instead the young doctor returned to the room with a huge black book, and began looking up diseases. Today when we visit the doctor, she begins by saying "What do you think you have?"

Julie has an unusually high degree of skill in doing research on the Internet. So when her podiatrist was stumped as to her foot disease, she diagnosed it using the Internet. "Do you have a health background?" he asked her. And when she wanted to present a letter to the local authorities, she researched the 'net before writing it. Asking an attorney to review her draft letter, he asked whether she had a legal background.

Indeed the Internet has destroyed the gatekeeping functions in society, forcing each and every one of us to develop the judgment skills needed to evaluate information on and offline.

21st Century Values

The root of today's value changes lies in the workplace, and the requirements of the knowledge workplace. The valued behaviors in the knowledge workplace differ so substantially and significantly from that of the factory and office that they are almost opposites. Just as the valued behaviors in the factory and office of the 20th century differed so substantially and significantly from that of the farm and agrarian way of life of the 19th century that they were almost opposites.

Collaboration

A central value of the 21st century is collaboration.

Now we have always had teamwork. We have always talked about working together. But the character and nature of that working together was very different in the 20th century.

In the 20th century, an individual largely worked alone. And the teamwork and working together came about as individuals largely did the same thing, conformed to the norm in the organization. The benefit was from all the supervisors in the organization doing the same kind of work, and of course all of the line workers in the factory doing the same work at the same time, in order to make the factory functional and effective.

But the contribution an individual made to the organization was almost totally his or her own individual effort. "Individual effort" was a key term.

Work was to be done alone, even when one was surrounded by others. If a person is seen standing by another person's desk, their supervisor (or anyone else) would first think that the two were engaged in social discussion, not work. "I'll leave you alone so you can work" is a common phrase.

In order to set the proper work, or school study, environment, the first thing we do is to create a separate space for the individual, a place where she or he can work.

In our 50s, we both cannot remember a time when we either worked or studied in school without both our feet planted firmly on the floor. We read books lying down or with our feet up, but serious study or work was almost never done in any other position other than sitting at a desk or table with both our feet on the ground.

By contrast, Marlene Tucker of Salt Lake City, Utah, told us, "When my 12-year-old is on the computer, she generally has a friend or two sitting next to her. How silly of me to set up a computer area with one nice chair by it for use. When I work on the computer, I am isolated and have the door closed. She comes in and chatters and I become frustrated.

She becomes confused because she feels she is helping."[7]

Donald Tapscott tells about the teacher Richard Ford of North York, Ontario, who insists his students ask everyone else in the class before they ask the teacher a question.

"The students learn to cooperate, work in teams, solve problems, and take responsibility for their own learning. If there's something they don't understand, they must ask everyone else in the class before they can ask the teacher. Right after the first class, one girl asks, 'What's a Web page?' Richard shrugs and says, 'I don't know.' Within a few days the kids have gotten the message. 'And who's the last person you ask for help?' says Richard. Everyone replies in unison, 'you are.'"[8]

Knowledge work of the 21st century demands something entirely different. The individual's contribution to the group is a distinct and often unique contribution, so much so that the contribution can best be made, sometimes only be made, in conjunction with the contributions of others.

So that working together not only means coordinating, but actually interfacing in real or asynchronous time, working with and changing each other's documents and work.

There are several reasons why collaborative work and study is fundamental for the 21st century:

- The world is so complicated, the solutions to problems so complex, that many problems, especially the biggest and most important ones, can no longer be solved by one person.
- The world is so diverse, with so much specialty and subspecialty, that no one person can know or grasp enough knowledge across a broad enough spectrum, to solve a problem or complete a major project without the collaborative input from others.
- That the process of finding out what others are doing, even as they are doing it, actually enhances and improves one's own learning and work.

University of Wyoming professor Kevin Lewis moved to having his students post their homework online instead of handing in papers. The posting of homework was done in an open environment, so that students could open each other's projects and see what others had submitted.

But the real change came, Professor Lewis reported, when students posted draft or partial projects online for review. Students looked at other students' work. And then each student's project improved. Sometimes a student would be challenged by another's work or sometimes took a technique and modified or enhanced it. The end result was neither mediocrity nor sameness, but enhanced and higher quality work.

Throughout the last century, and even at the time of this writing, this collaboration would be seen by most adults as clearly "cheating." In the knowledge workplace of this century, however, where the highest quality outcome can best be achieved by this kind of team work, cheating becomes collaboration.

P2P Takes Over

One of the values and behaviors accompanying collaboration is P2P, or peer-to-peer (P2P).

Peer-to-peer originally began as file sharing, or kids electronically sending each other information, commonly music files.

From there, the value of peers sharing information with each other began to emerge and grow.

Instead of relying on an authority such as a teacher to dispense all knowledge, we begin to see students as a source of knowledge and information for each other. In her book *Engaging Online Learners*, Dr. Rita-Marie Conrad of Florida State University advocates that teachers call upon the student to answer each other's questions, critique each other's papers, and even evaluate each other's contributions to group projects. No longer does a teacher need to be present to have learning take place. And when transferred to the work place, the initiative and skills involved in P2P make for greater productivity, more problem solving power, and greater self and group initiative.

There is an educational and work value of having students and workers share information, and see themselves as sharing information, teaching each other, solving problems together, critiquing each other, and facilitating group projects. The value of P2P is that it enhances learning, and makes work more productive.

One of the visible moral and value battles between the two centuries is the file sharing of music, movies and other files online.

Adults have tried to maintain that file sharing is immoral. In 2003 the president of the Motion Picture Association of America, Jack Valenti, went beyond calling the file sharing a "menace." He said, "This is more than just an economic problem or a legal problem or a constitutional problem. It is a moral problem... If you have young kids 18 to 23 making sure that moral compact is in a state of decay, then this country is in pretty sad shape."[9]

The kids argue that this is a moral issue as well. They point to multimillionaire Jack Valenti and say that his industry employs low cost sweatshop labor in other countries, that a few big rich companies control the majority of record and movie production. They charge that record companies regularly shortchange their artists and song writers on royalties, so that the lost royalties would not really go to the artists but to the corporations. They say that $20 for a CD with only one good song on it is not right, especially when a two-hour movie costs about the same. And they question how much of a young person's income the record industry should grab. In short, they question Mr. Valenti's moral values.

As of this writing, the kids are winning. File sharing appears to be growing and become commonplace. And a growing number of adults are downloading songs from the Internet now as well.

Outcomes Replace Inputs

In the last century, what you put into your work mattered. How much time you put in, how much energy, how much devotion, even pain was a highly respected input. And if you put your time in, and if you were busy and active, you were declared productive.

Office workers often describe what they have done in their progress report or staff report. They detail all the activities they undertook, everything they did. Be busy, put in your time.

Job descriptions of most factory and office workers consisted of activities, or things they do. One person answers the phone, another supervises, a third creates something, and so on. Few of their duties and responsibilities, however, specified and quantified what output, outcome or result was to be achieved. And virtually none of the jobs of full-time employees were measured by outcomes instead of inputs, namely time input.

Full-time jobs were of two types. First, there were hourly jobs. People were paid by the hour. After 40 hours, which was defined as full time, five days times 8 hours a day, a person was then paid overtime in order not to exploit them or overwork them without extra compensation. The type of work defined as hourly often involved repetitive or routine tasks, required some level of supervision, and did not involve significant decision making.

The other type was salaried. These were defined as having a broad range of responsibilities, often the person holding them had some level of college education, and quite often had some level of decision making or supervision involved. The work itself was regarded as neither repetitive nor routine.

The classic factory example was the union factory line production employee (hourly) and the supervisor management employee (salaried).

Salaried workers were expected to work 40 hours a week, sometimes more, rarely fewer, and there was no overtime pay. The reward was a higher pay level, plus greater independence and decision making.

Neither of these types of jobs, in and of themselves, specified quantifiable outcomes for evaluation. Sales positions were notable exceptions, although even here some sales jobs were salaried plus commission.

In today's work world in the knowledge sector, organizations have divided up work into "projects." A project has a start date, end date, and a quantifiable outcome. The organization places a value on a particular project, and then figures out how much it can afford to pay for having that project done. It is a set fee basis.

When the organization asks one or more people (employees, contract workers, etc.) to accomplish the project, the organization sets two requirements: first, the end result or outcome, outlined in quantifiable terms; and second, the deadline or due date.

The organization does not tell, nor even care to know, how the project is done, when the project is done, where the project is done, or even whether other people assist in getting the project done.

Projects are done with a minimum of meetings and other extraneous activity.

This is totally different than the work requirements of the organization of the last century. The organization of the last century measured work in terms of hours, not output. It did very much tell, and care, how the work was done, when the work was done, where the work was done, and whether other people were involved. Work was coordinated by a series of meetings and other auxiliary activity.

Behavior Becomes Secondary

Behavior in the pyramid organizational structure of the Industrial Age was important. How one dressed, what one said, how one worked was of the utmost importance.

And in schools, grades were, and often still are, tied to behavior.

Other kinds of school behavior directly impacted grades. It is not enough to know math... a student has to avoid disrupting the class, not make smart alecky remarks, obey the dress code, not be late, not leave early, not take too many bathroom breaks, not be too silent, not be too talkative, and much more. Thus, it is not enough to know one's math to get a good grade. One must also tuck one's shirt in, not wear a hat in school, not talk back to the teacher, bring one's textbook to class, and of course, show up every day.

In the factory and the office, behavior mattered because it influenced others' work as well as one's own.

But in the knowledge workplace, behavior is secondary to what a person does in his or her job. In the knowledge workplace of the 21st century, it matters very little the level of social skills a person has, whether they talk too much or too little, whether they adhere to the dress code, whether they show up on time.

All of that behavior is beside the point. As long as someone is producing results, that's what counts. If you know it, you know it, even if your hair is purple. If you did it, you did it, even if you can't get invited to a party.

And the proof is in the workplace. Boys, who starting in 1980 began to receive significantly poorer grades in schools (and are likely to do so until schools change), nevertheless are valued workers in the Information Age. Their skills gain them good jobs in the workplace. There is no evidence that poor behavior (with the obvious exception of illegal behavior) on the part of boys in school has any impact whatsoever on their ability to gain good employment.

Showing up.

In the last century, the famous comedian Woody Allen is reported to have said, "90% of success is just showing up." Attendance was a key to showing up. People were expected to show up; attendance was mandatory.

In universities, some deans have told us that they show up for meetings just in case their departments are discussed, just in case a decision is made.

In the 21st century, meetings often are time wasters, and decision making and work can be done at a distance, saving everyone precious time.

In the last century, it was not enough to show up, you had to show up on time. The factory started precisely on time. Not a minute after 7 am, not a minute before. Everyone had to be in place.

Early in the last century, people had to be taught to show up on time. Julie's father was rewarded in school with certificates for showing up on time. By the end of the century, the opposite occurred and our children were punished for not showing up on time.

In this century, showing up within one minute of being on time is totally irrelevant to producing an outcome. There are obviously some occasions when one needs to be precisely on time, or the plane will be missed.

Work at your own speed.

In an age when individual talents are valued, individual work styles have to be respected. That means individuals work at their own speed.

In the last century, we could expect and demand that every person conduct the same procedure in the same amount of time. In knowledge work, no such expectation can be demanded. Every knowledge task can be different, every job take a different amount of time. And the human brain is so varied and so different among people that we each work at a different rate of speed for highly complex knowledge tasks.

In school, the notion that every 14-year-old should be at the exact same level of knowledge in algebra at the same day of the same week as everyone else in class is totally unsubstantiated by experience and data.

We know that each of us learns at a different rate of speed and that we each are at different levels of knowledge about a particular subject.

Time becomes valuable.

In the last century, time was an input. The more time you put in, the more you produced, learned or earned. A Ph.D. was, in large measure, about "paying your dues," putting in time. Anyone who worked 12 or 14 hours was automatically deemed productive.

A continuing education unit (CEU) was measured by the amount of time an adult spent in a seat in a class. If one spent ten hours sitting in a class, one earned 1.0 CEUs. Now if someone spent 20 hours sitting in a class, the person earned 2.0 CEUs. Time as an input today is outmoded in two respects. Time put in does not equal results. There is no guarantee, no measurement, that someone sitting in a class for ten hours learned anything. There is no guarantee, and no measurement in and of itself, that someone working 12 hours produced anything of value.

And secondly, we reward someone for taking twice as long to accomplish something. Someone taking 20 hours to learn something is twice as rewarded as the person who only takes 10 hours to learn the same material.

In this century, conserving time is rewarded. If a project is accomplished in less time, the worker is rewarded by having additional time. It is a win-win situation as the organization gets the task accomplished sooner, and the worker gets extra time to either produce more, or have as leisure time.

Getting work done in a shorter amount of time is good. Getting work done quickly is rewarded.

The obvious contrast with the old view of time occurs in school and with homework. Smart students, and this is more true of boys than girls, often do not complete their homework. For smart boys (to generalize here) something should be learned and then one moves on. So doing repetitive homework simply for the sake of duplicating something one already knows is a waste of time. And it instills the wrong values.

They instinctively know that they will be rewarded for the opposite behavior in the workplace, and that in the workplace they will be rewarded for learning something quickly and moving on. So smart boys often will do poorly on a homework assignment yet do well on the test. They understand the test is the measurement of whether they learned something.

Self-discipline replaces supervision.

The last century and the Industrial Age were about supervision and external discipline. On the factory floor, the supervisor was called a "foreman." In the office, a supervisor was called "middle management." These people spent almost their entire day simply monitoring the work of other people, making sure other people got work done. This was effective for the Industrial Age, but it is an obsolete, financially unsustainable and ineffective method for the 21st century.

Work was not always monitored by external supervision. On the family farm of the Agrarian Age, the farmer and his wife were far more on their own. There was a tight-knit community and neighbors who provided encouragement and even help (barn raisings are the classic example). But on an hourly and daily basis, no one was looking over your shoulder.

In the Information Age, external supervision is too costly and too ineffective. It is too costly to pay people full time to monitor the work of others. It is also too ineffective. Work is so specialized and advanced that often it is not possible for another person to accurately gauge whether it is getting done or not. And with workers in varying locations, working at varying hours of the day, it is not feasible to provide the kind of external supervision that occurred in the last century.

That is not to say there is no accountability for one's work. There is actually more accountability for work being done in the 21st century. Because work is measured by outcomes rather than putting in one's time, work becomes more accountable. And monitoring work using an intranet or virtual office is more effective.

But in essence, the amount of self-discipline a worker must employ goes up substantially in the 21st century. The best way of monitoring one's work is to have self-discipline. This is possible. It is not easy to acquire, but children and adults will learn how to acquire self-discipline.

The process best begins in elementary school. From kindergarten through third grade, teachers are beginning to replace external supervision with teaching children how to manage their own day.

How Values Change

In the second part of this chapter, we look at the process of how attitudes, values and beliefs change.

The Jazz Singer

The first talking motion picture of the last century, or "talkie' as they were initially called, was released in 1927. It was *The Jazz Singer*, starring Al Jolson. It was the story of the changing values of the new century. The father is a man of God. He is not just religious, but his position in the community is as a cantor in the synagogue, or singer of sacred songs. He sang and led the congregation during the worship service. It was his job, but job seems like such a 20th century word. It was his life. His son, by contrast, growing up in the first decade of the 20th century, sings secular songs, popular music, jazz. He sneaks off from home and sings in cabarets or night clubs.

When he returns home, his father beats him. This is a clash not between generations, but between the Agrarian Age and the Industrial Age. For the father, beating his son is not just a duty, it is the best way to encourage proper behavior. And the sacred music represents a whole way of living, believing, and family. The son, of course, is a product of the Industrial Age, on his way to becoming a famous jazz singer on Broadway.

The telling line in the movie is when the mother tries in vain to make her husband understand, telling him about his son, "He thinks different." One hundred years later, as our children think differently from adults, it is again not just a clash of generations, but of economic and social eras. Today we jokingly say that our children are born with a silicon chip in their brains.

We are now coming to understand that the observation of the Jazz Singer's mother was rooted as much in nature as in nurture, having to do just as much with biology as environment. Today there is growing evidence that the brain adapts most readily to new circumstances, and that "thinking differently" is not just a voluntary attitude but a neurological and physical change in the brain.

A Man's Word

Attitudes and values are very much tied up with the economic and social circumstance in which one lived. "Ladies were not ladies anymore, and you couldn't trust a gentleman's word," moaned John Steinbeck in his classic book, *East of Eden*.[10] It is true that in the Agrarian Age a man's word was good. No written agreement was needed. But "a man's word was good" was not purely a product of higher morality and ethical behavior. In those days, illiteracy was high, lawyers were infrequent, and so a written agreement was expensive and difficult to obtain.

More importantly, the radius of a man's world was only 5 miles. One's whole world was inhabited by people one knew. One could not hide, one could not easily move to another town and take a job. One's assets were tied up in property, one's farm.

So it was not practically possible for a gentleman to go back on his word. In a tightly knit community where everyone knows everyone else, and where one's whole financial savings were in land, it was not possible to "cut and run."

Hicks and Hayseeds

At the time of this writing, the old obsolete values of the Industrial Age are still largely accepted and approved of by a majority of people in society. We are soon headed into a period of time, from 2005 to 2010 where those values will come into sharp conflict with the values of this century. And after 2010 the values of this century will gain the upper hand.

One of the necessary, though harsh, measures advocates of the new values will undertake is to portray the old values as "bad." The old values, of course, were not bad, just obsolete, out of date, and appropriate for an earlier time. But in order to establish the new values of the century, the old values will be deemed as inferior and bad.

We saw that in the last century. In 1900, half of all people in the country were farmers. Just twenty years later, however, farmers were referred to as hicks, hayseeds, country bumpkins, and of course, "farmer." We went from revering and respecting this most valuable profession to diminishing it as inferior, and farmers as being less intelligent than city folk. Society did that to get people off the farm. And to make them feel good about working in factories and offices.

Every society, every generation, needs nostalgia and sentimentality toward the good old days, often in part to accept and adjust to the current change and way of life.

In the last century, that nostalgia went not to the farm life, which in fact most people experienced. Instead, the nostalgia was created and generated for a way of life that practically no one had experienced, and was not even close to being as happy a life as that of the farmer: the cowboy.

Cowboys were in fact young boys aged 14 through around 22 who worked long hours doing dirty and unglamorous work. When they were paid much at all, it was at the end of the cattle drive. And within a week, most had spent all their cattle drive earnings (about three months' earnings) on liquor, gambling and prostitutes. Towns like Abilene, Kansas, sprung up at the end of the cattle line to take the cattle, but also to take the cowboy's money.

And yet in countless movies, television series, books and radio programs, the life of the cowboy is heralded as one of freedom, fighting for justice, taming the frontier, and just plain happiness. In recent decades, the legend of the cowboy has been transformed to that of the urban cowboy, the man with the values and upbringing of the rural west, competing successfully and with great sophistication in the urban city of the east.

Today a farmer hat denotes gullibility, mundane chores and a certain lack of intelligence. A cowboy hat denotes character, gallantry, bravery and freedom.

Once again we will demean the image of the typical worker of the previous century. It is part of the necessary process of distancing ourselves from last century behaviors and values, so that we can more readily adopt the new century's behaviors and values. It remains to be seen what will become nostalgic in our 21st century drive to put the past behind us.

Amish and Suburbanites

Now attitudes and values change much more slowly than behavior. It will take decades for the new 21st century values to be totally integrated into our psyche and value structure. There are telecommuters who show up on time, even at home. Eventually the vast majority of people will incorporate these new attitudes and values.

But not everyone. People still have a choice. And a few people will remain behind in the Industrial Age. We used to think of the Amish as being a) weird and holding very odd values; and b) being representative of a very small number of people, a sect if you will. We were wrong. The Amish are not weird or odd. And their values are not representative of just a small number of people.

The Amish, a small religious sect, still drive a horse and buggy, primarily farm as an occupation, and dress the way people did in the nineteenth century. "The Amish look like they stepped out of the nineteenth century," one Amish authority notes.[11]

In fact, the Amish way of life is very much the same as the majority of people in the nineteenth century. And the values and attitudes of the Amish are very much the same as those of your great grandparents. Your great grandparents would agree far more with the values of the Amish than they would agree with your values.

The Amish do not work on Sunday. They go to church. They do not believe in evolution. They value homegrown vegetables. They do not believe any education beyond the eighth grade is necessary. They do not put their elderly in retirement homes, but take care of them in the community.

The Amish have simply decided to remain in the Agrarian Age. They adhere to the values and attitudes of the Agrarian Age. They made a conscious decision not to adopt the values of the Industrial Age.

It is likely that some people will choose not to move into the Internet or Information Age. There will be a small minority of people who adhere to the values and attitudes of the Industrial Age. They will make a conscious decision not to adopt the new values of this century.

They will be called something like "suburbanites." They will live in suburbs, drive a station wagon or minivan to work, and continue to work in old-fashioned offices.

The men will wear leisure suits. And because competition was such a positive value of the last century, they will form factions that hold good natured rivalries from time to time. There will be the Cowboys, the Oilers, and, of course, the Packers.

Most people will be zipping along at 150 mph on a high speed train, staring down at the poor Suburbanites on potholed old highways, plodding along at 80 mph, a big orange triangle on the back of their minivans.

Before we leave the Amish and Surburbanites, we must say that these ways of living have much to their credit. Julie grew up in an agrarian society, and has some understanding of the virtues of the Amish way of life.

The Amish do not have to stress out over 401(k) retirement plans, agonize over what college their kids will attend, dash to make a plane flight, fight jet lag and time zones, spend three hours a day in traffic, shop til they drop, nor watch mindless television.

The Amish, we surmise based on Julie's upbringing, are focused on today, on the wind, air temperature, the dryness of the ground. They experience the immediacy of the smell of freshly picked fruit, the familiar nod of their horse's head. A problem is a broken harness, a leak in the barn roof, and while the problems are just as important as our rush-rush daily problems, they have an entirely different impact on the mind and the soul.

No More Tomboys

When she was growing up, Julie played first base with the boys playing sandlot baseball. And she rode horses, climbed trees. She was a "tomboy." In the last century, a girl could be a tomboy.

In this century, it is virtually impossible for a girl to be a tomboy. A girl could play hockey from a young age and never get that appellation. It's simply not possible for a girl to be a tomboy in this century.

The best a girl could do would be to be a geek or a nerd. If a girl got invited to a LAN party (a "local area network" party where kids cable their computers together and play games and share files) with 19 boys, she would be a geek.

A status symbol in the last century for women, it is also practically impossible today for a girl to be a "coed."

Thus, words and concepts change as well. In the Agrarian Age of the nineteenth century, one had scorcher, in the neck, upper ten, over the left, shad-bellied, plug-ugly, and dude.

New words such as "swell" and "so's your old man" were deemed distasteful and rude.

In the Industrial Age of the twentieth century, new words came into being, like receptionist, skyscraper, go-getter, hotsy-totsy, cat's pajamas, and heebie-jeebies.[12]

And words, connoting values of course, changed from positives to negatives. A "square" in the 19th century was something honest, fair and correct. Theodore Roosevelt, in fighting big corporate trusts, introduced legislation giving people "A Square Deal." By the mid-twentieth century, calling someone a "square" meant being old-fashioned and out of step with the current times.

The conflict of the new attitudes, values and behavior of the 21st century clashing against the old attitudes, values and behavior of the last century are best illustrated by the current state of boys in school.

Smart Boys, Bad Grades

There is a growing and widespread concern about the academic performance of boys in school. As few as 35% of today's college graduates are men,[13] down from 50% in 1981[14] and 76% a half century ago. But the problem doesn't begin in college, because only 35-40% of people entering college these days are men.[15] The problem of boys and young men and academic performance runs the gamut from secondary through higher education.

The issue is not confined or particular to the United States. A recent provincial report in Canada begins, "Over the last 15 years, it has become apparent that girls do better than boys at school, not only in Quebec but in most of the developed world."[16] A Guardian article in the United Kingdom on A-level results is headlined, "The trouble with boys: getting them to study is no easy matter."[17] It is a problem in New Zealand. And a special report on the issue in Australia called "The Education of Boys" states that "females dominate higher education enrollments."[18] There is a striking similarity in percentages and numerical differences in the studies in all post-industrial countries.

Here we look at some of the theories as to why boys under-perform in school, and then offer a different rationale for why boys under-perform in school, as well as suggest a solution to resolve the problem.

Chart 5 Marks by which Female Average TES exceeded Male Average TES 1981-1996

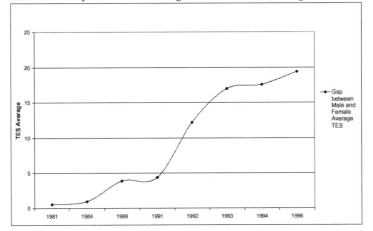

Source: MacCann, R., as featured in Buckingham (2000)

A chart from a study of Australian students showing the growing difference in scores between girls and boys between 1980 and 1998. The pattern is similar across post-industrial societies.

We are strictly concerned with the performance of boys in the upper half of their classes in terms of ability, test scores, grades and future work. While there are legitimate and serious concerns about boys in lower-income families, and those significantly behind their counterparts in school, that issue has been with us for a long time.

What is different now is that smart boys from upper socio-economic levels are falling behind their female counterparts. The Quebec research notes, "Given the same social origins, girls do better than boys at all levels of education." While the roots of the problem go back one to two decades, the issue has only recently surfaced and become an issue.

Ruling Out Other Theories
Here are other theories that do not hold up to scrutiny.

- Boys are inherently inferior academically. No educator or research has suggested this, and the data indicate otherwise. Indeed, as recently as 1998 boys in several achievement test studies did better than girls in computer studies, economics, math and science.[19]
- Parents are not raising their boys with good academic habits. No research indicates this is the case. The probability that parents would raise their female children with totally different standards and parental behavior than those from their male children is improbable, and unsupported by any data. On the other hand, there is evidence that in the same family a smart boy will get grades of about 20% lower than his similarly smart sister.
- The statistics are skewed because of changing participation of minority and low-income students. While this indeed is a problem in the United States, this alone would not explain the identical concern in other countries with very small minority populations, such as Australia and New Zealand, nor that of countries where minorities experience less discrimination, such as Canada.
- That the problem lies in recent social problems in families, particularly the increased number of single parent families and greater numbers of children from divorced parents. There are at least two problems with this theory. One is that girls are also affected by families under stress. The other is that the issue of academic underperformance of boys is well documented in two-parent traditional nuclear families where no family stress has occurred.
- There are psychological and/or behavioral issues with boys today. There are two indicators which suggest this is not the case. The first is that these psychological and/or behavioral issues are not found in

boys outside of the school setting. The second indicator is that young men who bypass further education for the work place do not exhibit these psychological and/or behavioral issues.

Some Important Data and Trends

In order to understand the real reason why boys are under-performing in school, it is necessary to understand some important data. They include:

1. This is a recent phenomenon.

It did not occur 30-60 years ago, when boys were roughly scholastically equal to girls. While girls overall have had better grades, the differences have been much slighter. In Australia, for example, the differences were marginal until 1981 when girls had 0.6 marks more than boys. This difference jumped to 19.4 marks, most noticeably in 1992 when the difference increased to 12.2 from 4.4 marks the previous year.[20] 1992 was also the first year after the invention of the World Wide Web.

2. There is no performance problem in the workforce.

For talented boys who go from secondary school into the workforce, bypassing higher education, there is no performance problem. Young men in technical jobs perform so well they are in high demand in today's economy. In a recent article, columnist Bob Weinstein says that boys are succeeding in the workforce, particularly if they have a computer certification.[21] Technically oriented young men recently found 7 jobs for every 1 qualified candidate. Technically oriented boys are not experiencing either behavioral problems or achievement problems in the workforce.

3. Intelligence is not the problem.

"See that boy," our son told Bill as we pulled up to the front of his middle school. "His name is Marvin. He's a genius but he's failing school." Later I asked my son to recall the incident and he replied, "I don't who it was exactly. There are lots of kids we could have said that about."

The stories are endless. A techie who shut down his middle school's computer system, who now has a top job as a computer and Internet technician. Boys being punished for exploring on computers and getting into school records, which should have been protected by school administrators.

When our oldest son was in high school, he was able to take college classes at the nearby university at the same time he was in high school. When he received his report card, we were initially puzzled that he was getting poor grades in high school and getting an 'A' in his college class.

Schools, Not Boys, Are the Problem

Teen crime is down to a 30-year record low. Teen pregnancy is down. School violence is at an all-time low. Teen drunken driving is down. Teen employment is up. Teen driving fatalities are down. Television viewing is down. Reading is up. Yet everyone knows boys are behaving poorly.

The primary battleground is in the nation's schools. Boys win hands-down on demerits and detention. Worse, boys are subject to more verbal punishment than ever before. "Today the girls were well behaved, and will get suckers," a middle school teacher stated in class recently. "The boys will get the broken suckers." "Everyone knows boys don't behave," she reported another time, reflecting a widely held view among educators and adults in general. Schools are failing to help boys learn, and blaming the boys.

The reason there is a war on against boys is that boys are into the Internet and technology. The Internet terrifies most teachers, and some boys know more about the Internet than do many educators. Boys also exhibit those accompanying attributes which go with a future dominated by the Internet, like taking risks, being entrepreneurial, and being collaborative. Thus they are leading society into the Internet Age.

On the other hand, what is bad behavior for boys in school is good behavior for young men in the workplace. The very same behaviors for which they are punished in school, boys are rewarded for when they enter the workforce. This is because taking risks, being entrepreneurial, being collaborative are all behaviors that lead to success in the workforce today.

Today's schools are bent on obsolete educational values such as conformity, discipline, and behavior totally unrelated to learning and academic achievement. The Wisconsin Public Schools, arguably one of the best in the nation, recently had a statewide advertising campaign where it proudly boasts of its ban on hats in school.[20] Wearing a hat, they claim, deters learning. By contrast, young men are often allowed to wear hats in the work setting, particularly in technology companies. A recent *New Yorker* cartoon, for example, has a young worker with a T-shirt and a baseball cap turned backwards telling an older worker dressed in a suit that he will need to change his dress code in order to remain at the company.

Schools and teachers fear technology, do not have a sufficient understanding of the Internet, and do not employ the web in their teaching. A recent National Center for Education Statistics report on what teachers feel most trained for is discipline (80% report feel adequately prepared). At the bottom of the list is the employment of technology, where only about 20% of teachers feel adequately prepared.

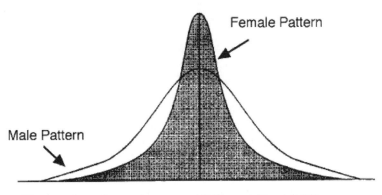

Illustration: Same Average, Different Variability

Judith Kleinfeld's work demonstrates the difference in the bell curves for males and females.

Indeed, teachers and schools are usually far behind their own male students in terms of technology. And the situation is further complicated by the fact that schools and teachers often refuse to learn from their technically skilled students, thus furthering the rift and suggesting to boys that school is no longer relevant for their present and future.

Both boys and girls perceive teachers as favoring girls over boys, according to The Metropolitan Life Survey of The American Teacher, 1997[23].

- Girls (57%) and boys (64%) say teachers pay more attention to girls.
- Girls who raise their hands see themselves as getting called on "often," by greater margins (72% vs. 66%), than boys.
- More boys than girls (31% vs. 19%) feel that it is "mostly true" that teachers do not listen to what they have to say.
- Boys demand more attention in class than girls, according to the majority (61%) of teachers.
- And teachers (47%) say that girls asked for more help after class.

When given a computer, however, so-called bad boys immediately turn into good behavior role models. On a recent school day, Julie observed boys in the computer lab so well behaved that there was no teacher in the room, nor one needed.

Boys are leading the technology revolution, the new economy, the Internet Age, and the workforce of the 21st century. But before they get there, they are being roundly punished.

Until our educational system is redesigned for the needs of the 21st century, the war against boys will continue.

It All Happened Once Before

This all happened once before, exactly 100 years ago, at the same time men were wimps and the Gibson Girl was the model female.[24]

Boys choose work.

Boys 100 years ago opted out of school and chose to work in factories 12 hours a day. Of child factory workers aged 10-15, 67% of them were boys.

Today boys opt for the workplace once again, especially the technology workplace, as soon as they get past the mandatory school age.

Boys are punished in school.

In the first decade of the last century, the Chicago child labor inspector surveyed over 500 teenage kids, asking them if their family did not need the money, would they prefer the factory or school. Some 80%

chose the factory. As one young boy noted about school:

"They hits you if ye don't learn, and they hits you if ye whisper, and they hits you if ye have string in yer pocket, and they hits you if yer seat sqeaks, and they hits you if ye scrape yer feet, and they hits you if ye don't stand up in time, and they hits you if yer late, and they hits you if ye forget the page."[25] Substitute "yell" for "hit;" verbal punishment for corporal punishment, and this is what too many boys experience once again in school.

Boys choose play.

Today boys choose to play with computers, video games, and the Internet. Only a few educators understand that play is learning, central to preparing one for the workplace.

Again, 100 years ago boys played with automobiles, which were thought in 1901 to be only a leisure play toy for rich people. No one thought the car had any value.

At that time, G. Stanley Hall, one of our nation's educational leaders and the President of Clark University wrote: "In play children both practice and train themselves for future vocations, and what is still more important, are rehearsing many, if not most, of the practical activities and vocations of the race. "So in right play-teaching we are working in the very depths and not in the shallows of the soul."[26]

By 1920 the school system was totally redesigned for the Industrial Age of the 20th century.

Industrial arts were incorporated into the secondary school curricula. Rural one-room schoolhouses were deemed inadequate for an industrial urban society. "The type of public school instruction is unsuited to the modern child," noted George W. Alger in 1921. "This is partly due to our inadequate system of rural schools: a school house which is an architectural miscarriage; a teaching force without normal training and hired at less than a janitor's pay... This is the combination the rural child laborer has to break if he is to break into the world of education. The effects of this impoverished system of rural school life are beginning to be felt by our educational statesmen and to be met by the modernized departments."[27] Indeed, the rural one room school house faded and was replaced by the unified or consolidated school district more relevant to the needs of an industrial society.

Until the industrial school system of the 20th century becomes web-based and meets the needs of society in the 21st century, boys will continue to be ill-served by schools. For example, boys may continue to do less well on achievement tests as the tests themselves become more obsolete. The SAT, for instance, was designed in 1901 for the newly industrialized schools and college entrance requirements. But the tests are based on the knowledge needs of the last century, not the current century. Just as we have a hard time passing a math test from the agrarian curriculum of 100 years ago, so technically and Internet oriented boys will find the industrial tests increasingly irrelevant to their learning needs. Here is a common math problem from schoolbooks of agrarian oriented schools of 100 years ago: "How many bushels of oats in a bin 12 feet long, 6 feet wide, and 8 feet deep?"[28] While few of us can answer that question today, it was an important, almost critical, knowledge skill for a society where more than half of the population resided and worked on the family farm. Internet oriented boys today are learning about the frame rate of video (35 frames per second) and other information vital to the Information Age, but found nowhere on today's outdated achievement tests.

Adding to the problem of achievement in school is that boys' social skills, never on a par with those of girls, are also changing, or 'worsening' by the standards of older generations. Julie, an authority on generational learning styles, says that boys use certain terms and vocal behaviors that are misperceived as being disrespectful. She notes that many boys end their sentences on a high note, which is misinterpreted as being disrespectful by older adults. And certain language is also misinterpreted. A common phrase among boys, "shut up," is a negative and disrespectful statement among adults, but has no such negative connotations among children. These changing mores and behaviors are not understood fully by adults and teachers.

Why Boys Are into Technology

While girls use the Internet as frequently as boys, boys are demonstrably more competent with new technology than girls. In several different studies in several different countries, boys score much higher on computer subjects, as well as the related math and science subjects.

Boys are naturally more into new technology than girls. Dr. Judith Kleinfeld, a professor at the University of Alaska at Fairbanks, in her groundbreaking article *The Myth That Schools Shortchange Girls*, provides the documentation on why this is so.[29]

She says boys have a greater variability in many human characteristics than do girls. So boys and girls have different bell shaped curves to describe their variability. Both curves have the same averages, she notes, but they have different peaks and slopes.

Girls have a much higher peaked curve than boys, putting girls much more in the middle or being similar in terms of human characteristics.

Boys, on the other hand, show a bell-shaped curve with much more variability, according to Kleinfeld. Thus, at the leading edge of the curve one finds more boys than girls. Applied to technology, there are more boys than girls engaged in the new technology and the accompanying behavior required in the new economy of the Internet Age.

This can be demonstrated by the numbers of young men in technology-related occupations.

To relate this to the 10,000-or-more-year span of human history, girls have been more likely to have taken the role of the keeper of the cave, which meant establishing and keeping relationships and holding the family and society together. Without women, everything would fall apart. To keep things together, women are more likely to be able to make things go better, and are better at adapting and keeping others in harmony. That means as students they not only are better able to respond to teachers' expectations for behavior, but also cluster together on the characteristics curve that Kleinfeld cites. This also means there is less variability to the female curve, with fewer 'stand-outs' at either end of the spectrum.

The male role over the last 10,000 years was more likely to have been the hunter and gatherer, going out of the cave and exploring new territory, trying new things, hunting, fighting and stealing. It is only 'natural' (either biologically or socially acculturated) that boys would explore the new technology first. Women are just as capable with technology, but do not explore new technology in the same ways as men nor at the same rate. For example, girls use the Internet just as much as boys, but in different ways than boys. And they are less apt to fix, explore, hack, take apart, or put back together as are boys. Thus, there is a biological reason why boys learn differently than girls, according to neurological development expert Michael Gurian.[30]

Gurian puts some percentages on the gender bell curves suggested by Kleinfeld. Gurian says that some 20% of girls are "cross-overs" and exhibit some of the traits of boys. Likewise, he notes that 20% of boys are cross-overs and exhibit some of the traits of girls. Thus, in terms of technology, some 80% of technical nerds can be expected to be boys, and 20% girls. Confirming those estimates, a recent study in the UK found that 21% of tech support people were women.[31] A study of students enrolled in high tech studies at a community college showed a similar ratio.[32]

Just as boys led the automobile movement and accompanying 20th century values, boys today are leading our societies into the Internet Age. They are developing the necessary skills to perform in the knowledge jobs they will be doing after their formal education. By 2020 these new values will be accepted by a majority of people in society.

Chapter 13
Half of All Learning is Online: Shift Eight

"You must do the thing that you think you cannot do."
— Eleanor Roosevelt

The Internet is the biggest technological change in education and learning since the advent of the printed book some 500 years ago. It is destroying the traditional classroom and replacing it with an even better way to learn and teach. And almost every learning situation will be totally altered, including training for business and industry, customer education, association conferences and meetings, continuing education, Sunday School classes, leisure learning, college degree programs, even elementary and secondary school education.

Learners learn more, while working at their own speed, time and manner, over the Internet. There is more interaction among teachers and learners than traditional in person presentations; daily quizzes can tell you exactly what you have mastered and what areas you still need to work on. Learners and teachers can come from all over the world, and they are able to form a virtual community that will kindle long-term relationships.

In the 21st century, online learning will constitute 50% of all learning and education. The rapid rise of learning on the Internet is occurring not because it is more convenient, cheaper, or faster, but because cognitive learning on the Internet is better than learning in-person. Of the growing number of experts seeing this development, Gerald Celente, author of the popular book *Trends 2000*, summarizes it most succinctly: "Interactive, on-line learning will revolutionize education. The education revolution will have as profound and as far-reaching an effect upon the world as the invention of printing. Not only will it affect where we learn; it also will influence how we learn and what we learn."[1] Recent research reported in the Washington *Post* cites studies showing that online learning is equally as effective as learning in-person. And note that we state "cognitive learning," not all learning.

It is still very early in the development of online learning. But the outlines of the potential of online learning are already emerging.

One hundred years ago, education went through dramatic changes between 1900 and 1920, providing a new system of education more suitable to the emerging Industrial Age. Prior to the tractor and automobile, one room schoolhouses were placed every six miles so that a child would have to walk at most three miles to school. The one room schoolhouse necessitated one teacher and multiple grade levels in one room. With the automobile, people moved into towns, and even rural residents could take buses to school, thus causing graded classrooms, school consolidation and the eventual all-but-extinction of the one-room schoolhouse. In the state of Washington, for example, between 1935 and 1939 almost 20% of rural one-room schoolhouses were closed.[2]

Today the 20th century model of education is obsolete. And when online learning is combined with a more interactive and facilitative in-person learning, it will easily out perform today's outmoded one-size-fits-all traditional lecture delivery system. "Digital media and Internet communications will transform learning practices," notes Peter J. Denning of George Mason University in his work *How We Will Learn.*[3]

Perhaps the most dramatic change is how the Internet is changing how we learn. Distance has nothing to do with "distance education." By this we mean that even when the teacher is in close proximity to the learners, the quality of the cognitive learning and teaching will be higher when the cognitive part of the learning is conducted over the Internet. Keoko University in Japan, for example, is already establishing online learning for its on-campus students.[4]

It is still very early in the development of online learning. But the outlines of the potential of online learning are already emerging. In this chapter we will outline what we already know and can forecast about how the Internet and online learning will change how we learn. We know that business will need its workers to learn more, more quickly, and at a lower cost, to remain competitive. We will show that these market forces will create the need and desirability for online learning.

Information Transfer

For most of history the standard educational setting has been an instructor (or teacher, leader, presenter, or speaker) standing in front of a group of people. This is the most common learning design in society, whether it be for college credit classes, noncredit courses, training in business and industry, high school instruction, or even a Sunday School class.

Basically, 90% of all education has been "information transfer," the process of transferring information and knowledge from the teacher's head into the heads of the learners. To do that, teachers have had to talk most of the time. And right up until today that mode of delivery has been the most effective, most efficient, most desirable way to learn.

But as educators we know that the traditional lecture is not the only way to learn. We as learners learn in many different ways, at different times, and from a variety of sources.[5] We also know that learning is not purely a cognitive process, but that it also involves the emotions and even the spirit.[6]

The Internet is destroying the traditional educational delivery system of an instructor speaking, lecturing or teaching in front of one or more learners.

The whole discipline of self-directed learning, variously called adult learning or adult education, has shown that the traditional delivery system is only one way to learn. The Internet represents the biggest technological aid helping people to learn in 500 years, according to many educators.[7] What the Internet is doing is to explode the traditional method of teaching into two parts — cognitive learning, which can be accomplished better with online learning; and affective learning, which can be accomplished better in a small group discussion setting.

Why cognitive learning can be done better on the Internet

Cognitive learning includes facts, data, knowledge, mental skills — what you can test. And information transfer and cognitive learning — even critical thinking skills — can be achieved faster, cheaper and better online.

There are several ways that online learning can be better than classroom learning, such as:

- A learner can learn during her or his peak learning time. Bill's peak learning time is from 10 am to noon. Our oldest son's peak learning time is between midnight and 3 am. He recently signed up for an Internet course and is looking for a couple more, because as he put it, "I have a lot of free time between midnight and 3 am." With traditional in-person classes, only some learners will be involved during their peak learning time. The rest will not fully benefit.

• A learner can learn at her or his own speed. With traditional classes, a learner has one chance to hear a concept, technique or piece of knowledge. With online learning, a learner can replay a portion of audio, reread a unit, review a video, and retest him or herself.

• A learner can focus on specific content areas. With traditional classes, each content area is covered and given the relative amount of emphasis and time that the teacher deems appropriate. But in a ten unit course, a given learner will not need to focus on each unit equally. For each of us, there will be some units we know already and some where we have little knowledge. With online learning, we as learners can focus more time, attention and energy on those units, modules or sections of the course where we need the most help and learning.

• A learner can test her or himself daily. With online learning, a learner can take quizzes and tests easily, instantly receiving the results and finding out how well she or he is doing in a course.

• A learner can interact more with the teacher. Contrary to common opinion today, online learning is more personal and more interactive than traditional classroom courses. In an online course, the instructor has to create the information transfer part of the course — lectures, graphics, text, video — only once. Once the course units or modules have been developed, there is need only for revisions later on. The instructor is then free to interact with participants in the course.

Learners can acquire the data and facts faster using the Internet. Officials at University Online Publishing, which has been involved in online learning more than most organizations, say that a typical 16-week college course, for example, can be cut to eight weeks because students learn more quickly online.[8]

Finally, technology has consistently driven down costs. Reports indicate that education costs continue to rise more than the annual inflation rate. For instance, education costs grew at over 5% for 1998, well above the 3% average for all other sectors of the economy. With education costs in the traditional system soaring, technological innovations promise the ability to deliver an education more cheaply.

Downward pressure is already being exerted on prices by online courses. Officials at Regents College in Albany, NY, which collects data on 8,000 distance learning courses, say that prices are dropping already.

One community college in Arizona, for example, offers online courses at just $32/credit hour for in-state residents, and $67/credit hour for out-of-state learners.

More Interaction Occurs with Online Learning

The heart and soul of an online course is not the lecture, the delivery, the audio or video. Rather, it is the interaction between the participants and the teacher, as well as the interaction among the participants themselves. This daily interaction among participants, for example, helps form what Hagel and Armstrong call a "virtual community,"[9] and what some educators call a "learning community."[10]

The next time you are in a course, count the number of questions asked of the teacher during a one-hour time period. Because of the instructor's need to convey information, the time able to be devoted to questions is very short. In an online course, everyone can ask questions, as many questions as each learner wants or needs.

There is more discussion. In an online course, there is more discussion. If there is a group discussion with thirty people and six to eight people make comments, that is a successful discussion that will take up almost a whole hour. And almost everyone in the group will agree it was lively. Now if you go into an asynchronous discussion forum on the Internet, and thirty people are there, all thirty people can be making comments, all at the same time.

Online, we can participate in discussions easily, absorbing more information in a much shorter time and engaging in more interaction, not less.

Top Ten Reasons

Here are our top ten reasons why cognitive learning on the Internet is BETTER than traditional in-person presentations:
10. You can learn at your own peak learning time of day.
9. You can learn at your own speed.
8. You can learn faster.
7. You can interact more with the teacher.
6. There is more discussion online.
5. Participants come from around the world.
4. You can learn from the foremost authorities and experts.
3. Online learning is less expensive and thus more accessible.
2. Internet links provide more resources.
1. You can form a virtual community.

The Forces Driving Online Learning

Online learning is popular and becoming more popular all the time. At the time of this writing, it is estimated that close to two million people are learning online. Many college students, including adult students, like online learning because it allows greater flexibility in the scheduling of their time. In 2000 the first high school, in Toronto, was reported to be requiring its students to take online courses.[11] In the same year, the first university, Farleigh Dickinson, was reported to be instituting a requirement that students take at least one online course a year.[12]

But this is just the beginning. There are several forces that are turning this scenario for online learning into reality, and turn it into reality very quickly. They include:

Business. Business is the biggest force. Business now understands that in order to remain competitive and profitable, it will need employees who are learning constantly. The only cost effective way for this to happen is with online learning.

So business will require its people to learn online, and it will look to recruit college graduates who can learn online. Colleges and universities will quickly adopt online learning because business will demand that capability from their graduates.

Youth. Our three children have never taken a basic computer course. And they never will. Because they are not just computer literate, they grew up in a digital culture. Young people want to learn online. They understand the future, because it is the world in which they must work and compete. Young students will choose online learning.

Marketplace. There are enormous opportunities created by online learning. There are subjects previously unavailable face-to-face that can now be offered successfully online. There are people in various localities that have not previously been served who can now take online courses. Competitors and other educational providers looking for new niches and markets are another force driving online learning.

The Impact of Online Learning

Online learning is rapidly becoming recognized as a valid learning delivery system. The number of part time students in higher education, to name just one educational system, now outnumbers full time students. A firm majority of colleges now offer some online courses and the number of online courses offered is growing. Online graduate programs and certificate programs have doubled in the last few years. Online learning has grown exponentially in the business sector, according to Elliot Masie of Saratoga Springs, NY, one of the foremost experts on online training in the workforce. Surveys by the American Society for Training and Development (ASTD) see online training replacing much of on-site training in the near future.

Online learning will do for society what the tractor did for food. A century ago food was expensive, in limited supply, and with very little variety. Today food is relatively cheap, in great supply in our society, and with tremendous variety. The Internet will do the same for education. More people will be able to learn more, for much less cost, and with a tremendous variety in choice of topics and subjects. It is something that societies of the past could only dream about. And it will come true for us in a very short time.

Learning in Person

As we have noted, about half of all learning will occur online. But that leaves the other half to be done in-person. But only a small portion of in-person will be the traditional lecture format we have today and that characterized almost all learning in the 20th century. Traditional lecture teaching, information transfer delivered in-person, will decline because it can be done more effectively online.

Most learning in-person will be very different from in-person learning today. In person learning will be focused around what the Internet cannot do. It will be oriented around the integrational aspects of learning. It will be learner-centered.

Now some learning, maybe 10-20%, can be done totally online. If you want to know about how to put a computer together, or maybe the history of the Civil War in the United States, you are interested in facts and data. You don't need a group discussion.

And some learning, maybe 10-20%, will be done entirely in-person. For example, if you want to learn how to make more ethical decisions as a business manager, you don't need a lot of facts and data. Instead, you will benefit from working with a teacher and perhaps other business managers dealing with the same issue.

And there will be a large portion of learning, maybe 60-80%, that will best be delivered using both online learning formats combined with integrative in-person discussion learning. Using both online and in-person formats, learners will gain the cognitive knowledge and facts from teachers online, and then meet with a facilitator teacher in-person to enhance and integrate their learning.

For example, a poetry writing class might involve an online module from a prize winning poet, combined with an in-person class with a local poetry instructor who can review the participants' work and make more personal and individual suggestions on writing poetry.

We actually know a lot less about how people will learn in-person than we do about how people will learn online. That is because online learning is almost entirely cognitive, and we have studied and practiced cognitive learning — transferring facts, information, data and knowledge — for thousands of years.

Integrative learning, the kind that will take place in-person, has been practiced much less because teachers have had to spend almost all of their time on information transfer, leaving precious little time for discussions, affective learning, unlearning, and other forms of integrative learning.

We can forecast that most in-person learning will take place with the participants and teacher sitting in chairs in a circle. This is the room arrangement most conducive to discussion and interaction.

And we know what we want in-person classes and meetings to accomplish. Here are some of the things that we will want in-person classes and meetings to accomplish:

- Help the participants learn how to learn.
- Encourage each learner, provide positive feedback and motivation.
- Deal with the emotions of learning.
- Help each person integrate the cognitive knowledge gained into his or her own life, the learner's own context, relevancy, and meaning.
- Address the spiritual aspects of learning.
- Help learners unlearn old ideas; assist them in "grieving for their old ideas," as adult educator Jerold Apps puts it.
- Measure the integrative learning needs of the learner.
- Assess the integrative learning outcomes.
- Advise learners on their own learning directions, their best learning styles.
- Create dissonance, challenging concepts and helping to stretch individuals' minds and frames of reference.
- Help learners ask the right questions.
- Relate learning to action, assisting participants to incorporate their new-found learning into a change in behavior, either individual behavior or social change actions.

- Physically transmit a bonding between learner and other learners, or between learner and teacher, to facilitate and heighten awareness and that "teachable moment."
- Create new learning as a group that could not be accomplished individually.

We are using the term "integrative learning" to encompass all of the above. Integrative learning implies incorporating one's learning into a greater system of understanding, making sense of the knowledge, being able to master it — not simply repeat it — internalize it, and use it.

The kind of teacher required for in-person learning will need to have very different skills and abilities from the kind of skills most teachers possess today. A cliche has already been created to summarize the transition: "The sage on the stage will be replaced by the guide on the side."

In-person teachers will need to know how to lead a good discussion, how to create dissonance and dialogue, how to summarize and bring things together, how to deal with the emotions of learning, how to advise learners, and most importantly, be more focused on the learners than on the subject matter. The in-person teacher will be a moderator, facilitator, adviser, counselor, broker, mentor.

The adult educator Jerry Apps has been an early pioneer in exploring this kind of learning. Here's what he says, "I emphasize an approach to teaching adults where you the teacher engage your entire personality, how you think, what you know and how you know it, and how you feel and why you feel that way. As a teacher, you ought to be prepared to help learners understand the meaning of what they are learning, help them explore and create, and help them critically analyze as well as think introspectively."[13]

The best role model for the in-person teacher we can think of is the elementary school teacher. When our youngest son was in grade school, each one of his teachers could sit down with us and spend a half hour talking about our son and his learning.

There is an old saying: "Elementary school teachers love their students; high school teachers love their subject matter; and college professors love themselves." That's not nice! That's probably not fair. But it does illustrate the strengths that elementary school teachers bring to their teaching. They do not pretend to be subject experts. Instead, they are focused around helping their students to learn, and their greatest expertise is understanding the learners themselves.

How Knowledge is Organized Online

Not only is learning online a different experience, but knowledge is actually organized differently on the Internet. This new structuring of knowledge changes the way educators construct content for their online courses.

Four new principles of how knowledge is organized online are:
1. Exploration of knowledge goes deeper, not down.
2. Knowledge content units or objects become reusable.
3. Original sources are accessed more for content.
4. Online courses become permanent, like a book.

There are several forces behind these changes. For one thing, there is a tremendous growth of knowledge and information. Today there is more information and knowledge than any one person, any group, any society, any organization could possibly acquire. And new knowledge and information is being created at a faster rate than ever before.

Adults over 40 grew up in a time when the amount of knowledge was more manageable, when one could start at the beginning and read to the end. So people growing up in the 20th century read left to right, top to bottom, start to finish. This is not how young people on the Internet read, says the father of a bright teenager interviewed by Margo Adler on National Public Radio.[14] Because there is too much information, reading on the Internet becomes a process of discovery.

A second and related force affecting how knowledge is organized online is the growing specialization and segmentation of knowledge and information.

New jobs are being created every day. New disciplines, subdisciplines, and areas of study are being created every day.

To cope, people in the workforce concentrate or focus on increasingly smaller areas of knowledge, or specialties. And people are segmented into narrower and narrower interest groups.

This increasing specialization means that one can take a course and divide it up into ten different parts and offer a whole course on each of the ten different parts. And then one can take each of the ten different parts, divide them again into subparts and offer a whole course on each of the one hundred subparts. On and on, more advanced, more specialized.

With so much information, so specialized, and changing so quickly, the Internet is becoming the primary source of information and cognitive knowledge. The Internet can store all this information, it can be updated, and it can be delivered instantly to anyone and everyone.

How information is organized on a web site

Information on a web site is organized like a complicated set of ladders, where you start at the top and go "deeper," choosing which ladder you want to use next. It is the very same method that students used to use to outline a report. The outline went like this:

I. xxxxx
II. xxxx
   A. xxxx
   B. xxxxx
     1. xxxx
     2. xxxx
       a) xxxx
       b) xxxxx, etc.

All items with the same type of designation (I, II, III, etc., A, B, C, etc.) have roughly the same equivalent importance and are distinct from each other. When items appear indented within a larger category (for example, B., followed by 1. and 2.) that means the items are within the same general category and are subtopics or specialized information.

This is how web sites are organized. Master web developer Cem Erdem designed a web site schema for us this way:

Home Page

    I   *II*   *III*

   A. *B.*   *A.* *B.* *C.*

   1. *2.*   *1.* *2.* *3.*

a) b) c) etc.

I, A. 2, c) would probably be something more in-depth and specific in the whole area of whatever information I,A is about.

A screen of copy for I A. 2, c) would be "deeper" than I. Or III B, for example. IA and IB would be more closely related in subject matter than IB and IIIB, for instance.

Course information is organized differently

Course information is also being organized differently. Susan Kirshbaum, head of online learning products for Oracle, a large software company involved with storing data and information, says that a course used to be thought of as a single identity, a huge "glob" as she calls it.[15]

Adds Guenther Weydauer, Vice President for New Product Development at LearningByte International, a content development company, "the worst kind of course content architecture is a bunch of HTML documents thrown together."[16] That is changing.

Knowledge is being broken apart and broken down. The once whole glob course is now composed of units or modules or lessons. Each unit is a separate entity, with a separate focus or theme or set of concepts or skills. Taken together the units make up a course. Broken down separately, each unit is itself an interesting almost-independent entity.

And units can be broken down further into subunits. A subunit might be a page of copy, on which there is a single central thought or idea.

Subunits are arranged in a way that makes sense and compose a unit. But subunits might be broken apart and each might be used again in a different course.

Here's how it breaks down:
- Curriculum (a set of related courses that compose the entire study)
- Course (a complete course of study, with a beginning and an end)
- Units (from 5 to 15 independent and different lessons, each with a different focus or theme)
- Subunits (a smaller breakdown of knowledge with a single focus or concept)

Reusable data

Instead of creating, rewriting and reinventing pieces of data or knowledge, eventually researchers, authors, professors and others will create subunits of knowledge or information.

Then anytime someone wants to use that subunit of information in a course, the information is available and can be used (probably for a price, but probably a pretty small price). Several benefits will then accrue:
- The best information and knowledge is available and widely used.
- It doesn't have to be recreated time and time again.
- It is presented in its best form, illustrated and conveyed in the best possible manner for maximum understanding and learning.

Weydauer says that the reusable units of data are organized into "shareable content objects," or SCOs. A shareable content object is content that is reusable and shareable, that is, can be used at different times in different courses sponsored by various institutions or providers.

According to Weydauer, a SCO:
- is 10-20 minutes of learning (in written, audio, video or other form)
- has 5-15 learning interactions taking place within it

- satisfies a small number of learning objectives
- has an interoperability connector which allows others to access the SCO.

An agency in the defense department of the United States government is heading up an effort to develop an industry-wide standard for shareable content objects. The specifications initials are SCORM.

The Creation of Metadata

To help find, access and determine the relevance of reusable date, a new kind of data has been created. This is data about data. It is called "metadata."

This data might be hidden, or be visible, but tells a person what the subunit or data is about.

Weydauer says that metadata act like "a card catalog in a library." For instance, it could convey:

- what you should learn first if you don't understand this subunit or data.
- what you should learn next if you do understand this subunit or data.
- what other subunits or data this piece of data is related to.
- what kinds of people (jobs, industries, interest areas) might be interested in this subunit or data.
- what kinds of courses this subunit or data might be used for.

Aiding in the creation of metadata is XML, or Extensible Mark-up Language, which has some advantages over HTML, or HyperText Mark-up Language. These new "set of tags on language" will make it easier to tag data in a variety of formats and delivery systems.

An example:

Putting the concepts of subunits, reusable data, and metadata together, here is an illustration of how this will be used in practice.

Let's create two different online courses:
- The History of Baseball
- The History of Race Relations

Here's a sample of the outline for the History of Baseball:
- The invention of baseball
- The early years
- The Black Sox scandal
- Babe Ruth
- Jackie Robinson and the color barrier

- The Yankees
- Baseball today, and so on

Here's a sample of the outline for the History of Race Relations:

- Slavery in America
- The Civil War
- Race relations in the early 20th century
- Eleanor Roosevelt and World War II
- Jackie Robinson and the color barrier
- The Civil Rights Movement
- Race relations today, and so on.

Did you see "Jackie Robinson and the color barrier" in both courses? This is an example of a unit that could be used in both courses. This unit could have the foremost authority on Jackie Robinson compose and write it. There could be interviews with his children or grandchildren. There could be photos and film and audio. It could be the best and most complete narration and elucidation about Jackie Robinson and his impact on the color barrier. It can be used again and again. And since it is the best, it is the best subunit for you and us to learn from.

This is an illustration of how subunits, reusable data, and metadata will be used in online learning.

Original Sources are Accessed More

As a result of the ability to create reusable SCOs and find them with metadata, one of the trends we are likely to see in the next few years is that original sources will be accessed more for content.

Instead of having an instructor talk about a prize winning poem, for example, the class will be able to access the poet talking about the poem.

Online Courses are Permanent

This new way of organizing knowledge on the Internet, and of shareable content objects, reusable data, and metadata, has changed the nature of courses and classes.

"All teaching becomes publishing," notes a copyright and intellectual property expert at a recent education conference.[17] "Every class is now a published work."

So an online course is a digitally fixed or permanent entity, unlike face-to-face classes which were transient and 'disappeared' after being offered. An online course can be accessed before, during and after the actual time of offering. The interactions and dialogue in the class become a permanent record. This is a fundamentally new way of approaching the development of education, and it offers exciting possibilities for enhancing quality and serving students better.

How Young People Learn Online

People born after 1980 have more of the online learning attributes than older people. It doesn't mean they will get better grades online, or that older adults cannot learn online. But it does mean that they come to the situation with a better aptitude for the skills needed to learn online.

Those born after 2000 will already have these aptitudes built into their systems. For those of us who spent most of our lives in the last century, we will want to unlearn as much as we can and adopt new ways of thinking about our learning when we go online.

If you are a young person and the following is duh (obvious in the terminology of young people circa 2000-2005), move on. Or think about how you will handle it when there is an even younger generation than yours online and you will need to learn from them, just as your elders need to learn from you now.

Here are some of the learning characteristics of young people online:

1. Technology is good.

Almost universally young people see technology as good. Adults often are cautious, wary or see the downside of the Internet. For young people, the Internet is good. What the Internet can do might be scary, but one need not be afraid of the technology, nor see it as posing uncontrollable risks or dangers.

Unquestionably, if one sees the Internet as good, then one will be more able to learn effectively online.

2. Learn by discovery.

The "discovery" method of learning is different than how adults have been taught to learn. The discovery method is more immediate, more task or outcome driven, seeks relevance, and involves trial and experimentation (discovery).

In one of our online courses, an adult participant exasperatingly exclaimed about the numerous participant comments in the discussion forum, "There's too much information here." That is exactly the point of why online learning is necessary: the world has too much information. And if you do not have any idea of what you want to learn, you will be deluged by too much information. To reiterate the Cheshire Cat's response to

Russian girls gather around a computer at a Moscow educational institution. Internet behavior and attitudes of young people today are similar across post-industrial societies. Photo by the authors.

Alice in *Alice in Wonderland*, if you don't know where you want to go, then any road will be fine.

To cope with too much information, adopt the Discovery method and find out what you need to know when you need it.

If we expect to start at the beginning, and wind up at the end, we will become hopelessly bogged down with too much information.

3. Scan, don't read.

This is a skill we need to apply online when we begin to learn by discovery. We are actually very good at it when we read a newspaper. But somehow we don't apply the same approach to our learning.

Online, scan, don't read. Use the built-in keyword search software capabilities to find what you are looking for.

When you read a book, read. When you are on the Internet, scan.

4. Chat is natural.

Typing in comments online comes much more naturally to young people than it does to adults. Only about 35% of adults feel comfortable making comments online, while about twice that percentage (close to 70%) of young people feel comfortable making comments online, according to our first hand research. And this percentage will grow to 90% or more.

Making comments online is not only critical to your learning online, it will also be required in the near future as we begin to work online.

5. Netiquette is important.

Young people understand that in order to have successful conversations online, there have to be some rules, an element of politeness, and concern for others. Since they are young people, they may break those rules or test the limits, but they know when they are doing that as well.

6. Learning is also visual and auditory.

More than adults over 30, who learn primarily by text, young people are more visual learners. We will see much more dynamic visuals, including animation and simulations, in online learning in the near future.

7. Trust your judgment online.

There used to be 'gatekeepers' in the world of knowledge. They could tell you what was right, what was wrong, what was reasonable, what wasn't, what the most outstanding novels of a particular century were, and so on.

But on the Internet, anyone can say or post or declare anything. The Internet is full of false misleading information. It is full of opinion. There are a lot of intentional spoofs. And there are some heretical ideas that most of us would consider false today that in 25 years will be almost universally acclaimed as true.

So who do you trust online? Primarily, you have to develop the skill and the assurance to trust your judgment online. This involves developing a few skill sets. A good technique is recommended in Don Tapscott's *Growing Up Digital*, 'consider the source.' Researching the source of the information is one such way to help you develop your online judgment.

8. Face-to-face is good too.

Adults over 30 were brought up believing in either/or. Something was either true or false, either yes or no, either right or wrong, either red or blue. Adults over 30 often place technology and online learning in that either/or situation; online learning is either good or bad; they see themselves as either online learners, or in-person learners.

Young people see technology as being in balance with face-to-face encounters and learning. For them, online and off-line is both/and rather than either/or.

So face-to-face learning is valid, good, and has an important place in their lives. They are not spending 98% of their lives on the Internet. They see more balance in life than that.

9. Interconnectedness is different.

Adults over 30 often view computers and the Internet as isolating individuals, and separating them. For them, face-to-face encounters establish relationships and interconnectedness.

When we visited our home town recently, we went to the public library. Downstairs, in the adult section, there was one adult per computer on the Internet. When we went upstairs, to the children's section of the library, we found two, three, sometimes four young people on a computer on the Internet. While adults see computers as isolating people, young people do not experience or behave that way. The Internet is a socializing experience for them as well. They play together online.

Likewise, they have a better sense of how we are interconnected on the Internet. We exist in relationships online, in a community, relating to each other. It is a new way, an unfamiliar way for most adults over 30, but that interconnectedness is there. Young people see relationships and interconnectedness online.

Young people also learn via online gaming. Computer games are good for you, say researchers. Professor Talmadge Wright and colleagues at Loyola University in Chicago studied computer games and interviewed gamers. Professor Wright found that online gaming increased complex thinking skills. He also found that there is an important social side to online gaming. Games that rely on trust and cooperation give rise to strong communities and good friendships, Wright says.[18] Online gaming also enhances a superior way of problem solving, what some call 'clever crowds' or 'smart mobs.' It turns out that online communities that band together to solve puzzles could provide clues to the next big step in social development, the rise and superiority of collaborative thinking. This novel form of problem solving is emerging because the Internet makes it easy for people to keep in constant touch, and to bring together people with very high skills in a variety of different areas, reports BBC technology correspondent Mark Ward. He reports that the combined thinking power of groups of people exceed that of any one individual. As an example, he reports on a game in which the winner was predicted to solve the puzzle in thirty days. A collaborative group surprised the game's developers by solving the puzzle in just three days.[19]

Professor Rod Riegle of Illinois State University goes so far as to state that if a skill or knowledge cannot be gained online, it is not necessary knowing it for working and living in the 21st century.[20]

The way we learn online is evolving out of the new requirements for how we work successfully in the Information Age of the 21st century. In the Information Age, successful work is even more dependent on successful learning than ever before. The skills for success are the same for both work and learning.

In the previous era shift, the restructure of education followed the requirements of the new factory and office workplace. In today's shift, learning and work are so intertwined that it seems as though as much of the change in behavior skills is being initiated first in schools as it is in the work environment. But the overriding and most critical point is that once again the education and work sectors are working hand in hand. The same 21st century skills are required for success in both school and work.

This transformation in how we learn and teach is therefore changing education dramatically between 2000 and 2020. To serve students who will spend most of their lives in the 21st century, schools and colleges will have to be designed totally different than they were in the last century.

Chapter 14
Education Becomes
Web-based: Shift Nine

"It is a terrible thing to see and have no vision."
— Helen Keller

All successful organizations in the 21st century will be web-based. By that, we do not mean that organizations will be virtual, or totally online. What we mean is that the fundamental functions of communications, decision making and information work will be done online.

One way organizations can measure whether they are web-based is by comparing infrastructure expenditures on technology with those expenditures on facilities. When an organization spends more on technology than it does on physical facilities, it has become web-based.

Education, from kindergarten through college, will certainly be decidedly web-based by around 2020. Education is currently in the process of becoming web-based. A case can be made that in the Information Age, education is leading rather than following the business sector in becoming web based.

But clearly education will be modeled after the primary work sector in the 21st century, just as in previous economic ages where education was modeled after the primary work sector. For this century education in advanced societies will by necessity need to prepare youth for knowledge work, and thus education will be formatted to resemble the knowledge work setting for which it is preparing its students.

Here we review how education will resemble the work place in some very basic ways. And then we will proceed to detail some education-specific characteristics of schools and higher education in this century.

Schools and colleges in the first decade of the 21st century are obsolete and out of date, preparing students for a work (manufacturing) that does not exist anymore. Schools are deteriorating in effectiveness, and will continue to decline until they are restructured around the requirements of the Information Age.

Moreover, it is not just educational structures that are changing. The pedagogy of the 21st century is also significantly different from that of the last century.

The fundamental requirements of education for this century are exactly the same as the requirements for the successful knowledge-based work place. They include:

1. Work done online.

Communications, decision making and information work in schools is done online, using an intranet. For example, all homework is posted online for students and parents to see. Test scores, progress reports and grades are posted online. This is done in a secure manner so that only the student and his or her parents can have access to them.

2. Information delivered online.

Information and cognitive-based knowledge and content is presented more effectively online than in-person. The teacher's role in information transfer declines. The teacher's role in teaching and helping students learn increases.

3. Learning takes place in more than one location.

School buildings still exist. But the concept that learning can only take place in one building disappears. Students have a variety of facilities available to them in which to learn, including libraries and the home.

4. Learning is 24X7.

Teachers are not working 24 hours a day, seven days a week. But students can learn anytime, day or night, week day or weekend. Based on a given student's peak learning time, educational activities are timed to respond most effectively.

5. Individual choice expands.

Students have the choice of how they learn, the rate of speed in which they learn, and to some extent the teaching style that matches best their own learning style.

6. F2F focus is learner oriented.

More face-to-face (F2F) time with the teacher is spent in helping students to learn, in motivation and emotional support, and responding to individual learning needs.

All of these fundamental changes in education mirror the same changes in the workplace, and provide necessary preparation for youth as they enter the work world.

Now let's dispel some of the myths surrounding educational change right now:

Teachers will not disappear, or even decline.

In a knowledge society, we need more teachers, not fewer. The Internet does not replace teachers. It does allow teachers to spend more time interacting with students and helping them learn.

Teacher quality is not the issue.

Teacher quality is not the basic reason why education today is not working. While the upward mobility of women over the past half-century has allowed talented women to move into many other professions other than teaching, nevertheless we have teachers of sufficient talent and ability.

Money is not the issue.

Education does take money. And a knowledge society will spend more money on education than an industrial society. Yet the fundamental issue with the financing of education relates to the misallocation of funds toward buildings, overhead and non-educational activities that schools provide. When these industrial era priorities are replaced by putting our financial resources on the priorities of the 21st century (technology and intellectual capital such as teachers), the money issues will be resolved.

Students and parents are not the issue.

Every generation, every age, has its own characteristics, weaknesses and strengths.[1] However, the ability of our students to learn has never been higher.[2] Parenting, overall, has never been better. Kids are not the problem.

Save Space

Buildings are the albatross, the burden, the biggest threat to educational institutions in the 21st century. The mandate is clear: stop building buildings.

For higher education, here are the top ways space can be reduced and reallocated to enhance student learning and educational effectiveness.

1. The lecture hall is obsolete.

The classroom lecture is now poor pedagogy, and can be done better online. The lecture does not respond to learners' peak learning times. Live in-person lectures cannot be revisited or heard again. They waste student time. Valuable teaching time is lost repeating lectures. There is not enough interaction in a typical lecture.

2. Offices are wasted space.

Millions of dollars could be saved by eliminating faculty offices. Faculty have led society in working at home. They can be more productive working at home and enjoy it more. Professors can meet students in lounges, homes, classrooms or group offices.

3. Existing classrooms must be refitted.

Some classroom space is needed. But the classroom needs to be turned into a discussion room where faculty and groups of students can hold discussions, dialogue and engage in meaningful in-person learning. And every area of every educational building needs to be fitted for wireless Internet connectivity. That means refitting existing classrooms into spaces where chairs can be set up in a circle, with carpeting and good lighting.

4. Computer labs are obsolete.

Every student needs to have a laptop in a wireless environment. Computers must be portable. Students need access to their computers at all times, whether in the classroom, studying at school, or studying at home. A "computer lab" makes as much sense in this century as a "pencil lab" would have made in the last century.[3]

5. Buildings eat up capital expenditures.

By using limited and valuable capital investment dollars for buildings, institutions mortgage their futures. Institutions cannot afford both technology and buildings. They stand to lose their effectiveness and competitive edge, unable to afford the best technology and top quality faculty, as they increase their budgets and expenditures for building maintenance. It is estimated that a typical institution spends almost 10% of its annual budget on facilities and the staff to run those facilities. In business, 10% is often the difference between success and failure. On top of that, buildings often compose most or even all of capital expenditures, so institutions waste millions on building new facilities.[4]

6. Existing facilities should be maximized.

More than half of college students are now adults. With the mix of ages from 18 on up, students of different demographic groups have varied time schedules and time needs. Classroom space could and should be used up to 18 hours a day, from early morning to late at night.

About the only organization that uses buildings profitably are hotels, where meeting, dining and sleeping rooms are used 18 hours a day.

Space that is used 18 hours a day is valuable and important. But space that is used only half-time is unaffordable.

7. Non-educational facilities should be reviewed.

Some proponents of the brick-and-mortar Industrial Age college argue that college life is not about education, it is about social experiences. This notion, that education is not about education, was feasible in the last century. But if push comes to shove, if education has to be only about education, then non-educational facilities should be reviewed.

For example, the University of Chicago and Marquette University are just two universities that maintain high academic standards and reputation without having a football team. The majority of us like college sports, stadiums, big libraries, student unions that border on shopping malls, theaters, and the other amenities of traditional 18- to 22-year-old college life.

How many non-academic buildings a college or university can afford will be a difficult, contentious but necessary question to be asked.

K-12 Space

For elementary and secondary schools, here are the top ways space can be reduced and reallocated to enhance student learning and educational endeavors.

1. Combine resources.

Library and physical education resources can be combined.

In every city, there is a library in every elementary school, every middle school, every high school. Then there is at least one public library. And if there is a technical institute, community college, or state university in town, there are additional libraries.

Each library is understaffed and lacks sufficient materials, books, magazines and other physical resources. Often, the same reference books are in all of the same libraries.

Each library also limits its hours of operations, so that many students do not have access during their peak learning time. Our local community library, for example, closes at 8 pm on school nights, and 6 pm on weekends, being unavailable to teenagers during their peak learning times. Of course, the school libraries are also closed during the evening. Teenagers are effectively shut-out of libraries during the times when they would benefit from them most.

By combining libraries both children and the general public would be better served. There would be more books, greater variety and resources available, and librarians could specialize and provide even greater service to library patrons.

The situation with physical education facilities is the same. Every school has a gymnasium, often there are more than one swimming pool, and yet various sectors of the school-age or general public still do not have access to adequate recreation and fitness facilities.

Combining school and community resources makes sense from a number of different levels.

- Pedagogically, children should see learning as taking place in the community, not in a single building.
- Financially, taxpayers are more likely to support facilities to which they have access.
- Economically, a bigger bang for the buck can be provided to students.

2. Become community centers.

A friend of ours who is a medical economics consultant in Des Moines, Iowa, works out of his home. He told us he uses two buildings very frequently — Kinkos copy shop, and the public library. He uses the library not just for research but as a temporary downtown office in between meetings. During the day, he says, there are two types of people who use the library consistently — homeless people, and consultants and other professionals like himself.

Just as the public library serves a variety of community functions and needs, public schools can do the same.

By adding community services, including community education classes for adults, recreation and fitness activities, public school buildings can be maximized, receive greater taxpayer support, and also be justified financially and economically.

Two of those services that make sense are community education classes for adults, and recreation and fitness activities using school gymnasiums, swimming pools, and fields.

In the last 25 years we have lived in two homes in two different states, both located within a block of an elementary school. In neither case has the school gymnasium been available to us during the evening for basketball or any other recreation or leisure activity. It simply makes little sense to deny adults, especially those without children in public schools, access to facilities which they pay for, and which stand idle during parts of the day and weekend.

Like hotels, schools need to be used for 18 hours a day. We pay for schools, including heating, lighting and utilities, around the clock.

By making school facilities available to adults during the day and evening hours, schools will gain needed taxpayer support.

In the 1960s, two-thirds of adults had one or more children in the public schools. Two-thirds is more than 50%, the necessary margin needed to win bond referendums, mill levies, and other tax votes for schools. By the mid 1990s only 26% of adults had one or more children in public school. Follow the numbers now: 26% is less than 50%. That's one reason why schools are having greater difficulty obtaining increased financial support. Unless schools begin serving the 74% of the population without school age children, schools will be hard pressed to gain the necessary support for maintaining quality education for our nation's children.

By providing community education, recreation and other services to adults, schools gain broader taxpayer support for the schools. Here's an example.

When the schools in Manhattan, Kansas, wanted an indoor swimming pool attached to the high school, they held a referendum. They asked the voters to approve the pool so that the students could have swimming lessons. Maybe adults could use the pool, but that was not clear. The indoor swimming pool referendum failed.

In Fond du Lac, Wisconsin, by contrast, the public school also wanted a swimming pool at the high school for its students. There they asked for a pool so that adults, especially older adults, could engage in therapeutic swimming and other adults could have recreational swimming year round. And yes, the high school students would be able to use the pool as well. The referendum passed, the school gained an indoor swimming pool, and adults were provided access.

Utilizing school facilities for community activities is a win-win situation.

3. Establish independent learning and sharing.

At the secondary level, beginning in sixth grade and continuing through high school, students need to develop the self-discipline to study and work independently. At the same time, they also need to be able to work collaboratively with other students. They need to mentor, tutor and teach other students. They need to share experiences in solving problems. They need to be able to work together on group projects.

At the secondary level, students should not be forced into only one mode of learning all day, while teachers are forced into one mode of teaching all day. The idea that learning can only take place when 30 students are sitting in rows in desks with a teacher at the front of the classroom is simply obsolete and not borne out by educational research.

At the secondary level, students can spend part of their day working and studying independently. They can spend another part of their day working and studying together with other students in small groups. That allows teachers to engage students in small groups and increase the quality time with students. It also requires far less classroom space.

While elementary schools come closest to maximum usage during the day, secondary schools put too many resources into buildings. Secondary schools need to model the type of learning environments that students will find in college, and in the workplace.

Elementary Education

As compared to secondary and post-secondary schools, elementary schools will see the least amount of change.

There are at least two reasons for this. First, elementary schools appear to serve the vast majority of children most adequately, and the gap in educational attainment between boys and girls is the least. And second, the elementary school teacher represents the model teacher for the 21st century.[5]

The elementary school teacher, by and large, focuses primarily on helping students learn, rather than delivering subject matter. When our son was in elementary school, we as parents would have the traditional teacher-parent meetings. The teachers would be able to speak for a half hour about our child. They probably could have gone on longer, but that was the time limit for the conferences. They could tell us about our child's academic strengths, weaknesses, progress, and much more.

This is because elementary schools are structured to be focused on the children rather than subject matter. Few elementary school teachers would claim to be experts in the subjects in which they teach. What they can claim is to be experts — the foremost authority in fact — on each one of the children they teach.

When children move into middle or junior high school, the teachers shift from a student to subject centered approach to teaching. And their knowledge of each student declines significantly.

The most significant changes in elementary education are likely to be:

- The Internet is used more by children for study and gaining information. Children will have laptops and elementary schools will have wireless Internet connections.
- Teachers will need to be better versed in utilizing the Internet for teaching resources and be able themselves to learn in cyberspace.
- The process of learning self-discipline needs to begin in elementary school. Teachers there need to begin an entirely different mode of instilling accountability in students, even at these young ages.
- Students need to be able to learn at their own rate of speed, have their own individual learning objectives, and have their own learning styles positively reinforced and aided.

Secondary Education

As we move from elementary school to secondary school, education changes its focus from what a child has learned, to what a child has not learned. All the fun goes away. The balloons come down, the posters aren't as colorful.

Behavior now becomes as important as learning. In fact, behavior equals learning. If one speaks out of turn, or has an extended illness preventing one to attend class regularly, one's grade goes down. Not only is behavior rather than knowledge a primary goal, but that behavior has to be lock-step with all other students. We all have to turn in homework assignment 587 on Thursday, regardless of whether a student is ahead, behind, ill, or out of town. The factory model becomes dominant. Sitting in a chair in class is defined as meeting educational requirements. Talking about going to Mexico in class is learning. Actually going to Mexico and speaking Spanish is defined as skipping school.

To prepare youth for working in a factory job that no longer exists, students are required to show up at factory times, beginning at 7:30 am. This despite medical research showing that teenagers should be sleeping early in the morning, and that when school starts at 8:30 or 9:00 am student achievement goes up.[6]

To enforce the lock-step behavior the yelling starts. The punishment begins. Here are some of the multiple ways that schools have of meting out punishment:

- **Tardy slips.** Even being a minute late warrants a tardy slip. Too many tardy slips and additional punishment is administered.
- **Demerits.** Students get demerits for nonconforming behavior, but good behavior cannot reduce the number of demerits. Too many demerits and access to recess or participation in the annual picnic is denied.
- **No recess.** Behavior, like chewing gum or wearing a hat, can result in denial of recess, an important physical stimulant to learning.
- **Suspension.** While those students with problems need more learning and attention, schools prohibit students with problems from learning, thus worsening the situation.
- **Expulsion.** If you really want to create an outcast from society and increase the prison population, this is the way to do it.
- **Law suits.** Schools and teachers do threaten and occasionally bring law suits against students and parents.
- **Court fines.** One student was fined by a judge for raising his voice in school.
- **ISL.** This is the equivalent of solitary confinement. A student is taken out of class and isolated and shamed.
- **Detention.** Staying after school, while no research has provided statistically valid positive benefits, is a popular punishment.
- **Arrest.** Humiliation is a primary punishment here where students are arrested in school, even when the charges are dropped, even for legal behavior that occurs outside of school time and outside of school property.
- **Absenteeism.** A student cannot learn unless she or he is in class. If a student is sick, for example, yet gets "As" on all her tests, that nevertheless warrants failure.

- **Truancy.** We have a whole different term of humiliation for one who is absent too often, even if the student is not responsible.
- **Yelling.** Yelling is not an official school punishment, but it is the most common. It takes various forms, but is the equivalent of corporal punishment some hundred years ago in terms of its demeaning and counterproductive effect on self esteem, motivation, and preparing one to learn.

To place blame on the student for not conforming to the one-size-fits-all norm of behavior and learning, teachers use a variety of punishing phrases, including:

- "Take responsibility for yourself."
- "Focus."
- "If you had listened the first time…"
- "Step up to the plate."
- "Just apply yourself."
- "Everybody else got it."
- "Pay attention."

With all the time and effort devoted to regulating lock-step behavior, middle and high school educators have significantly reduced time for actual teaching and learning.

The entire Industrial Age model for secondary schools is now so obsolete that it is disintegrating in terms of positive educational outcomes for students. Today's secondary schools nowhere come near expectations and requirements for their students in the 21st century.

The notion that all 14-year-olds can and must learn exactly the same subject matter, at the same rate of speed, taught by a single teaching style regardless of their own learning style, all at the same hour of the day regardless of the individual's peak learning time, has been totally discredited.

This obsolete system is in the process of breaking down. There has been a growth of alternatives outside of public schools, including home schooling and private schools. There is a rapid growth of alternatives within the public school system, including magnet schools, Montessori schools, renaissance schools for those children with problems, specialized schools by subject focus, specialized schools by learning disability, and virtual schools. These schools not only are an attempt to give students and parents a choice based on the needs of the child. They are also a clear indication that the main school model is broke.

At the same time, mainline schools are increasingly adopting 21st century practices and technology.

Is this a school or a factory? The school of the 20th century was based on the model of the factory. Schools will continue to model the economic age of which they are a part.

Private schools and schools run by for-profit companies are temporary band aids, but are not long term solutions.[7] For-profit companies have a bottom line, and that is profit. There is profit in serving the top 20% of the families that are well off financially. There is no profit, and no savings, from serving the other 80% of society. This is why we have nonprofit organizations and government. The likelihood that most schools will be run by for-profit companies is very low.[8] The likelihood that public schools will transition from the outmoded factory model to becoming web-based is very high. And it is happening right now.

There are five major areas of redesign that will constitute the secondary school of the 21st century.

1. Teacher web sites.

Teachers are moving quite quickly to develop web sites where students access learning resources and where teachers communicate with parents and students. Some of the things that go on a teacher's web site include:

- Homework assignments. Students and parents can access homework assignments on a daily basis, so they always can find out easily what is required and due.
- Grades. Students and parents can find out on a daily basis how well the child is doing on tests, projects and homework assignments. For example, our son took a test at 9 am one day and by 2 pm we were able to log on and find out his test score.
- Learning resources. The web is full of web sites, articles, pictures, animations, simulations, audio lectures and other content that provide a growing core of learning resources for students.
- Completed assignments. Students can e-mail or post papers, essays, worksheets and other home assignments online. Parents can verify that assignments have been turned in. Students can have access to their work for study and corrections. Teachers can actually grade and comment upon online papers faster than marking hard copy papers. And online papers don't get lost.[9]
- Self quizzes. Students can test themselves frequently to measure their own progress without any grade implications.

These are just a few of the ways teachers are enhancing learning, making teaching more time effective, and reorganizing class time to allow for increased time on the more important teaching and learning activities. The tools to accomplish the above functions are already available and so reasonably priced that teachers are developing their web sites with little additional resources required. Once built, these web site features actually

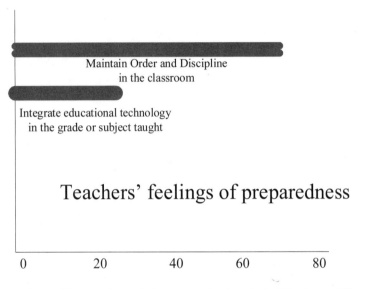

Maintain Order and Discipline
in the classroom

Integrate educational technology
in the grade or subject taught

Teachers' feelings of preparedness

| 0 | 20 | 40 | 60 | 80 |

Source: U.S. Department of Education, National Center for Education Statistics, 1998

Teachers' feelings of preparedness indicate 20th century skills, with teachers themselves ranking their preparedness for maintaining order highest, and their preparedness with technology lowest, among a variety of different teaching skills.

Source: National Center for Educational Statistics.

reduce teacher time in content preparation, communication and grading.

2. Technology infrastructure.

Creating the necessary technology infrastructure for our secondary schools requires financial and educational leadership and commitment. It is also a decision that has to be made at the school or district level, with all teachers committing to it.

The main components of the technology infrastructure required are:

Laptops.

Every student needs a portable laptop computer which can be used in school and taken home.[10] The laptop provides access to the Internet and learning resources. It provides communication with the teacher. And of course it produces papers, essays and other assignments.

Laptops are used in class, as teachers refer to learning resources on the Internet, and teach using the resources of the Web. Laptops are used in study hall and between classes, as students learn independently on the web, print out papers, and communicate. And laptops are used at home for homework and study and writing and test preparation.[11]

Wireless connections.

Every school will have wireless Internet connections so that students, teachers and administrators can do work, whether it be learning, teaching or administration.

The wireless connections allow students and teachers to have Internet connections without any cords, and so that the Web can be accessed anywhere in the school.

Servers.

Every school will need to have its operations and capabilities on servers. Those servers might be in each school. They might be housed at the district level. Or they might be housed by a company with a "server farm."

Technical support.

Professional technical support is required at least at the district level to support and maintain the technology infrastructure, and to train teachers.

The technology infrastructure involves a major commitment of money for each school district. It is unclear whether this investment can be accomplished while maintaining huge brick-and-mortar facilities, many of the expenses of which go for duplicated space, underutilized space, and unnecessary space. It is unclear whether this investment can be accomplished while maintaining costly non-educational features of the school system, such as sports teams and facilities, or bus transportation systems. It is unclear whether this investment can be accomplished without raising taxes.

What is clear is that a technology infrastructure is absolutely essential and required, and that schools will fall further and further behind without it. Every child today requires this technology support system in order to learn and to prepare for the world of work in the 21st century.

3. Curriculum restructured.

When teachers have web sites and a technology infrastructure is built, it then becomes clear that curriculum goes online and becomes restructured.

The curriculum gets divided into modules or units, which are usually done in weekly time periods. The curriculum moves from nondescriptive terms like "Chapter 7" to knowledge concepts and skills, with greater definition and outcomes specified.

Homework and other projects will move from a daily due date to a weekly due date. This will allow students greater flexibility and take into consideration the normal daily ups and downs of life. It will also be one way in which students learn self-discipline.

A greater mix of outcomes and work will be incorporated, including group projects, PowerPoint presentations, online discussion, individual projects, role playing, debates and other measures of knowledge achievement.

With self-quizzes, students will be able to quiz-out of those subunits and areas where they are already accomplished, and be able to reallocate valuable time on the areas where they need additional attention and study.

And behavior will be taken out of the equation and will become irrelevant to the educational process.

4. Place and time changes.

As the first three changes occur, then educators will start to redesign the place and time in which education at the secondary level takes place.

In the obsolete industrial model, education can only take place in one location: the designated school. Obviously learning is an activity, not a place. Just like work will take place in many different locations, learning will take place in many different locations.

This will happen because each person has a slightly different optimal physical learning environment. Variation and multiple options in place of learning will prepare youth for the world of work in the 21st century. And it may very well be that educational resources are located in more than one location.

In the obsolete industrial model, education can only take place during first shift factory hours, from 7:30 am to around 3:00 pm. This is an optimal work time for most adults. But it is a terrible work time for the biological clock that controls most teenagers, whose physical health and growth is better served by later hours of study.

A one-time-fits-all also does not respond to the individual differences in peak learning time among youth.

In terms of pedagogy, expanding the options of time and place for learning enhances learning. Educators are coming to understand that student learning is enhanced by at least three interactions or educational engagements.

One interaction is between the student and teacher. Another interaction is among the students themselves, particularly with a buddy or tutor, and in small groups. A third educational engagement is between the student and the educational resources, which means studying or working online.

Classes will eventually evolve to utilizing all three interactions in more equal portions and with greater educational efficiencies. Thus, a typical class might see some students in small groups helping each other, other students engaged in study alone, and the rest of the class spending time with the teacher.

One positive effect of this is that the teacher will be able to spend more time with an individual student, more quality or instructional time, and in smaller groups. Thus, in effect, "class size" will become smaller.

Once you begin to see classroom set-ups change from desks in a row to chairs in a circle, this will be a primary indication that this change is underway.

5. Learning becomes customized.

In the obsolete industrial model, all students learn the same thing, at the same pace, at the same time, in the same manner, by the same teacher, at the same age.

The Internet makes it possible for each student to have an individual learning plan. This learning plan maximizes each student's learning strengths and addresses each student's learning weaknesses. It helps each student get from point A to point B in the best way possible. It creates "choice."

We know that:

• Boys learn differently than girls.
• People learn at different rates and speeds.
• Some people learn one subject faster than others, and fall behind the normative curve on other subjects.
• People have different learning styles.
• Teachers have different teaching styles.
• People in different cultures have different learning characteristics.

There is currently an evolution in a particular kind of software called a Learner Management System, or LMS. This software records what an individual learner currently knows; records what the parents, teachers and youth determine is a future subject matter curriculum (where we're going); and then denotes what units and modules the student needs to master in order to pass or complete the curriculum.

The Learner Management System can also be used to provide resources based on the youth's learning style, and match the student to teachers whose teaching styles will best benefit the student.[12]

Given the bell curve nature of humankind, it is unlikely that customizing learning will lead to chaos. We are not suggesting all teachers will need to be available at 3 am, that students will wander off to innumerable locations to study, that there will be a thousand totally different variations on schooling.

The nature of human beings suggests there will be a few very different patterns, and that within those basic patterns a student might have a minor individual variation. There might be one hour spent differently, or one location, or one subject, or a student listening to a lecture rather than reading it, or another student be assigned a part-time mentor from her home culture half-way around the world.

These variations can be managed using a Learner Management System. The end result is that each student, each learner, will come out of school with unique knowledge skills and attributes that will match the requirements of the work world, a work world that cannot value employees with all the same skills, a work world that benefits from and profits from a workforce made up of employees with individually distinct talents and abilities.

Higher Education

Nowhere does the advent of online learning and the Internet have a more profound and cataclysmic impact than on higher education, which is being transformed dramatically here in the 21st century.

Higher education based on the "bricks and mortar" model of the last century is breaking down. It will soon collapse. When it does, there will be winners and losers. Some institutions that have positioned themselves for the 21st century and begun to change early in the game (before 2010) will be winners. Those that wait may have waited too long. It is likely that some of the institutions of higher education will disappear or merge within the next twenty years.

The Industrial Age institution of higher education is currently sagging under the weight of the demands being asked of it. Only a handful of institutions will be able to remain based on the Industrial Age model. Harvard University, for example, has enough financial reserves to do anything it likes, although Harvard has already begun the process of transitioning to becoming web based for academic reasons and to stay a premier provider of higher learning. And a few "retro-look" institutions will cater to those families who continue to support the values of the last century. But establishing a foothold as one of the remaining holdouts of last century education will be very risky, and competitive. It is not easy being the last of anything.

Just a few of the signs and symptoms that higher education has to change include:

- The cost of higher education now exceeds the increase in inflation, numerous other indices, and in some cases parallels the excessive cost rise of health care.
- The average student in 2000 left college with more than $20,000 in college debts, triple the average debt a student incurred just nine years earlier.
- Access to state institutions is being challenged at a time when more youth, not fewer, need higher education opportunities.
- State funding of public universities has decreased from more than 50% of the universities' funding down to around 33%, with some universities seeing their state funding fall even further, to around 25%.

Here are some of the main features of 21st century higher education which seem most apparent.

1. Attendance grows significantly.

Structural changes will occur as a result of moving from having only one-third of the population with a four year college degree to giving the vast majority of citizens a four year college degree.

Colleges and universities will need to double their enrollments. At the same time they will have to lower tuition significantly to make college affordable.

2. All classes are online.

We know that classes on the Internet are superior to totally face-to-face (F2F) classes.

This does not mean that classes will not meet in person. Many courses, perhaps the majority for undergraduate students, will also meet F2F. They will be composed of a hybrid or mix of online and F2F components.[13]

3. Virtual communities form.

Students will relate to each other on two levels. They will have very local and small communities that involve F2F contact. At the same time, they will participate in one or more much larger virtual communities with people from around the world.[14]

Virtual communities will be organized by all kinds of characteristics. There will be communities by culture and ethnicity, by subject matter, by learning style, by avocational interest, and much more.

Virtual communities will be support groups to help the student academically, socially and emotionally. Faculty will lead or participate in virtual communities as well as a means of maintaining their scholarship, research and teaching relevancy.

4. Courses become syndicated.

Currently only 1,000-2,000 subjects are taught at the college level.[15] Most of the subjects are taught simultaneously at a majority of the 4,000 campuses in the United States.

To improve quality and efficiency, courses will become syndicated. A foremost authority will originate and develop a course, and that online course will be made available to other institutions.

The result will be that the number of subjects offered will dramatically increase to 10,000 or so subjects. Courses that currently have too little interest on a single campus, or no expert faculty, will be able to be offered. The religion of the Druids, seventeenth century French poetry, the life of Adlai Stevenson, the care of mango trees, and thousands of other legitimate academic subjects will become available.[16]

5. Faculty are dispersed.

Being web based, colleges will communicate and operate using an intranet and online classrooms. This will allow some or many faculty to be located in widely dispersed geographic areas.

Some may teach only at a distance. Others may visit the campus frequently for F2F meetings with students. But the key advantage is that a college can recruit specialists and scholars to enhance its particular strengths, emphasis and unique leadership in academia.

6. Graduate specialties proliferate.

For graduate study, totally online degrees will proliferate. Graduate specialties will proliferate because advanced professional training is increasingly required for success in the business and professional world. Another reason is that the number of subspecialties and occupational specialties continues to increase, creating increasingly specialized areas of study, scholarship and practice.

Another reason why online graduate degrees will proliferate is that there are numerous professions where there are only a few practitioners in a given local geographic area. Newspaper editors, museum curators, city managers, and professionals in a thousand other fields simply do not have enough numbers in a geographic area for a class. Relocation is not an option for someone who needs to keep her or his job. Online graduate degrees meet the requirements of these professionals.

All colleges and universities will be web based. They will be run via intranets and online classrooms. They will have enormous investments in technology, software and technical support. Where they have buildings and campuses, they will be wireless. All students will be required to have laptops.

Young college students may continue to need and desire an intense personal F2F experience on campus. Residential and commuter campuses may continue to thrive, although they too will have to become web based.

Community colleges are likely to partner with one or more four year institutions and offer the last two years of a four year degree online. This will allow more students to acquire a four year degree without leaving jobs or moving away from home.

Universities are likely to become distinguished by graduate degrees and specialties in offerings.

The changes in education toward a web-based delivery system are actually happening fairly quickly. Business leaders are advocating for more learning about technology in schools.[17] Virtual schools and other alternatives to Industrial Age schools are growing. A growing percentage of teachers are becoming receptive to professional development in using the Internet in their teaching. Parents and students want more online learning in schools. In higher education, every year a few more campuses go wireless.[18] In colleges and universities, the use of the Internet and online learning in classes is only a few years away from being common and commonly accepted.

With education central to a knowledge society, the positive transformation of education is also a causal force for change in the work place environment.

Only the Beginning

There is annual, and sometimes monthly progress for almost all of the nine shifts we have described (the shift from cars to trains is the one most difficult to ascertain progress). There is continual growth in the number of people working at home,[19] and interest in virtual offices. The debates on 21st century public policy, social infrastructures and values get louder each year.

All nine shifts are happening. By 2020 all nine shifts will be evident, and evidently superior to the industrial ways of the last century. To invert F. Scott Fitzgerald's lyric phrasing, evitable is becoming inevitable.[20] It is an exciting time. It is one of the more critical time periods in this century, a time to create a better society for our children and grandchildren. Thanks for being a part of *Nine Shift*. Enjoy the 21st century.

References

Introduction

1. *The Big Change*, by Frederick Lewis Allen, Harper & Brothers, New York, 1952, page 187.

2. Kathleen McMonigal, University of Washington, Seattle, speech before the 17th Annual Distance Teaching and Learning Conference, Madison, Wisconsin, 2001.

3. Peter F. Drucker, *Managing in the Next Society*, Truman Talley Books, New York, 2002, page 296. It is interesting to note that Frederick Allen, writing about the changes 100 years ago in *The Big Change*, acknowledges the work of Peter Drucker in summarizing proceedings from a conference in 1951 that led to Allen's undertaking of his history.

4. Ibid, page 129.

5. Ibid, page 299.

6. Richard Thieme is a futurist and technology expert from Milwaukee, Wisconsin. We first heard his comment about the future in 1996 in a speech in Chicago for an American Society of Association Executives conference. His web site is *www.thiemeworks.com.*

Chapter 1. The End of the World, As We Know It

1. *The 20th Century is Almost Over*, by Steve Goodman, 1977, Big Ears Music Inc./Red Pajamas Music, Inc. ASCAP.

2. From a paper and presentation before the River Falls, Wisconsin, Rotary Club in November 1999, by professor Clyde Smith, a retired history professor at the University of Wisconsin – River Falls. It was not clear to the authors whether the account actually happened, or whether it was a story that people in the 11th century told after the second millennium had occurred.

3. From a newspaper account of how Americans failed to celebrate the new millennium, by British reporter Mark Steyn, *The Sunday Telegraph*, London, January 2, 2000, page 12.

4. Dr. Jerold Apps is a retired professor of adult education from The University of Wisconsin. His concepts of grieving the loss of old ideas and unlearning are contained in his book, *The Mastering of Teaching Adults*, by Krieger Publishing, Melbourne, Florida, 1991.

5. This interpretation of *The Wizard of Oz* is from a lecture by history professor Dr. Robert Luehrs of Fort Hays State University, Hays, Kansas, 1992, funded by the Kansas Committee for the Humanities, and attended by the authors. The authors recognize that there are other interpretations of *The Wizard of Oz*.

6. *Ladies Home Journal*, December 1900. The quote was part of a display by the State Historical Society of Wisconsin, Madison, 2000.

7. *Platteville* (Wisconsin) *Journal*, January 11, 1901, as cited in *Yesterday's Future, The Twentieth Century Begins*, edited by Michael E. Stevens, State Historical Society of Wisconsin, Madison, 1999.

8. *The Big Change*, by Frederick Lewis Allen, page 187.

9. From *The Music Man*, by Meredith Willson, music and lyrics by Meredith Willson, based on a story by Meredith Willson and Franklin Lacey, 1957.

10. From *Main Street*, by Sinclair Lewis, Harcourt Brace Jovanovich, Inc., New York, 1920, forward.

11. Ibid, page 19 and 39.

12. Ibid, page 401.

13. Ibid, page 432. Lewis' observations on society at the turn of the 20th century is confirmed by contemporary novelist Tracy Chevalier, whose main character thinks to herself, "It is only eleven hours into the twentieth century, yet I know very well that nothing has changed but a number." (*Falling Angels*, by Tracy Chevalier, Plume, New York, NY, 2001, page 2.)

14. Wisconsin State Historical Society Museum, survey of museum attendees, August 2000.

15. From a story on traffic lanes and transportation in the *Milwaukee Journal Sentinel*, August 6, 2002.

16. *The Social Life of Information*, by John Seely Brown and Paul Druguid, Harvard Business School Press, 2000, 2002, quotes from Chapter 3, 'Home Alone.'

17. Brochure for Heleker Brothers Department Store, Frankfort, Kansas, 1907, discovered in an antique store in Texas by Timothy Draves.

18. Authors' interview with June Warren, Frankfort, Kansas, librarian and town historian, September 1996. It was this interview, and her answer of "eleven miles," that was one of the conceptual turning points in our understanding of the impact of the Internet on society in the 21st century.

19. For background information about the plow and tractor, the authors are indebted to Andrew Barkley, Department of Agricultural Economics, Kansas State University, Manhattan, Kansas.

Chapter 2. The Auto and the Internet

1. *Net Gain*, by John Hagel III and Arthur G. Armstrong, Harvard Business School Press, Boston, MA, 1996. A seminal work in understanding networks and the changing economics brought about by the Internet.

2. *Cybercorp, the new business revolution*, by James Martin, Amacom, New York, NY, 1996. Another important conceptual book from the de-

cade of the 1990s that helped the intellectual fervor and outlining of how the Internet is changing society.

3. *The Centerless Corporation*, by Bruce A. Pasternack and Albert J. Viscio, Simon & Schuster, New York, NY, 1998. Our understanding of business units is based on this book and the work of Peter Drucker.

4. *The Great Crossover, personal confidence in the age of the microchip*, by Dan Sullivan, Babs Smith, Michel Neray, The Strategic Coach, Toronto, Canada, © 1994-1997. Given to the authors by CPA Tom Hintz, this was important to us in explaining how organizations, and life, have been organized as a pyramid, and how that affects each one of us personally and professionally.

5. *Cyberville, clicks, culture, and the creation of an online town*, by Stacy Horn, Warner Books, New York, NY, 1998. One of the first books to describe in detail how the Internet impacts cultural and social relationships.

6. Statistical History of the U.S., Fairfield Publishers, page 74.

7. In June 2003, the Department of Labor, Bureau of Labor Statistics reported manufacturing employment at 14.7 million, down from 17.3 million in 2000, according to a *USA Today* chart in *The Reporter*, Fond du Lac, Wisconsin, page A1. The 14.7 million figure would be just under 15% of the work force.

A similar estimate was provided by economist Raj Aggarwal, Firestone Chair and Professor of Finance, Kent State University, Kent, Ohio, in an e-mail dated April 11, 2002, to the authors following an interview with Dr. Aggarwal on National Public Radio. Aggarwal put the percentage at less than 18%.

While Aggarwal confirmed the growth of knowledge workers, he noted the current difficulty in providing estimates on the number of knowledge workers, noting in his e-mail to the authors, "I am not sure if we have reliable estimates of the number of knowledge workers. As one somewhat extreme example, how do you classify a ceramic artist who adds intellectual content to a piece of clay?"

8. *Statistical Abstract of the U.S.*, National Data Book, 1996, page 410.

9. *The Essential Drucker*, by Peter F. Drucker, Harper Collins Publishers, New York, NY, 2001, pages 304-305.

10. Allen, page 7.

11. Ibid, page 7.

12. *The American Family Educator*, A.B. Kuhlman Company, Chicago, IL, 1904, page 28.

13. *Robert M. LaFollette*, by Belle Case LaFollette and Fola LaFollette, The Macmillan Company, New York, 1953, Volume I, page 184.

14. *Standard Reference Work*, 1908, Volume II, Carriage. The books do not have page numbers.

15. *The Horse & Buggy Age in New England*, Edwin Valentine Mitchell, Coward-McCann, Inc., New York, 1937, page 4.

16. Standard Reference Work, Carriage entry.

17. 1910 Census, "Thirteenth Census," as found in *19th Century American Carriages: Their Manufacture, Decoration and Use*, by The Museums of Stony Brook (no authors given), Stony Brook, 1987, page 505.

18. Ibid.

19. Ibid.

20. "The Dawn of the Truck," by Leonard S. Reich, *Invention & Technology* magazine, Fall 2000, page 18.

21. Obituary of Robert H. Rimmer, New York Times, August 11, 2001.

Chapter 3. Your Pyramid is Collapsing

1. *We Are Our Work*, by Joseph French Johnson, The American Viewpoint Society, Inc., New York, NY, 1928, page 152.

2. Smithsonian Institution web site, *http://educate.si.edu/scitech/carbons/*

3. *The American Adventure, A History of the United States, Volume II, From the Civil War*, by David Saville Muzzey, Harper & Brothers, New York and London, 1927, page 476.

4. See, for example, *The Age of the Automobile*, by George Bishop, Hamlyn, London, 1977. Interestingly, the Ford jokes continue into the 21st century. For a sample, do a Google search for "Ford jokes."

5. Muzzey, page 487.

6. Ibid, page 499.

7. *America Enters the World. A People's History of The Progressive Era and World War I*, by Paige Smith, McGraw-Hill, New York, NY, 1985, page 311.

8. Ibid, page 329.

9. From a speech by Peter Cochrane, British Telecom, London, England, at the 15th Annual Distance Learning and Teaching Conference, Madison, Wisconsin, August 1999.

10. From a speech by Jaron Lanier, at Online Learning 2000, Denver, Colorado, September 2000.

11. *Faster, the acceleration of just about everything*, by James Glick, Pantheon Books, New York, 1999, page 124.

12. Muzzey, page 474.

13. Ibid, page 471.

14. Authors' conversation with Ralph Hughes, author of *The History of John Deere Buggies and Carriages*, conversation held March 14, 2000.

15. *The Great Gatsby*, by F. Scott Fitzgerald, Charles Scribner's Sons, New York, 1925.

Chapter 4. Homer Simpson and The Gibson Girl

1. This is an emoticon of Homer Simpson: (_8^(l) To see Homer, hold the book sideways..

2. See, for example, a web site about Charles Dana Gibson at *http:// cdgibson.com.*

3. Allen, page 9.

4. Frederick Allen, *Only Yesterday*, Harper & Brothers, New York, NY, 1931, page 2.

5. Authors' interview with Alice Thorkelson, who told us the meaning of "It" in the It Girl, December 2001.

6. Authors' interview with Y.A. Taylor, Julie's father, of Black Mountain, North Carolina, July 2001.

7. *The Reckless Decade, America in the 1890s*, by H.W. Brands, St. Martin's Press, New York, 1995, page 3.

8. Ibid, jacket cover copy.

9. *Lady Chatterly's Lover*, by D.H. Lawrence, Grove Press, New York, 1928, pages 203 and 205.

10. Ibid, page 206.

11. Ibid, page 111.

12. Ibid, page 146.

13. Y.A. Taylor interview.

14. *The Music Man*, by Meredith Willson, music and lyrics by Meredith Willson, based on a story by Meredith Willson and Franklin Lacey, 1957.

15. *Self-taught young techies don't see point of college*, by Bob Weinstein, King Features Syndicate, February 2001.

16. *The Myth That Schools Shortchange Girls: Social Science in the Service of Deception*, by Dr. Judith Kleinfeld, University of Alaska, Fairbanks, 1998.

17. *The Twilight of American Culture*, by Morris Berman, W.W. Norton and Company, New York, NY, 2000, page 69.

18. From the diary of William A. Draves II, 1904, unpublished, in the authors' library.

19. *Burma-Shave, the rhymes, the signs, the times*, by Bill Vossler, North Star Press of St. Cloud, Inc., St. Cloud, Minnesota, 1997, page 106.

20. Keynote address, by Jaron Lanier, Online Learning 2000, Denver, September, 2000.

21. *Growing Up Digital: The Rise of the Net Generation*, by Donald Tapscott, McGraw-Hill, New York, 1998, page 36.

22. BBC radio report, March 11, 2003.

23. *Managing Transitions, Making the Most of Change*, by William Bridges, Perseus Books, Reading, Massachusetts, 1991, page 70.

24. *The Future of Success*, by Robert B. Reich, Vintage Books, New York, 2000, page 252.

25. George Carlin, comedy routine, performed in Manhattan, Kansas, 1984.

26. Reich, page 14.

Chapter 5. Somebody Does Something

1. From an article, "Master of Disaster," by John Cassidy, in *The New Yorker*, July 15, 2002, page 84.

2. From *Globalization and Its Discontents*, by Joseph Stiglitz, quoted in *The New Yorker*, July 15, 2002, page 84.

3. Paige Smith, page 9

4. Muzzey, page 480.

5. Ibid, page 480.

6. Allen, page 56.

7. *Marketplace* (public radio program), with David Broncaccio, August 28, 2002. See *www.Marketplace.org.*

8. From an afterword by Emory Elliott to *The Jungle*, by Upton Sinclair, Signet Classic, 1990 edition, page 344.

9. Ibid, pages 343-344.

10. Allen, page 68.

11. *A Synopsis of American History,* by Charles Sellers and Henry May, Rand McNally & Co, 1963, Chicago, page 280.

12. Muzzey, page 402.

13. Sellers and May, page 280.

14. *Great Issues in American History*, edited by Richard Hoftstadter and Beatrice K. Hofstadter, Vintage Books, New York, 1958, 1982, page 273.

15. Ibid, page 273.

16. LaFollette, page 172.

17. Smith, page 23.

18. Ibid, page 325.

19. Muzzey, page 482.

Chapter 6. People Work from Home: Shift One

1. Peter Leyden, keynote speech, LERN Annual Convention, San Francisco, December 4, 2001.

2. *The Essential Drucker*, by Peter F. Drucker, HarperCollins, New York, NY, 2002, page 303; first published as *Emergence of the Knowledge Society, Management in a Time of Great Change*, 1995.

3. Ibid, pages 304-305.

4. *FDR: The War President*, by Kenneth S. Davis, Random House, New York, 2000, page 415.

5. Source: 2002 Society for Human Resource Management survey of 531 human resource professionals, as reported by Adrienne Lewis in *USA Today*, March 30, 2002.

6. *Telecommuting on the rise in U.S.*, MSNBC, *msnbc.com/news*, June 16, 2002.

7. Ibid.

8. "Telecommuting's Big Experiment," by Jonathan D. Glater, *The New York Times*, May 9, 2001.

9. MSNBC.

10. "Breaking up the Central Office," by Amy Harmon, *The New York Times*, October 29, 2001.

11. *Should I Mow the Lawn or Make a Sale*, speech by Jim Bennett, Starwood Hotels & Resorts, and Brian Richey, ConferenceDirect, at PCMA Annual Convention, January 7, 2002, Nashville, TN.

12. "Working at home today?" by Katie Hafner, *The New York Times*, November 2, 2000.

13. *The Social Life of Information*, by John Seely Brown and Paul Drugid, Harvard Business School Press, Boston, Massachusetts, 2002, page 63.

14. Drucker, page 307.

15. "The Economist Intelligence Unit (EIU) surveyed 237 senior executives worldwide for AT&T and determined that by 2005, 80% of companies around the world will have employees who telecommute (termed "telework" by the EIU) — rising from 54% by the end of this year. The EIU explains that economic pressures as well as technological developments will push more companies to allow for telecommuting." From "Business Benefits of Telecommuting," *BizReport*, Denmark, July 17, 2003.

Chapter 7. Intranets Replace Offices: Shift Two

1. *How the Internet Works*, by Preston Gralla, Que, Indianapolis, Indiana, 1999, page 253.

2. Ibid.

3. See for example, *The Corporate Intranet*, by Ryan Bernard, John Wiley & Sons, Inc., New York, 1996; and *Intranets* by Stephen J. Vaughan-Nichols, Academic Press, Inc., Boston, 1997.

4. *Survey: Broadband Access Boosts Teleworker Productivity*, by Allen Bernard, April 29, 2003, Austraila.Internet.com

5. "Home, Sweet Office," by Matt Glynn, *The Buffalo News*, Buffalo, New York, May 4, 2003.

6. See for example, "Badly designed intranets cost employers thousands," by Ross Wigham, *PersonnelToday.uk*, April 30, 2003.

7. California Cedar Products Company, e-mail to the authors, April 8, 2002.

8. "A remedy for doctors' handwriting," by Joe Manning, *The Milwaukee Journal-Sentinel*, December 25, 2002, page 1A and 17A.

9. Source: Kepner-Tregoe, reported in *USA Today* by Anne R. Carey and Genevieve Lynn, October 3, 2001.

Chapter 8. Networks Replace the Pyramid: Shift Three

1. *The Great Crossover*, by Dan Sullivan, The Strategic Coach, Toronto, Canada, 1994, page 16.

2. *Managing for the Future*, by Peter F. Drucker, Truman Talley Books, 1992, New York, page 157.

3. Ibid, page 161.

4. "The Coming of the New Organization," by Peter F. Drucker, in *Harvard Business Review on Knowledge Management*, 1998, Cambridge, MA, page 3, originally published in the January-February 1988 issue of *Harvard Business Review*.

5. Ibid, page 6.

6. Ibid, pages 10-11.

7. Peter Leyden, former managing editor of *Wired* magazine, and business consultant, from a speech in San Francisco November 29, 2001, reported in "New leadership skill key in 21st century," *LERN Magazine*, February 2002, page 9.

8. Ibid.

9. *The Centerless Corporation*, Bruce A. Pasternack and Albert J. Viscio, Simon & Schuster, New York, NY, 1998, page 24.

10. Ibid, page 34.

11. *FDR: The War President*, by Kenneth S. Davis, Random House, New York, 2000, page 397.

12. *Advertising and the Motor-Car*, by Michael Frostick, Lund Humphries, London, England, 1971, page 43.

13. Leyden.

Chapter 9. Trains Replace Cars: Shift Four

1. "The Primacy of the Car is Over, California Governor Declares," by James Sterngold, T*he New York Times*, August 20, 2001.

2. Authors' discussion with limousine driver, San Francisco Marriott Hotel, November 2001.

3. Conversation with Wm. Draves, Abu Dhabi, United Arab Emirates, April 16, 2001.

4. *Faster*, by James Gleick, Pantheon Books, New York, 1999, pages 123-124.

5. Editorial, "Destroy a Freeway, Save a City," by Charles Lockwood, *The New York Times*, August 23, 2001.

6. *Mobiles worse than drink-driving*, BBC-News Online, March 22, 2002.

7. "Wrong Turn," by Malcolm Gladwell, *The New Yorker*, June 11, 2001, page 55.

8. Ibid, page 55

9. Ibid, page 50

10. *New Departures: Rethinking Rail Passenger Policy in the Twenty First Century*, by Anthony Perl, The University Press of Kentucky, Lexington, KY, 2002, page 5.

11. Ibid, page 239.

12. Ibid, page 239.

13. Ibid, page 253.

14. *Transportation — A Major Player in Smart Growth*, by Ted Mondale, ITE Journal, November 2000, page 940, quoting a 1999 University of Minnesota Center for Survey Research study.

15. Perl, page 224, citing *http://www.smartgrowthamerica.com/poll.pdf.*

16. *FDR: The War President*, by Kenneth S. Davis, page 438.

17. "Big Three take big hit, fall below 60%," by James R. Healey, *USA Today*, September 6, 2001, page A01.

18. See the web site of the locomotive division of General Motors at *http://www.gmemd.com/en/locomotive/.*

19. Source: New York City transit authority, as quoted in *The New York Times*, May 20, 2002.

20. "Acela speeds through airlines' shuttle customer base," by Marilyn Adams, *USA Today*, April 16, 2002, page B05.

21. *http://www.cahighspeedrail.ca.gov*, February 1, 2003. See also *http://www. Amtrakwest.com/califuture/5yearplan.htm*, March 19, 2001.

22. "The bullet train concept is picking up speed," by Martin Kasindorf, *USA Today* October 11, 2002, page A07.

23. Conversation with authors, Manhattan, Kansas, country club, 1995.

24. Authors' conversation with Manhattan Steel and Pipe CEO Jack Goldstein, Manhattan, Kansas, Rotary Club, 1996. He also noted that river barge is one-third the cost of train shipping.

Chapter 10. Communities Become Dense: Shift Five

1. "Sprawl-Weary Los Angeles Builds Up and In," by Timothy Egan, *The New York Times*, March 10, 2002.

2. "Five Rooms, Gucci View," by William L. Hamilton, *The New York Times*, February 21, 2002.

3. "Living Downtown," by Laura Taxel, *Continental* magazine, April 2003, page 25.

4. "Good Morning, New York: Eggs Over Easy, Business on the Side," by Florence Fabricant, *The New York Times*, March 19, 2003.

5. "Clearer Skies for IT," by Colin Brace, *Holland Herald*, June 2003, page 73.

6. "Low-income housing goes wireless," Associated Press, February 24, 2003.

7. Hamilton.

8. *Bowling Alone: The Collapse and Revival of American Community*, by Robert D. Putnam, Simon & Schuster, New York, 2000, page 212.

9. Ibid.

10. Ibid.

11. Ibid, page 213. Putnam's source is analyses of DDB Needham Life Style, Roper Social and Political Trends, and Americans' Use of Time survey archives.

12. Ibid.

13. Ibid, page 403.

14. Ibid.

15. "From Parking To Taxes, a Push to Get Answers Online," by Rebecca Fairley Raney, *The New York Times*, April 4, 2002.

16. Ibid.

17. "eGovernment: Local government web sites are failing," by John Cradden, April 15, 2003, ElectricNews.net, *http://www.enn.ie/news.html?code=9355411*.

18. "How to Escape an Office With No Walls," by Lawrence Van Gelder, *The New York Times*, June 14, 2003.

Chapter 11. New Societal Infrastructures Evolve: Shift Six

1. *America's Coming-of-Age*, by Van Wyck Brooks, The Viking Press, New York, 1915, pages 177-178.

2. See, for example, "1% of total U.S. income goes to 400," *The New York Times*, June 26, 2003. According to the article, "The 400 wealthiest taxpayers accounted for more than 1% of all the income in the United States in the year 2000, more than double their share just eight years earlier, according to new data from the Internal Revenue Service."

3. "When no job is safe," *On Point* public radio program, with Tom Ashbrook, aired July 24, 2003.

4. Ibid.

5. "US Feeling is That Technology Jobs Should Go to Americans," Lesley Stones, *Business Day* (Johannesburg, South Africa), July 24, 2003.

6. "IBM 'outsourcing' indicative of trend," by Jonathan Ment, *Freeman*, Kingston, New York, July 24, 2003.

7. Stones, *Business Day*.

8. Ashbrook, *On Point*.

9. *Why the American Century?* By Olivier Zunz, University of Chicago Press, Chicago, Illinois, 2000.

10. For instance, the first unemployment benefits case filed by a telecommuter pointed out the inadequacy of current unemployment law for telecommuters. See "Telecommuter Zapped on Benefits," CBS News, July 3, 2003.

11. "The Marx Brother: how a philosopher from Slovenia became an international star," by Rebecca Mead, *The New Yorker*, May 5, 2003, page 40.

12. "The Money Note: Can the record business survive?" by John Seabrook, *New Yorker Magazine*, July 7, 2003 (quotes from pages 49 and 51).

13. Stephen Downes, Senior Researcher, Canadian Research Council, eLearning Group, Monckton, New Brunswick, interviewed by the authors for an online conference in June 2003.

14. From the July 2003 web site of the Electronic Privacy Information Center (EPIC), *http://www.epic.org*.

15. See, for example, "Privacy Law Hurt Plasma Case," by John Tuohy and Diana Penner, *Indianapolis Star*, July 19, 2003. The writers note, "Laws intended to protect the privacy of HIV carriers helped delay by more than a year state health officials' efforts to identify some of the five people accused of selling tainted plasma."

16. Australia, for example, has a national privacy act that specifies what organizations can, and cannot do, with information. Policy makers at the time of this writing were debating whether pictures should be covered in the privacy law. See, for example, *Every Step You Take*, by Nicole Manktelow, Icon, July 19, 2003.

17. Wisconsin Public Radio, July 2003

18. *Wealth and Democracy*, by Kevin Phillips, Random House, New York, 2002, page 110.

19. Source: National Center for Education Statistics, Department of Education, US Government, 1997.

20. "Only the Minimum," Bob Herbert, *The New York Times*, June 27, 2002.

21. "Some students require a hand on the way up," by Richard Rothstein, *The New York Times*, October 4, 2000.

22. "Put College on Line," William A. Draves, *The New York Times*, September 2, 1997.

23. "Hard drive," by Peter Cochrane, *London Daily Telegraph*, July 7, 2000.

24. "Tuition increase called 'modest'," by Sharif Durhams, *Milwaukee Journal Sentinel*, October 17, 2000.

25. *What the Public Wants From Higher Education: Workforce Implications*, by Don A. Dillman, Washington State University, Pullman, Washington, from a 1995 National Survey available from the Social & Economic Sciences Research Center, Washington State University, Pullman, WA ,Technical Report #95–52.

26. United States Office of Personnel Management, *http://www.opm.gov/ hrd/lead/ILA/ilaguide.asp#what*, web page sourced, May 15, 2003.

27. "However, Ministers have said that they are fully committed to developing a replacement ILA style scheme and a consultation with a range of key stakeholders is currently taking place," reported Lynne Robinson, Department for Education and Skills, in 2002. Source: *http:// www.helpisathand.gov.uk/news/2002/ila/*

28. Statistics compiled and averaged to the nearest million people from two statistical charts in the Statistical Abstract of the US 1997: *The National Data Book*, by the US Census Bureau, pages 160 and 470.

29. Individual Learning Account Pilot Initiative, A Learning Tool for the 21st Century, Appendix A, OPM Federal ILA Pilot Initiative Guidelines, *http://www.opm.gov/hrd/lead/ILA/ilarpt-A.asp#Background2*.

Chapter 12. Cheating Becomes Collaboration: Shift Seven

1. *The Death of Character*, by James Davison Hunter, Basic Books, New York, NY, 2000, page 3.

2. Ibid.

3. Ibid, page 7

4. Direct wording from *An A-Z of Cosmonautics*, an English translation of the history of space by V. Gor'kov and Yu Avdeev, Mir Publishers, Moscow, 1989, page 190.

5. Walter Cronkite, in a radio broadcast on National Public Radio, October 7, 2002, commemorating the 45th anniversary of Sputnik.

6. Coalition of Lifelong Learning Organizations, Spring 1997, One DuPont Circle, Washington, D.C.

7. Marlene Tucker, comment in the authors' online course, May 2001, reported in *Teaching OntheNet* e-mail newsletter, August 2001.

8. Tapscott, page 155.

9. "R-rated films are sent to back of ticket line," by Andy Seiler, *USA Today*, March 5, 2003, page D01.

10. *East of Eden*, by John Steinbeck, Penguin Books, New York, NY, 1952, page 129.

11. See *http://www.800padutch.com/amish*.

12. Examples from *Supplement One, The American Language*, by H.L. Mencken, Knopf, New York, 1945, pages 325-330.

13. University of Wisconsin – River Falls Graduation, River Falls, Wisconsin, December 2000.

14. Degrees conferred by institutions of higher education, by level of degree and sex of student, 1949-50 to 1993-94, National Center for Education Statistics, Earned Degrees Conferred.

15. "Where the boys aren't," by Brendan I. Koerner, *U.S. News*, February 8, 1999.

16. "Improving Boys' and Girls' Academic Achievement," Conseil Superier de L'Education, Government of Quebec, Canada.

17. "The Trouble with Boys," *The Guardian*, August 21, 2000.

18. The Education of Boys, Department of Education, Training and Youth Affairs, Australian Government, August 2000.

19. Ibid.

20. Ibid.

21. *Self-taught young techies don't see point of college*, by Bob Weinstein, King Features Syndicate, February 2001.

22. Wisconsin Public Schools radio advertisement, Fall 2000.

23. Metropolitan Life Survey of The American Teacher 1997, as reported by Dr. Judith Kleinfeld in *The Myth That Schools Shortchange Girls*.

24. *The Americans, A Social History of the United States 1587-1914*, by J. C. Furnas, G.P. Putnam's, New York, 1969, pages 886-887.

25. United States Congress, House Committee on the Judiciary, March 28, 1924. Child Labor, compiled by Julia E. Johnsen, HW Wilson Company, New York, 1924, page 145.

26. G. Stanley Hall, President of Clarkson University, in *The Home Teacher*, The Chautauqua Industrial Art Desk, Lewis E. Myers and Company, 1903, page 120. G. Stanley Hall was called "America's Foremost Teacher" (The Standard Reference Work, 1920).

27. Owen R. Lovejoy, National Child Labor Committee, in *Child Labor*.

28. *The Standard Educator*, page 238, Welles Brothers Publishing Company, Minneapolis and Chicago, 1919.

29. *The Myth That Schools ShortChange Girls: Social Science in the Service of Deception*, by Dr. Judith Kleinfeld, University of Alaska, Fairbanks, 1998.

30. *Boys and Girls Learn Differently!* by Michael Gurian, Jossey-Bass, 2001.

31. "Women are under-represented in the information technology industry in the UK, accounting for just 21% of the workforce," according to the story "Women Offered a Taste of Tech," BBC News, Thursday, January 30, 2003.

32. Statistics from high tech enrollments in the division of continuing education, Harper College, Palatine, Illinois, Russ Mills, Vice President for Continuing Education, 2003.

Chapter 13. Half of All Learning is Online: Shift Eight

1. *Trends 2000*, by Gerald Celente, Warner Books, New York, NY, 1997, p. 249.

2. *Encyclopedia Britannica*, University of Chicago, Chicago, Illinois, 1945, Volume 23, page 389.

3. *How We Will Learn*, Peter J. Denning, George Mason University, paper, 1996, page 2.

4. "Japan Shuts Down Its Education Assembly Line," by Gale Eisenstodt, *Fast Company* magazine, Feburary/March 1997, pages 40-42.

5. *The Adult Learner: A Neglected Species*, by Malcolm Knowles, Gulf Publishing, Houston, Texas, 1973, page 42.

6. *Mastering the Teaching of Adults*, by Jerold Apps, Krieger Publishing Company, Melbourne, Florida, 1991.

7. Richard Thieme, consultant and futurist, Fox Point, Wisconsin, from a speech at the Metcom conference, April 4, 1996, Chicago, sponsored by the American Society for Association Executives and the Professional Convention Management Association.

8. Authors conversation with Dees Stallings, University Online Publishing, Fairfax, Virginia, 2000.

9. Hagel and Armstrong.

10. *Building Learning Communities in Cyberspace*, by Rena M. Palloff and Keith Pratt, Jossey-Bass Publishers, San Francisco, 1999.

11. Authors conversation with Ken Harvey, Principal, Distance Education School, Greater Vancouver Public Schools, Vancouver, BC, January 2001.

12. Reported by the *Chronicle of Higher Education*, September 15, 2000.

13. Apps, page 1.

14. Margo Adler, National Public Radio, April 28, 2000.

15. "Customizing the Learning Experience with Reusable Content Objects," Susan Kirshbaum, Oracle Corporation, in a speech April 23, 2000, St. Paul, Minnesota, sponsored by LearningByte International.

16. "The Future of Online Content," Guenther Weydauer, Vice President for New Product Development at LearningByte International, Keynote address, Learning Online 2001 conference, June 25, 2001, Minneapolis, sponsored by the Learning Resources Network (LERN).

17. Copyright and Intellectual Property panel discussion, World Education Market conference, Vancouver, Canada, May 24-26, 2001.

18. "Gaming is good for you," by Mark Ward, BBC News online, Wednesday, February 12, 2003.

19. "Think tanks for gamers," by Mark Ward, BBC News online, Monday, February 10, 2003.

20. Professor Rod Riegle, Illinois State University, in a presentation at the Distance Learning and Teaching Conference, Madison, Wisconsin, August 15, 2002.

Chapter 14. Education Becomes Web-based: Shift Nine

1. See *Generational Learning Styles*, by Julie Coates, Learning Resources Network publishers, River Falls, Wisconsin, 2004.

2. For example, SAT test questions are periodically made more difficult to adjust to the increasing student abilities over the generations. When a 92-year-old teacher was asked what the difference was between students in 2000 and previous generations, she replied that students are much smarter today.

3. We are indebted to Richard Thieme (speech, December 4, 2000, Chicago) for the comparison of the modern day computer lab with a fictional pencil lab of yesteryear.

4. In 2003, for example, Brooke Scharlott, an administrator at Myers University in Cleveland, Ohio, a university with a comparatively high degree of online courses, reported to us (Seattle, June 12, 2003) that the institution had downsized a new classroom building from seven stories to three stories, and significantly reduced space in an administration building, thus becoming one of the first universities to begin reallocating resources from buildings to technology.

5. For more on andragogy and the principles of helping people to learn, see *How to Teach Adults*, by William A. Draves, Learning Resources Network publishers, River Falls, Wisconsin, 1984 (first edition) and 1998 (second edition).

6. Source: Minnesota Medical Association. The research was used by the Minneapolis Public Schools to change starting times from 7:30 am to 8:30 am. The school district reports that grades and student achievement went up as a result of the later morning start time.

7. For more on the limitations of for-profit schools see, for instance, "Edison Schools' Founder to Take It Private," by Diana B. Henriques, *The New York Times*, July 15, 2003.

8. In the area of higher education, for example, an official of the for-profit and virtual Capella University told us (interview, May 2002, Minneapolis, Minnesota) that he projected that for-profit virtual institutions would not get above 10% of the total student market.

9. For more on online grading, see such sites as *www.mygradebook.com*.

10. In 2003, the sale of laptops exceeded the sale of desktop computers for the first time, according to an Associated Press story, "Laptop sales beat desktops for first time," reported in *The New York Times*, July 3, 2003.

11. In 2003 the State of Maine became the first state to announce that it would provide laptops to all 7th graders in the state. See "A governor

would give every student a laptop," *The New York Times*, March 2, 2003.

12. For more on learner management systems, see Brandon Hall's comprehensive work, *Learner Management Systems*, by Brandon Hall, Brandon-hall.com, Sunnyvale, California, 2000.

13. For example, in 2003 learning technology expert Les Howles of the University of Wisconsin-Madison's department of information technology reported to the authors that a majority of professors requesting technical assistance wanted to integrate the Internet in their traditional classrooms (so-called hybrid or mixed courses) rather than teach totally online.

14. Kim Roberts, Director of Outreach, University of Western Australia, Nedlands, Australia, speech, Providence, Rhode Island, June 14, 2002.

15. Source: Marketing Data Retrieval, Chicago, Illinois, Higher Education Lists directory, 2003.

16. For more explanation on how the syndication of online courses works in higher education, see Chapter 26 in the second edition of *Teaching Online*, by William A. Draves, Learning Resources Network publishers, River Falls, Wisconsin, 2002.

17. See, for example, "Education Leads Silicon Valley Wish List," *The New York Times*, January 22, 2001.

18. The move to a wireless campus is not limited, nor even apparently led, by universities with greater financial resources or status. For example, in 2003 the University of Wisconsin – Stout, in Menominee, Wisconsin, a campus of around 5,000 students, went wireless.

19. In 2003, the number of telecommuters in the United States was reported to be 28 million, National Public Radio, July 3, 2003.

20. From *Tender is the Night*, by F. Scott Fitzgerald, Charles Scribner's Sons, New York, NY, 1933. The original phrasing was "inevitable became evitable".

Annotated Bibliography

The following are those books which the authors found particularly valuable or pioneering or provided unique contributions to our understanding of the societal transition from one economic era to another.

The Big Change, by Frederick Lewis Allen, Harper & Brothers, New York, 1952.

One of the most comprehensive treatments of the societal change from the agrarian society to the industrial society, Allen also demonstrates an awareness of the transition as a phenomenon taking place in just two decades.

For our work, Allen saw the same transition 100 years ago as the one we witness today. The parallels and information Allen provided were immensely supportive and instructive.

The Essential Drucker, by Peter F. Drucker, HarperCollins, New York, NY, 2002.

There are so many excellent Drucker books on management and economic organization, we recommend any and all of his work. Drucker's wisdom and foresight are so deep that his work will continue to be relevant and innovative for many years to come.

For our work, Drucker has changed our organization and work lives several times with his guidance and organizational prescriptions. His historical perspective, plus his role in Allen's work, are rich treats as well.

Growing Up Digital: The Rise of the Net Generation, by Donald Tapscott, McGraw-Hll, New York, 1998.

Donald Tapscott was one of the first people to understand the impact of the World Wide Web on the first generations of the 21st century, and to illuminate some of the implications for learning, behavior and culture.

For our work, his notion of "lapping" was insightful for understanding how adults and children approach the world of the web differently.

Net Gain, by John Hagel III and Arthur G. Armstrong, Harvard Business School Press, Bostom, MA, 1996.

This is a seminal work in our understanding of networks and the changing economics brought about by the Internet. Hagel and Armstrong also provide an early and prescient treatment of the emerging and central concept of virtual community for life in this century.

We have been exploring, struggling and enjoying our attempts at creating and participating in virtual communities ever since reading it.

The Great Crossover, by Dan Sullivan, Babs Smith, and Michel Neray, The Strategic Coach, Toronto, Canada, 1994-1997.

This is a pioneering work in dissecting the organization chart and pyramid as an organizational focal point for life in the last century. As an increasing number of phenomena are now defined in terms of the network model, *The Great Crossover* stands out for its explanation of the transition from the pyramid to the network.

For our work, *The Great Crossover* provided more than one revelation. It also helped us understand the personal and individual transition each of us as adults can make.

FDR: Volumes 1-5, by Kenneth S. Davis, Random House, New York (*Volume 5, The War President*, copyright 2000).

Franklin Delano Roosevelt has been repeatedly named the most important president of the United States during the 20th century, and Davis has been cited as the best biographer of FDR. He lived during the FDR era, traveled with Eisenhower during World War II, was a speechwriter for Adlai Stevenson, and spent decades researching FDR.

Fascinating reading, Davis uniquely analyzes the turning points in creating a social infrastructure in the 1930s for the nation. An underlying theme is the tug and pull of technology versus human endeavor.

Bowling Alone: The Collapse and Revival of American Community, by Robert D. Putnam, Simon & Schuster, New York, 2000.

The most comprehensive, objective and statistical documentation of the decline in the sense of community in the United States in the last half of the 20th century. The scope and detail of Putnam's research is revealing, and the illumination of the problems he provides is insightful.

From our perspective, he does not provide viable solutions to the "revival" of American community, yet his delineation of the problem is in itself a major contribution.

Robert M. LaFollette, by Belle Case LaFollette and Fola LaFollette, The Macmillan Company, New York, 1953.

The twin benefits of this book, about one of the more effective progressive change agents in the 20th century, written from the perspective of his wife and daughter, who were intimately involved in helping to make those changes happen.

The result of these twin benefits is that this biography shines an irrepressible optimism from those who were involved in the losses as well as the few wins about the worth of fighting for social gains in society. The result is an emotional and psychological how-to manual for improving society.

Child Labor, compiled by Julia E. Johnsen, HW Wilson Company, New York, 1924.

A rare insight into the viewpoint of those living in the early part of the 20th century, filled with fascinating statistics, interviews, and revealing perspectives on the nature of those times.

In the original telling of their times one finds a more reliable social guide to the prospects for societal change in our times.

Wealth and Democracy, by Kevin Phillips, Random House, New York, 2002.

Kevin Phillips provides an up-to-date analysis of the relationship between wealth and democracy. He notes the issues facing America in the early 21st century, and draws parallels and relevance to the wealth and democracy issues in our history, including most strikingly the similarities at the turn of the 20th century.

The Centerless Corporation, by Bruce A. Pasternack and Albert J. Viscio, Simon & Schuster, New York, NY, 1998.

A pioneering critique of the outmoded pyramid structure of business organization, and introduces the concept of business units and a networked structure for business organizations in this century, which they call a "centerless corporation."

Main Street, by Sinclair Lewis, Harcourt Brace Jovanovich, Inc., New York, 1920.

This well known and celebrated novel is worth another look for its clarity as well as clairvoyance. Lewis provides an all-encompassing description of how life was for most Americans, as well as clues and insights to its disintegration.

About the Authors

Julie Coates is Vice President for Information Services for the Learning Resources Network, where she is editor of Course Trends magazine and does consulting.

Julie was born and raised in Black Mountain, North Carolina. She attended Cornell University, North Carolina State University, and pursued graduate study in public administration and adult education at Kansas State University, from which she earned her Masters Degree .

She was active in the civil rights movement in the 1960s, being a target of the Ku Klux Klan and participating in sit-ins and other civil rights activities in Greensboro, NC.

In Manhattan, Kansas, she ran one of the nation's premiere lifelong learning programs. She also was a community organizer, initiating the statewide folk life program for Kansas, a day-care center, avocational programs for adults with disabilities, and community-wide volunteer clearinghouse.

Julie is a well-known authority and speaker on demographics and brochure design, having done keynotes and seminars in Russia, Germany, Australia, Mexico, Canada and throughout the U.S. She also teaches online courses as part of a graduate program with the University of South Dakota. Her newest book is *Generational Learning Styles*.

William A. Draves, CAE, is an internationally recognized teacher, author and consultant and President of the LERN.

He is one of the most quoted experts on lifelong learning and online learning by the nation's media, having been interviewed by *The New York Times*, *Los Angeles Times*, *Washington Post*, *Wall Street Journal*, National Public Radio, NBC Nightly News, and Wired.com.

Bill holds a master's degree in adult education from The George Washington University in Washington, D.C. He has authored six books, and does speaking throughout the world. Maureen Geddes, vice president of the Ontario Speakers Association calls Bill "a world-class speaker" and Phil Housel of Kerrville, Texas, says, "I'd trample my grandma to hear Draves speak." More info is at *www.WilliamDraves.com*.

For More Information

For more information about *Nine Shift*, check out the book's web site at *www.NineShift.com.*

The authors are available for conference speaking engagements, in-house staff training, consulting, and offer online courses on the subject.

Our permanent web site address is *www.lern.org.*

Spread the Word

Help spread the word about *Nine Shift*. Send e-mails to 10 people and we'll put your name on our web site as a supporter. Check out *www.NineShift.com* or e-mail *info@lern.org* for details.

If you want to do more to spread this important message to your organization or community, e-mail us at *info@lern.org.*

About LERN

The Learning Resources Network (LERN) is the leading association in the world in lifelong learning programming, serving more than 10,000 professionals every year in 20 countries.

Begun in 1974, LERN offers information and consulting to providers of lifelong learning programs, including for-profit and non-profit organizations, such as universities, community colleges, public schools, recreation departments, training providers, associations and others.

LERN provides practical, how-to information on marketing, finances, management, product development, teaching and course design. It is information not available anywhere else.

A specialty area of expertise is online learning and teaching, with LERN being the leading provider of online professional development for faculty and teachers using the Internet.

LERN is a nonprofit, tax-exempt, educational organization. We are led by a Board of Directors, with daily operations carried out by a staff and consultants located in eight states. With a mission to extend lifelong learning to all, our slogan is "Information That Works!" ®

Share Nine Shift
with your colleagues

For your office: 10 copies, just $99 (only $9.90 each)
(Price subject to change.)

_____
Name

_____
Title or Department (if any)

_____
Organization

_____
Address

_____
City, State/Province, ZIP/Postal Code

_____
E-mail Address   Phone #

Please check one:

____One copy, $20 plus $5 shipping = $25 total

____Ten copies, $99 plus $10 shipping = $109 total

For other quantities, send e-mail to _info@lern.org_ for shipping costs.

Please check one:

____Payment enclosed.

____Charge my credit card.

For overnight shipping or
more information, call LERN
at 800-678-5376 or send
e-mail to _info@lern.org_.

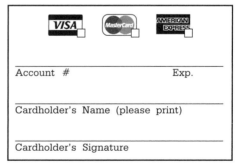

Account #   Exp.

_____

Cardholder's Name (please print)

_____

Cardholder's Signature

To Order Nine Shift

Call: 800-678-5376 (US and Canada)
Fax, toll-free: 888-234-8633 (toll-free worldwide)
E-mail: info@lern.org
Web: www.nineshift.com or www.lern.org
Mail to: LERN Books, PO Box 9, River Falls, WI 54022 USA